Hammersley, Martyn.

Classroom ethnography.

CLASSROOM ETHNOGRAPHY
Empirical and
Methodological Essays

MODERN EDUCATIONAL THOUGHT
Series Editor: Professor Andy Hargreaves,
            Ontario Institute for Studies in Education

This important new series contains some of the very best of modern educational thought that will stimulate interest and controversy among teachers and educationalists alike.

It brings together writers of distinction and originality within educational studies who have made significant contributions to policy and practice. The writers are all scholars of international standing who are recognized authorities in their own particular field and who are still actively researching and advancing knowledge in that field.

The series represents some of their best and most distinctive writing as a set of provocative, interrelated essays addressing a specific theme of contemporary importance. A unique feature of the series is that each collection includes a critical introduction to the author's work written by another influential figure in the field.

Current titles:

Roger Dale: *The State and Education Policy*
Andy Hargreaves: *Curriculum and Assessment Reform*
Martyn Hammersley: *Classroom Ethnography*

Forthcoming titles include:

Stephen Ball: *Education and Political Process*
Michael Fullan: *Implementation and Change in Education*
Ivor Goodson: *Pupils, Pedagogy and Power*
David Hargreaves: *Teaching*
Jean Rudduck: *Innovation, Involvement and Understanding*

Classroom Ethnography
Empirical and Methodological Essays

MARTYN HAMMERSLEY

OPEN UNIVERSITY PRESS
Milton Keynes · Philadelphia

Open University Press
Celtic Court
22 Ballmoor
Buckingham MK18 1XW

and

1900 Frost Road, Suite 101
Bristol, PA 19007, USA

First Published 1990

British Library Cataloguing-in-Publication Data

Hammersley, Martyn
   Classroom ethnography: empirical and methodological
     essays — (Modern educational thought).
   1. Education. Research. Applications of ethnography
   I. Title   II. Series
   370.78

   ISBN 0-335-09236-5
   ISBN 0-335-09235-7 (pbk)

Library of Congress Cataloging-in-Publication Data

Hammersley, Martyn.
   Classroom ethnography: empirical and methodological essays
   Martyn Hammersley.
      p.   cm. – (Modern educational thought)
   Includes bibliographical references.
   ISBN 0-335-09236-5. – ISBN 0-335-09235-7 (pbk.)
   1. Education – Research.   2. Classroom environment – Research.
   I. Title.   II. Series.
   LB1028.H314   1990
   370'.7'8 – dc20

                         89–48887CIP

Typeset by Inforum Typesetting, Portsmouth
Printed in Great Britain by St Edmundsbury Press Ltd
Bury St Edmunds, Suffolk

Contents

Preface

This book is the product of an intellectual journey, one that is not yet completed. It collects together a selection of my work over the past 15 years, both substantive and methodological. The most striking theme is probably the gradual shift in my methodological attitude: from a fairly conventional ethnographic approach to my current view that ethnography suffers from disabling problems and requires major reconstruction.

This is a personal story; it certainly does not match the development of the whole field of ethnographic research on classroom interaction, though developments in that field touch upon it at many points. My own work began in the early 1970s. This was a time of ferment in the sociology of education in Britain. Like many others at this time, I believed that previous sociological work on education had failed for both theoretical and methodological reasons. Theoretically, it had placed too much emphasis on the social determination of human behaviour and not enough on the ability of individuals and groups to transform the social world. This not only misrepresented the nature of human social life but also served to preserve the political status quo. Methodologically, sociologists had generally failed to employ methods that captured the perspectives and activities of teachers and pupils, being concerned with correlations between input and output variables of schools and of the educational system as a whole.[1]* There was virtually no sociological work on classrooms. Furthermore, what educational research there had been in this area was primarily concerned with categorizing behaviour in terms of concepts pre-defined by the researcher. As a result, I and others felt, this too failed to understand the social processes involved in classroom interaction. These criticisms of previous work in the field formed the basis for a variety of attempts to develop a more effective sociology of education. One of the most prominent symbols of this change was the book *Knowledge and Control*, announcing what came to be called 'the new sociology of education'.[2]

---

* Superscript numerals refer to numbered notes at the end of the book.

From the beginning, though, this 'new sociology of education' was frag-
mented. There were three broad approaches. First, there were those who
engaged in collaborative work with teachers to help them put progressive
educational ideas into practice in the classroom, and who used qualitative
methods to serve this purpose. Second, there were researchers who were
concerned with bringing about radical educational and social change, and who
became increasingly concerned to analyse the constraints placed upon teachers
by wider social structures. Finally, there were those who were strongly influenced by symbolic interactionism, and who placed primary emphasis on exploring and documenting the world of school life largely for its own sake.[3]
Most research showed a mixture of these approaches, but in different
proportions.

I was closest to the last of these approaches. This was the most productive of
the three strands in terms of the amount of published empirical research.
Various aspects of the process of schooling were studied: teachers' and pupils'
perspectives and strategies; the curriculum in the classroom; staffroom and
meeting talk; teachers' careers, etc.[4] My own work began .with a study of
patterns of teacher and pupil adaptation in an inner-city school that I called
Downtown.[5] This was a boys' secondary modern school[6] that had acquired a
reputation in the 1950s and 1960s as one of the few academically successful
secondary moderns in the city in which it was located. As a result it had
attracted many pupils from outside its catchment area, including middle-class
pupils from the suburbs. By the early 1970s, when I studied it, however,
Downtown was no longer entering pupils for GCE examinations, and its entry
was creamed by two new schools nearby. In this later period its pupil popu-
lation reflected the composition of its catchment area much more closely, with
a roughly equal mixture of pupils of white working-class, Afro-Caribbean and
Asian backgrounds. Most of the teachers had been at the school for many years,
witnessing what they regarded as its decline. They were committed to a very
traditional conception of teaching, and my aim was to document the nature
and consequences of this teaching ideology.

More recently, I have been involved, with John Scarth and Sue Webb, in
research on the effects of assessment regimes (particularly public examinations)
on secondary school teaching.[7] This focused on the work of 11 teachers in five
schools, four comprehensives and a grammar school. It was largely out of this
second research experience that my doubts about the methodological viability
of ethnography emerged. This work forced us to spend a considerable amount
of time trying to clarify and resolve fundamental methodological problems
facing ethnographic research (indeed facing all social research), of which I had
previously been largely unaware.

However, there were other catalysts for my methodological doubts. One
was my early contact with ethnomethodology. As I have explained elsewhere,[8]
my contact with ethnomethodology was salutary because it forced me to
recognize that many of the criticisms that interactionists directed at conventional sociology were equally applicable to their own work. In particular, I was
impressed by the ethnomethodologists' emphasis on the rigorous description

and analysis of processes of social interaction. Some of my early articles reflect this, for example applying Sacks' analysis of turn-taking procedures in conversation to the process of classroom interaction.[9]

Another important stimulus to methodological reflection was working on an Open University research methods course.[10] This required me to present and justify ethnographic method, both to a course team who were not ethnographers and who were a little suspicious of it and to undergraduate students. That task continued and developed when Paul Atkinson and I collaborated to produce an introductory text on ethnographic method.[11] In doing this work I found that I had to present and defend ethnographic method without reliance on the many assumptions that ethnographers take for granted. And once I began to be aware of those assumptions and to think about them, I came to realize that some of them were untenable.

As a result of these experiences, I have spent considerable time thinking and writing about the nature of ethnographic research: about the relationship between different approaches to the study of classroom processes;[12] and about the requirements that ethnography must meet, how its products should be evaluated and whether the criteria differ from those appropriate to other forms of social research.[13] One of the main conclusions that I came to was that conventional ethnographic research does not provide an effective basis for the development and testing of sociological theory. While it often claims to be concerned with theory, there is ambiguity about whether or not theory development takes the same form as it does in other kinds of social research.[14] And no more than other kinds of sociological research does ethnographic work display cumulative theoretical development.[15]

Max Weber argues that methodological reflection is of value only when there is a crisis that prevents the successful pursuit of research. A concern with methodological issues can too easily take on a life of its own, becoming a substitute for doing the research that it is supposed to facilitate. This is undoubtedly true. But Weber devoted a considerable amount of effort to methodological discussions because he believed that at the time when he was writing, the early years of this century, there was a serious methodological crisis that needed resolving before research could progress.[16] It seems to me that much the same is true for us today. And, ironically, it is the same crisis (in the sense of the same issues) that preoccupies us. Those issues, about the nature of theory in the social sciences and how it is to be produced, about the relationship between concepts and data, etc., have persisted from his time to ours, resurfacing every so often, and then slipping out of sight, only to return. The progress of research, on classrooms and in other areas too, requires their resolution.

The first part of this book presents some of the fruits of my ethnographic research. The first three articles arise from my work at Downtown (two of them have been published elsewhere, the other appears here for the first time). I have left these articles substantially as they were originally written. I have not sought to bring them into line with my current methodological thinking. Indeed, this would not be possible. Whatever merits they may possess, my view now is that the form of research that they represent is ill-conceived. This is not to say that such work has no value, simply that it has less value than I once thought. The fourth article in this section comes from the examinations research, and represents an overview of our findings to date. As is clear from the briefest glance, the character of this research was quite different from the earlier study. The most obvious difference is that it involves a substantial quantitative element. Equally important, though, the research was specifically designed to develop and test a theory. As we emphasize, the results are tentative, and it must be said that up to now this research has been more notable for the methodological problems that it has generated than for its results. None the less, I believe that the methodological thinking on which it was based is sound as far as it went, and this research has been extraordinarily productive in enabling me to push my methodological ideas further.

The second part of the book focuses directly on theoretical and methodological reflections about ethnographic research on classrooms. The first, 'Putting competence into action', dates from a time when I was still operating within a relatively conventional view of the nature and value of ethnographic research; though it does not misrepresent my current views about the theoretical approaches that inform classroom research today. The other papers document my departure from a conventional position towards a more radical questioning of the ethnographic enterprise. There are two main areas where I have come to believe that modifications of current practice are required. First, the selection of cases for investigation must provide variation of the theoretical variable(s) and at least partial control of relevant extraneous variables. Second, the operationalization of concepts must be made more rigorous. Chapters 6 and 8 deal with both these issues. The former discusses one of the few examples of ethnographic research that approximates these requirements. The latter spells out in greater depth what I believe to be required for there to be theoretical progress in ethnographic research on classrooms. Chapter 7 focuses on the problem of operationalizing concepts in ethnographic research, dealing with this issue in some detail.

I must emphasize that I do not pretend that these discussions resolve all the problems that they raise, even to my satisfaction. Some readers may find this disconcerting. After all, having raised all these problems, and assuming that they are as serious as I say they are, do I not have a responsibility to show how they can be solved? The answer to this question must be affirmative. However, being committed to finding solutions to problems and succeeding in finding them are very different. As I said at the beginning of this Preface, my intellectual journey is not over. None the less, I hope that this book may help others on their way; at the very least it may show which paths are to be avoided.

Acknowledgements

I was very pleased when Louis Smith agreed to write the Critical Introduction to this book. We have met only once or twice, and then only briefly; but I have come to admire his work (and especially what I would call his disciplined eclecticism), while recognizing the geographical and intellectual distance between us. I hoped that he would provide an interesting slant on the articles presented here; I was not disappointed. I am very grateful to him (and his students) for providing a reaction to my work.

There are others whose contributions, of various kinds, to what is reported here should be acknowledged. There are the teachers and pupils in several schools who welcomed me into their classrooms and talked to me about their experiences and views. There are many colleagues who have encouraged me and sharpened my ideas, of whom I can mention only a few: Isabel Emmett, Douglas Barnes, Peter Woods, Andy Hargreaves, Paul Atkinson, Sara Delamont, Stephen Ball, Colin Lacey, Barry Cooper and especially John Scarth. I must also thank Andy Hargreaves, as Editor, and John Skelton of Open University Press for inviting me to contribute to the series. I hope that they feel the product justifies their commitment. My family have, of course, borne some of the costs of the work reported here – I thank Joan, Rachel and Paul for everything.

The essays in this collection come from the following sources, to whose publishers grateful acknowledgement is made:

Ch. 1 *Sociological Review*, **22**, 3, 1974, pp. 355–69.
Ch. 2 P. Woods and M. Hammersley (eds), *School Experience*, London, Croom Helm, 1977, pp. 57–86.
Ch. 4 *British Educational Research Journal*, **14**, 3, 1988, pp. 231–49.
Ch. 5 P. French and M. MacLure (eds), *Adult–Child Conversation*, London, Croom Helm, 1981, pp. 47–58.
Ch. 6 *Sociology*, **19**, 2, 1986, pp. 244–57.
Ch. 7 M. Hammersley (ed.), *Case Studies in Classroom Research*, Milton Keynes, Open University Press, 1986, pp. 49–60.
Ch. 8 *British Educational Research Journal*, **13**, 3, 1987, pp. 283–96.

Critical Introduction: Whither Classroom Ethnography?[1]

LOUIS M. SMITH

Finding a footing

An 'Introduction' to a book seems, like teaching, to fall somewhere in between the forms of science and art. It quickly becomes entangled with other similar exercises – prologues, forewords and prefaces. When asked to write this introduction I felt flattered. But I seemed also an unlikely candidate. Although I had met Martyn at a meeting or two, I did not know him or his work well. I had done a careful reading and review of *Ethnography, Principles in Practice*, which he had written with Paul Atkinson. Also, I had reviewed the collection of papers he had edited with Peter Woods.[2]

The invitation came as I was preparing the syllabus for my course, Education 5292, 'Field Methods in the Study of Groups, Organizations and Communities'. I felt badly that I had already ordered Goetz and LeCompte and could not introduce my class to his general text.[3] A class session or two on a couple of the Hammersley papers in this collection seemed reasonable for discussion in the course. I presented the idea at the first meeting and found everyone responsive. A humorous comment or two about the class doing my work for me arose from several students whom I had known previously. As I began to read the papers carefully to select the ones for class discussion, I was struck by the fact that Martyn and I both had been doing classroom ethnography for a couple of decades, but that we have been living in two different cultures if not worlds. That seemed an anomaly of some proportion for we are both well read and we footnote extensively. Opening a more formal dialogue arose as an idea for the form of this 'Introduction'. Involving my students, and what I do with them, seemed to specify more concretely the scope of the idea. It seemed an unusual but potentially creative and productive vehicle.

Ethnography is ethnography is ethnography???

Ethnography as social science is fractured along national lines (e.g. USA, UK and the Commonwealth), disciplines (e.g. education, sociology and anthropology), substantive interests (e.g. classroom analysis, innovation and evaluation), smaller interpersonal University groups (e.g. Stanford, Manchester, East Anglia, etc.), paradigmatic perspectives (e.g. neo-positivists, interpretivists and critical theorists) and commitment to action and reform (action researchers versus more academic interpreters and analysts).

The outline and the references of my syllabus contrast with Hammersley's chapter outline and the references from each of his essays. The overall structure of Hammersley's book falls into two sections, empirical research and reflections on theory and methodology. The empirical part splits, roughly, into a concern for the social organizational aspects of a classroom, i.e. participation and order, and the intellectual aspects of a classroom, i.e. the prerequisites to answering questions in classroom discussion and the impact of examinations. All are important issues from my perspective. The second section contains discussions of models, programmes of research, measurement and the cumulative development of theory. Also good and important problems, I believe. I want my students to be aware of and knowledgeable about all this. Most importantly, I want them to be able to put the ideas and skills into the practice of doing original research – at a beginner's level in my course but ultimately, for some, into dissertations and profesional publications.

The exciting anomaly falls in the virtual non-overlap of scholars, their publications, and their references my students read to get to where Hammersley is, and those he has read and cited. Exploring that anomaly requires a more careful account of each strand. The most fundamental position in my course resides in the work and thought of an eminent American sociologist, George Homans. In my self-taught route into classroom ethnography, I found Homans' *The Human Group* the most stimulating book of social science I had ever read.[4] It became a model for our first ethnographic study, *The Complexities of an Urban Classroom*.[5] In that book we were trying for an educational case study to add to his book of cases. Both Hammersley and I were immersed in urban education early in our work, and the first three of his essays here recount his early research. But more of that later.

The Human Group has a number of interesting features. First it is a collection of case studies. A brief bit on an Irish farm family from Arensberg and Kimball[6] opens the discussion and starts the cumulative theory development, a problem Hammersley confronts directly in his eighth essay. Homans moves next to a long discussion of the 'Bank Wiring group' from Roethlisberger and Dickson's early study of *Management and the Worker*.[7] Unusual and imaginative glimpses of Willis' 'lads' and 'earoles', grown up and ethnic American, appear on the bank wiring shop floor.[8] Even more relevant are excerpts of the 'Norton Street Gang', the corner boys from William Foote Whyte's *Street Corner Society*,[9] which is the third piece of ethnography raised by Homans. In reporting these studies, Homans does several things. First he describes the group in common-sense, lay language. 'Experience near' would be Clifford Geertz's label for such an account.[10] Then Homans makes a theoretical analysis of the events that have been described, an 'experience distant' account. Further, he uses the concepts developed in the earlier case studies and extends the theoretical repertory as necessary to handle new phenomena. Finally, he patterns the concepts into hypotheses and miniature theories.

The last of his case studies we raise in Ed 5292 is the 'Electrical Equipment Company' from the Arensberg and MacGregor industrial consulting files.[11] This study enables Homans to deal with organizations and all the complications of 'groups' of that sort, with the nature of social conflict, including its antecedents and consequences, and with history, the changes in the organization over time. Later he moves into a chapter on 'leadership'. Manifestly, the chapter builds on the earlier cases, but latently, in my judgement, it grows out of his four years of experience in the Second World War when he captained a small warship as a line officer in the navy. That experience appeared as a powerful piece of 'action research', published originally in 1946 and reprinted in a collection of his essays entitled *Sentiments and Activities*.[12] The 'practical' nature of his principles, reasoning and advice, despite his self-avowed hard determinism and positivism, in that essay and in the leadership chapter, give me an image of a symbolic interactionist at work. The latent image, again in my judgement, runs throughout *The Human Group* as he talks to the reader as guide and teacher.

The syllabus moves into a short unit on alternative approaches to ethnography. We discuss several chapters from Smith and Geoffrey's study, one that was intended to be an educational case to accompany Homans' cases. We introduce the Hammersley materials as a direct substantive contrast to *Complexities* and an indirect contrast to Homans. Finally, we consider Clifford Geertz's classic essay on ethnography as thick description and the classic substantive contribution on the Bali cockfight.[13] The students get a glimpse of one of the best American interpretive cultural anthropologists. On occasion in the past, I have used some of Howard Becker's work or Alan Peshkin's school and community studies. This semester individual students have been guided into *Boys in White* and *Imperfect Union*, as these studies were explicitly relevant to their projects.[14]

The final unit, 'The General and the Particular', weaves Goetz and LeCompte's handbook with the students' own projects. In my view Goetz and LeCompte know considerably less British literature than Hammersley and Atkinson know of the American literature. I have not content analysed the references for independence and overlap, nor have I tried to teach from both at the same time. Goetz and LeCompte cite none of Martyn's research.

The group towards whom these materials and ideas are directed is quite diverse. Most are Ph.D. students, although three are post-doctoral, one is an undergraduate, and a couple are M.A. students. Three different institutions are represented – Washington University, University of Missouri, St Louis, and Maryville College. Most are majoring in various sub-fields of Education (administration, curriculum and instruction psychology and adult education), but a few are from departments of sociology, social work and human resource management. Hammersley's 'classroom ethnography' is directly pertinent to a major subset of the group. Diversity, specialization and independence exist to a surprising degree among students interested in 'ethnography'. That remains a puzzlement for me.

A classroom experience

On 3 April I had assigned and 'taught' Hammersley's Table of Contents, Intro-duction, Chapter 2 and Chapter 8. It proved to be an unusual and unexpected experience. Picking only a couple of his essays constrained the discussion. The reasons for the particular selections seemed simple and reasonably straight-forward. We could not do all of them. The introductory materials set the stage for Hammersley's discussion, the Downtown study paralleled *Complexities* which we had spent a period discussing, and the 'Cumulation of Theory' essay repres-ented one of the major points I had been stressing from Homans' materials. I thought we were all set – but, oh the beguiling nature of teaching.

After spending some time recounting tales from AERA, whose annual meet-ing I had attended the week before, I opened the discussion with Hammersley's introductory comments on his hope that ethnography would address some of the large limitations in earlier forms of educational sociology – too deterministic, preservation of the status quo, failing to capture the perspective of the actors, and researcher's pre-set categorization. All were points that I agreed with. Two or three probes of a 'What do you think?' variety precipitated no reaction from what is usually a very talkative, questioning and opinion-expressing group. I had that sinking feeling: 'It's going to be a long evening.'

One of the students moved us to Hammersley's next paragraph as he raised the question of where I thought *Complexities* fitted into Hammersley's point about the fragmentation of the early ethnographic research into three broad trends. My answer began as a process of elimination and seemed to set the tone for what became a long and vigorous discussion. I argued that *Complexities* was not radical, but that we were concerned with constraints from the various levels of increasingly macro items – the faculty peer group which was very important in controlling Geoffrey's action in the Washington School, the principal as both a position and an incumbent, and the Office with its edicts and formal doctrine. Next I argued that we were not introducing progressive practices in the sense of action research, but that the study was assuredly collaborative, more so than most ethnographies. Finally, I noted that we proba-bly best fitted the third category but even here we had trouble for we had not started as symbolic interactionists, rather we had ended essentially there with our decision-making model of teaching. But further we were not exploring school life for its own sake; rather, we were on the hunt for understandings that would inform my pre-service, in-service and Ph.D. students. Audience always seems on my mind. Particular cases seem to elude suggested patterns or tradi-tions in ethnography.[15] In turn, that elusiveness suggests that crucial cuts are not being made in the construals.

A flood of discussion came when one of the students indicated that she had read the materials a couple of times and just did not understand what Ham-mersley was trying to say. Others followed suit. To my comment that his essays were dense, others added 'disjointed' and still others indicated that they were having trouble with cross-national particulars, e.g. 'GCE', 'caning' and 'clouting'. An Indian student in social work was very helpful here. She knew

British schooling directly. One student indicated later and privately that she had been upset with the amount of corporal punishment and that as a parent she had been in conflict with local schools over those issues. We had not raised those ethical problems in the class discussion.

But the student whose comment had opened the flood also pinpointed the problems with 'theory', as we had been using it, as Homans used the term, and as she was trying to use it in her project. At that point, as teacher, I flipped my mental coin and elected to move directly to Hammersley's Chapter 8 on the development, cumulation and testing of theory, rather than taking up his essay on Downtown School, which had been my original intention regarding sequencing the discussion. Here I argued that for me, development was more similar to Glaser and Strauss' 'generation' of theory,[16] cumulation was the adding and integrating of concepts and propositions in the form of Homans, and testing or falsification of theory was taking Hammersley toward more traditional research methods. To illustrate, I moved directly to his discussion of 'survival strategies' and to the alternative sets of antecedents from Woods' research and from Hargreaves' research. I did my 'chalk and talk' thing in making a case for Zetterberg's several ways of formatting hypotheses, about which we had talked on an earlier day.[17] We noted several key problems. First, the two inventories of determinants, as presented by Hammersley, were very different. Is Woods right? Or is Hargreaves? Or are they complementary in some sense? Secondly, is there a way of reducing the terms definitionally? Thirdly, how would one go about testing the sets of hypotheses? Another case study or set of case studies? A kind of 'experimental anthropology' in which one selects one's next case to illuminate a specific hypothesis? A move to more traditional survey or experimental formats? Hammersley suggests each of these as possibilities, but he seems to lean towards a rapprochement with traditional methods because these methods were originally devised for this kind of question. This latter alternative seems a significant move away from ethnography, a move with telling consequences.

During this discussion, I reintroduced our 'teacher awareness' study in which we had gone from a classroom anecdote to a miniature theory of teacher awareness in *Complexities* and then to a correlational study of teacher awareness.[18] We measured awareness by the teachers' ability to reproduce the sociometric hierarchy in their classrooms. We sought the relationship of 'awareness' to 'pupil esteem for the teacher'. The latter was measured with a pupil questionnaire from a factor-analysed Leader Behavior Description Questionnaire (LBDQ) which was popular in American social psychology several decades ago. That study illustrated well some of Hammersley's remarks about measurement. While I have always liked what we did with the instruments and the 60 or 70 teachers and their classrooms, I remained less convinced that that was the way I wanted to think about issues. I have never become involved with other such studies, even though that had been a part of my earlier agenda. Now Martyn seemed to be arguing for more of that kind of work. And I'm still not convinced. Why?

Woven into, or perhaps better, veering off from, this discussion was another brief set of comments. As Martyn spelled out four kinds of activity implied within 'theory development', I was reminded of Robert Merton's penetrating essays on 'the bearing of theory on empirical research' and 'the bearing of research on theory'. It had been years since I had read those chapters (2 and 3) from his *Social Theory and Social Structure*, but at the time I had thought them to be major contributions.[19] My jammed schedule had kept me from reviewing them before class, but I alluded to them briefly. Since then I have put one of the sociology graduate students on to them and I have re-read them. They elaborate Martyn's arguments significantly.

In this short introduction I cannot give all the details of the class discussion, nor do I really want to go back to the tape-recording we made and try to pick up the nuances. Rather, I will report on a couple more key issues we raised. We had considerable difficulty with the dichotomy between 'survival strategies' and 'teaching'. As we discussed this we came to no resolution but thought it an awkward construction. Most seemed to feel that survival strategies belonged as part of a concept of teaching. Some of this got elaborated with another student comment in the form of outcomes of survival strategies – whether they were really defensive items toward making the teacher's job easier or whether they were part of the teacher's attempt to develop a climate where learning could occur. This cued similarities to and differences from 'Big Nurse' in Kenneth Kesey's *One Flew Over the Cuckoo's Nest*.[20] I despaired that I had not continued more carefully the kind of glossary I had started with Geoffrey in *Complexities*. Theoretical and operational definitions and indices were part of that agenda. Would it be helpful to accumulate Martyn's concepts and those from his citations with that original list of concepts in the glossary? Is that a kind of theory accumulation?

After a coffee break in our two-and-a-half-hour class period, we returned to a discussion of the Downtown study, Chapter 2. I fumbled around a bit trying to find a way to grab hold of this essay, which I thought was brilliant. The students were more sceptical. One noted his view that there was not much theory in the essay and asked whether Hammersley raised more of it later. I countered that I thought it was full of theory. And we were off and running once again. We skipped lightly through the illustrative material, noting for the moment the vividness of the data. But I called attention to one of the differences of data from here and the data from *Complexities*. Benefits accrue from having several teachers and their classrooms under observations and analysis, but losses also accrue. A better picture of the school arises from Hammersley's tack, but when the analysis focuses on pupil behaviour in the classroom, to have a single 'natural' unit, a case, such as Geoffrey's classroom, seems stronger. For example, in *Complexities*, Sam's behaviour, we argued, is much clearer if one knows him to be playing the role of 'court jester', a way of viewing that is dependent on considering the classroom as its own small group, and not isolating or abstracting Sam from that particular setting. Case studies *qua* case studies rather than qualitative or ethnographic or participant observation or field studies seemed to be at the heart of this cut. More and more I believe this to be a significant empirical and analytical point of departure.

Then we explored Hammersley's view of coercive strategies and their use –

suspension, caning, slapping and the threats of one or another. Coercive strategies were contrasted with his multiple kinds of justification strategies – appeals to civility, to conversational rules, to age and to gender. He did this contrast nicely and persuasively. I found myself back in Redl and Wineman, and Redl and Wattenberg.[21] They have very sophisticated accounts of 'interference' or 'influence' techniques. Very clearly – and I could not remember all of the scheme at the time – they spoke of 'supporting self control', 'situational assistance', 'reality and value appraisals' (Hammersley's main point on 'legitimizing rhetorics') and 'invoking the pleasure–pain principle'. The Redl scheme is built on a neo-psychoanalytic framework, which gives a major theoretical justification in accounting for Pioneer House, their residential treatment centre, or for extrapolation to the classroom events of Hammersley. Further, I am struck that a creative follow-up of the Redl materials appears in a long series of articles and a book, *Discipline and Group Management*, by Jack Kounin who takes many of the ideas, adds his own, and subjects them to more careful quantitative experimental and correlational analysis.[22] He works off of a neo-Kurt Lewin kind of field theory. Questions in the sociology of science arise: why do I know these things and think them so important while Martyn doesn't know them or thinks them not worthy of comment nor integration into his scheme? I assume it is partially the cross-national communities, for he could do the same kind of analysis and critique on anything I have done, so I am not being personally negative in any sense. In addition, I assume it is partially our different training in psychology and sociology, and maybe the groups we teach and the kind of theory we want to build. Perhaps we need a year in each other's institution? Or we need to do a book together? Or?

Along the way in this two-and-a-half-hour discussion I started some more chalk and talk over the similarities and differences between Hammersley and Smith in general and between *Complexities* and *Classroom Ethnography* in particular. I began as a quantitative test and measurement psychologist with a dissertation published as 'The concurrent validity of six personality and adjustment tests for children'.[23] Another way of describing my training might be 'atheoretical' in what is called the 'dustbowl empiricism' of the University of Minnesota's psychology department. We were deterministic and positivistic applied scientists. Empirical predictions were more important than understandings. Who cares why Lincoln is more important than Washington, as long as such a test item discriminates between two significant groups? My problems started when I tried to teach this kind of educational psychology to teachers and found that they were interested in other kinds of help. Since then I have moved towards more qualitative case studies, with an interpretive or symbolic interactionist perspective. Now I find I am moving further towards a reflexive and normative if not critical kind of theory. In contrast, as I read Hammersley he is moving from an interpretive kind of ethnography towards a more traditional, if not neo-positivistic, kind of social science. He argues this has occurred because ethnography has troubles with non-conscious kinds of data and theories, with integrating macro events, and with difficulties in cumulating and testing theory. He wants to go where I have been. And I am not quite ready to go back. So what do we do? Our class ended with concerns such as these. And now as I write this Introduction, I find that if I were sufficiently clever, I could reanalyse this section in terms of the content of several of Martyn's essays – questions, cultural resources and the move from ethnography to theory. Perhaps he, or you as readers, will do that.

Further lessons from Martyn

For some years now I have been enamoured of the phrase, 'Lessons from . . .'. To me it conveys the message that an article, a monograph or a book someone has written has taught me something. Connotatively, the term 'lesson' seems broader and more significant than simple facts, although they can be part of the learning. More usually, there is an insight which occasions the reaction, 'I wish I had thought of that.' Or an implicit way of looking at a phenomenon exists that I had missed or had not been clever enough to have seen for myself. 'Lessons from' is a difficult criterion, at least as I apply it. Now I would like to return to the several papers in this collection and begin another strand of dialogue. Because of space, the conversation will be more illustrative than exhaustive.

In Chapter 1 'The Organization of Pupil Participation', Hammersley captures what a lesson is all about from the teacher's point of view. I found myself saying, 'Yes, yes, that's what I do.' Or when I am talking with teachers or teachers-to-be, I find myself saying 'you need to worry about attention, about discipline, about pupils raising their hands, about the kind of difficulties and dilemmas you get into if you do this or that'. And then Martyn drops in the insights: 'Pupils' "failure" to conform fully to the participation rules is not to be explained in terms of their perversity or on the grounds that they are operating on the basis of values opposite to those of the school' (p. 19). Or later, 'The teacher always starts the topic talk and his right to do so is never challenged . . .' (p. 21) strikes me as a formidable generalization that raises innumerable additional questions that Martyn takes on systematically. Pupils 'cultural resources' and 'cultural competence' become important and necessary concepts. At this point I really wanted to shift from the 'monologues' into a more direct dialogue. I wanted to try out our pictorial 'theoretical models', a slightly more formal theorizing that we did at great length in *Complexities*. We had found those so helpful in getting us towards one of his major goals of cumulating theories. I wanted to do a miniature theory of the antecedents of cultural competence, for I believe that it would both clarify and extend the insights that he has presented. Or at least that is the argument that I wanted to make in the discussion. In the end notes, we find Martyn reflecting and talking with himself and implicitly with us as readers about the limits and possibilities of what he is about. These introductory comments of mine are a kind of 'end notes to the end notes'.

Chapter 2, 'School Learning', opens up the intellectual life of the classroom, again from the perspective of the teacher who is trying to teach something to a group of pupils. It nicely complements the prior discussions of participation and order in 'Downtown School'. The 'tall story' excerpt is both provocative and hilarious, one worthy of extended analysis. In the 'commentary', as he calls it, Martyn introduces concept upon concept as he reflects on the lesson: breaking down a problem, producing the right answer, suspending evaluation, exploring pupils' thinking, interrupting, consensual formulating, climbing the ladder of knowledge, organizing the lesson in the nature of a crescendo, covering moves, and on and on. The concepts come so fast, it is hard to capture them in a first reading, much less accumulate them into more organized systems of hypotheses. He then moves toward a breadth and depth of general literature (e.g. Schutz) and problems, (e.g. teachers versus people in general) that I found mind-boggling. And it is not that there were not points of interpretation that I would want to discuss, e.g. interruptions as vicarious teaching versus interruptions as checks. Or to cite another illustration, seeing 'crescendos' as elements in a larger dramatic metaphor of teaching. Interpretations upon interpretations. I missed the teacher's view of how his lesson had gone, and I missed that very difficult set of data, the pupils' views of what had happened. Ken Beittel's alternative ways of doing art education research on the creative drawing process is a point of view that Martyn and I need to talk about in this specific context.[24] Beittel collects these kinds of data, and he conceptualizes the events and processes in a very creative manner. Martyn's later essays raise some of these complications.

I am still puzzled by why I believe this essay is the best short piece of ethnography I have ever read. Perhaps because he has taught me how to do what Pat Brock and I had wanted to do and never seemed to be able to pull off in the way we wanted.[25] Solving someone's 20-year-old problem is not a minor accolade.

Chapter 4, on examinations and teaching, tries to answer the question of the hypothesized control of teaching 'the facts' by public examinations. Also, the essay demonstrates that Martyn wants to do important educational research other than ethnography. He gathers data which suggests that exams do not control the teaching of information. He answers that question tentatively but convincingly, even though he worries about samples, measures and statistical tests. But because he was not doing a model-building or theory-generating ethnographic study, he has not created multiple hypotheses regarding the antecedents of 'fact transmission teaching', a problem that remains unexplained. Different questions, different designs, and different canons and criteria of research!

Chapter 5, 'Putting Competence into Action', is one of those 'Where were you Martyn when I needed you?' statements. Transcripts of lessons, whether tape-recorded and reproduced as typescripts or tallied on an pre-set observational schedule, are behavioural items and do not deal with classroom interaction which involves intentions and behaviour. In America, the legacy of Flanders and Medley and Mitzel was long and very strong. In a very abstract discussion, Martyn carries the discussion further as he argues for two kinds of models of non-behaviourist analysis: 'Competence theories are concerned with explaining social order, action theories with detecting and accounting for patterns of social control.' Eventually, he subsumes the competence models into the action models. This kind of theoretical synthesizing I find both difficult and important.

Interestingly, Martyn does this with someone else's ethnographic data. Homans would applaud. Also, this is a very different kind of intellectual effort than the previous essay, his hypothesis testing effort.

Chapter 6, 'From Ethnography to Theory', is a long and powerful gauntlet-throwing manifesto. The first paragraph states an interrelated series of assertions. I would paraphrase them: (1) We have a wealth of theoretical ideas in sociology; (2) but a paucity of theories; (3) the theoretical ideas are rarely developed into an explicit and coherent form; (4) and even more rarely are they subjected to systematic testing; (5) etc., etc., etc. And away he goes for 15 pages of carefully argued text. Homans would agree with items 1–3. But Clifford Geertz would be hesitant and talk of thick description, especially regarding item 4. My colleagues and I would extend the argument with the neologism of 'thick(er) description' in regard to our return to the Kensington School and the theoretical problems of the 'anatomy of educational innovation'. The latter was the problem and the title of our book the first time, and, even though we did not recognize it immediately, it was still the problem 15 years later.[26] One might argue that our follow-up research was an alternative programme and paradigm in the sociology of education, to use the subtitle of Martyn's essay. He hears the siren call of the neo-positivists, and we seem to hear a Geertzian refrain. And that is a huge item for the dialogue. My interpretive aside summarizing my notes to his essay was 'powerful model'.

In Chapter 7, 'Measurement in Ethnography', I find him continuing to take exemplary studies and to rework them into his cumulating point of view. Once again, I have alternatives to pose. Paul Pohland and I worried along our adaptation of Campbell and Fiske's 'convergent and discriminant validation' ideas, Cronbach and Meehl's 'construct validity' and Denzin's 'triangulation' into what we called, lovingly, the 'Validity of Participant Observation: a Multimethod, Multiperson, Multisituation, and Multivariable Matrix'.[27] Need I say more to move the discussion along a step in another, but only slightly different, direction.

In sum, each of the essays in this volume triggered other conjectures and alternative interpretations of the sort I have presented. I commend these essays to the reader and only wish I could continue this part of the dialogue at greater length. Martyn's style of worrying an issue to the point of exhaustion I find exhilarating. But I have another broader issue to raise.

'Cutting nature at the joints': Ideas toward a theory of classroom ethnography

'Cutting nature at the joints' is an old expression, attributed by Kaplan to Plato.[28] While it carries connotations of a strong realism and naturalism, I find that it captures metaphorically the idea of the potency of one's theoretical analysis. Much of the recent worldwide debate regarding the theory, assumptions and metatheory of ethnography cuts into the issues in ways I have not found productive. Reading the Hammersley papers suggests some points of agreement and disagreement which continue, hopefully profitably, the dialogue.

We share a concern for the continuing attempt at integration of manifestly diverse methods of inquiry. As commonsense problem solving is made more sophisticated, as different issues are central, and as different investigators with different backgrounds, skills and interests approach these issues, different methods and analytic approaches arise. The similarities and differences in approaches to research are open for continuous reflection.

We differ somewhat on the degree to which inquiry should be discipline-based or practice-based. As I read Martyn's work, for example, on subcultures and teacher strategies, I find him generating new work from the theories *per se* rather than generating new work from new problems of practice. As one moves towards one or the other end of such a continuum, I believe that profound changes begin to occur in the research. Discipline-based work tends to run towards more context-free inquiry. And this has its strengths and weaknesses.

The relative emphasis on what I call an 'intact', 'natural' or 'ongoing' group versus some kind of sampled set of pupils, teachers, classes, curricula or schools also seems very important. I believe that this is what some of the case study advocates mean by 'case'. I have tended to stay with 'cases', which then permit a kind of integrated theorizing within the group and between the group and its environment. Implications arise over the degree to which one wants a 'strong narrative' with an employment of human drama as part of one's social science. I tend to think yes on this issue. Martyn's work ranges more freely here. Our shared desire to move towards something akin to verification and falsification takes on quite different means at this point – a return to another case analysis versus a move towards surveys and experiments. I feel I may be cluttering several issues here which need separate and disentangled analytical treatment.

In recent years, a re-reading of Robert Redfield and C. Wright Mills[29] and our Kensington Revisited project[30] has moved me toward a view of the similarities and the possibilities of an integration of ethnography, history and biography as methods of educational inquiry. In part this continues a concern with 'process', seeing events over time. Problems in school innovation and improvement seem to require such an enlarged view. This collection of Martyn's essays tend towards a more contemporaneous analysis.

Geertz's distinction between 'experience near' and 'experience distant' accounts of groups under study reflects the degree to which one concentrates on conceptions used by the people in the setting and conceptions reflecting the investigator's beginnings or endings.[31] I find myself wanting to be reflexive, moving back and forth between the two, each enlightening the other. Sometimes this occurs within and sometimes between research projects. Martyn does this too, although he seems again to be a bit more discipline-oriented and experience-distant.

Audience becomes an additional concept in a theory of ethnographic methodology. By happenstance early, and deliberate choice later, I find myself in an Education Department, teaching pre-service and in-service courses for teachers. I no longer maintain a joint appointment in psychology (although I have acquired a courtesy appointment in anthropology). The psychologists seem to not only think differently (experimentally rather than ethnographically) but have different audiences than me. Martyn seems to remain very much a sociologist. Gains and losses occur from the stance one takes here.

I believe that it is important to conceptualize the behaviour, action and interaction of the researcher with the same theoretical concepts and theories that one uses to conceptualize the behaviour, action and interaction of the subjects in the research setting. I find the lack of this a fatal flaw in behaviourism and some forms of sociological functionalism. It has led me towards a kind of symbolic interactionism. At root, Martyn and I seem to be in a similar camp here, although we may be moving in different directions from this similar point of departure.

Finally, a growing concern with ethical issues in ethnographic fieldwork has left me with different kinds of discomfort with some of the research I have done over the years. The pieces I have felt best about were those which tended towards a variant of what is now called action research. The involvement with at least some of the individuals in the setting as co-participants, co-investigators and co-authors seems to fit the way I want to live a large part of my professional life. Inextricably, the larger issues of education as a value-laden activity requiring a value-laden theory surface here as well as at other points. Once again, I am not arguing for one right way. Rather I am trying to highlight significant issues in the construal of ethnography. None of the essays in this volume brings ethical issues to the forefront (nor is the word indexed in Hammersley and Atkinson).[32]

Whether these methodological issues cut 'nature at its joints', or even whether that is a provocative metaphor, I will leave to Martyn, to the methodological theorists, and to each of you, the readers of this collection of essays. The essays themselves are done so powerfully that they force one to keep examining in more and more depth one's own research practices.

Conclusion

This essay has taken on an unusual form, occasioned by the particular timing of the task, the cultural context, the interestingly separate but intertwined intellectual interests we have, the flux existing within educational ethnography, and the mutual dependency of these items. My overall intent has been to heighten the dialogue, initially between Martyn and me, then between him and my students, and now among the readers of this collection of his papers. I believe that this dialogue is important, for Martyn is one of the most acute observers and analysts of the classroom scene and one of the most intense reflectors upon his experience as an ethnographer. It is rare to find someone who does first-rate fieldwork, who knows so much of the literature, and who has such insight into the process. It has been a pleasure to join in and to learn with him.

PART 1

Empirical Research

1 The Organization of Pupil Participation[1]

This article was one of the first detailed studies of the organization of classroom talk. It was a product of my research on an inner-city secondary modern school (Downtown), focusing in particular on the hierarchical structure of classroom interaction and the assumptions about knowledge, learning and intelligence built into it. The teachers at Downtown adopted an extremely 'traditional' pedagogy, in which whole-class question and answer sessions played a major part. Their views about the nature of education were also very traditional. My analysis in this article takes the form of an implicit comparison of the structure of interaction at Downtown with that which is characteristic of ordinary conversation.

The purpose of this chapter is largely descriptive: to give an account of an aspect of the order that the teachers in one school seek to impose on classroom interaction.[2] Analysis of that order is essential for any satisfactory account of pupil actions. The explanation of pupil orientations in terms of 'background' or even 'subculture' is premature without detailed attention to the organization of the school and particularly to the nature of the 'teaching' in classrooms.

Attention to teachers' classroom activities is also important for any account of schools as 'socializing' agencies seeking to mould pupils in terms of a particular version of cultural competence. It is in relation to some such notions of competence and achievement that pupils are judged by teachers to be 'bright', 'stupid', etc. Assessments of a person's intelligence are based on evaluations of his performances at particular activities and in particular circumstances. Whatever the claims of those doing the assessment, it is essential to investigate the conditions under which those who are being evaluated must act if they are to be seen as 'intelligent', and the conception of intelligence in terms of which they are being judged – the activities that are taken as crucial and the criteria of 'success' or 'intelligent attempt' that are applied. Schools are agencies assigning particular importance to certain activities and able to a considerable degree to impose a particular definition of achievement on pupils.

My focus here is the way in which the teachers in a particular school work to organize pupil participation in classrooms and the relevance of that organization for the 'intelligence' pupils are required to show. The nature of the knowledge which the teachers present, in terms of which pupils must display their 'intelligence', is an equally important topic, but, like the overall organization of the school, will have to be left to another paper.

The teachers set out to establish and maintain the 'proper attention' of pupils to official proceedings in the classroom.[3] Pupils are to watch and listen to the teacher when he is at the front talking and to 'follow' what he says. When written work is set they are to get on with it 'sensibly', 'carefully' and at a 'reasonable' speed. The teacher monitors pupil behaviour and sometimes when he detects inattention he will look up from working at his desk or interrupt his discourse in order to demand attention.

However, the establishment and maintenance of attention is only one element of the teachers' concern with 'discipline' in the classroom. They do not merely require pupils to pay attention but also to participate. Pupil participation, though, should conform to certain rules: the teacher tries to reduce classroom interaction to a two-party format, with himself as one speaker and one or another pupil acting as the other. Furthermore, he reserves for himself the right to talk to the whole class and to produce extended utterances, often ruling pupil initiatives out of order. He is therefore faced with the problem of making pupils behave as one, subordinate, participant.

The teacher provides for pupil participation by asking questions. However, problems necessarily arise since only one slot is provided for the participation of a large number of pupils. Potentially, some 17 speakers are competing for one answer slot. From the point of view of the teachers, the classroom encounter as an interaction system, focused on and co-ordinated from the front, can just as easily disintegrate as a result of 'over-participation' by pupils as it can by escalating inattention. The teachers seek a solution to this problem by insisting that they select answerers, either directly or indirectly. Direct selection involves tagging a question with a name or 'One of you four', 'You', combined with pointing, etc.

(a) T: First of all let's have a, a little bit of revision, on what
                     we've done so far since Christmas. Our friend Leach can
                     tell us what we *need*, to make iron
     P: Iron?
     T: Yes iron
     P: Sir is it carbon sir?
     P: Sir   Sir
                          (
     T: Dear me, tell us
                     Richardson in a clear voice
                          (
                          Sir
     P: Sir y'use iron ore sir an' put it in a blast furnace y'need
                     coke, iron-coke
     P: Limestone
     P: Limestone and iron ore sir

T:	Good, in what kind of furnace Short?
P: ,	Blast
P:	Ehr blast furnace
T:	In a *blast* furnace. Good. What type of temperature do we need? (H)

More frequently, teachers enforce indirect selection: the teacher asks a question, calls for 'hands up' or waits for hands to go up automatically, and then appoints an answerer by naming, pointing, nodding, looking or whatever, from among those with raised hands.

(b)　T:　　If you listened carefully to that story yesterday you'll have noticed that two things in the story created terror, anybody remember what they were?

　　P:　　Sir

　　T:　　Don't sir just put your hand up. Campbell?

　　P:　　Head–headless horse, headless horses pulling a wagon sir
　　　　　(

　　T:　　　　　　　Headless horses pulling a carriage yes that's one very good
　　　　　　　　　(

　　P:　　　　　　· Sir
　　　　　((Pause, then the teacher appoints))

　　P:　　The castle

　　T:　　The castle, I don't think so may 'ave done but may alright we'll accept the castle

　　P:　　(Laughing) sir

　　P: ((appointed))　When he saw the knight

　　T:　　When he saw the knight yes but there was something before then
　　　　　　　　(

　　P:　　　　　Sir

　　T:　　I think there was the headless horseman which is something that he *saw*

　　P:　　Sir

　　P:　　Sir
　　　　　　　(

　　P:　　　　　Sir

　　P: ((appointed))　When he heard that laughing sound

　　T:　　Yes the noise, the laughter (W)

Selection of answerers is backed up with demands that pupils 'don't "sir" ', 'don't shout out', speak 'one at a time', etc. As with the maintenance of 'attention', the preservation of 'one speaker at a time' is a continuous concern, the teacher issuing demands for 'disciplined' participation when he judges things to be getting out of hand. At times, however, the teachers seem to worsen the problem of 'over-participation' by refusing to ask those with their hands up, clamouring to answer:

(c) T: What, in what way Crick, in what way was the river a
                 bit of a problem to them a problem or a
                                                    (
     P: (Washing)
     T: nuisance
                 (
     P: Sir
     P: Sir
     P: Sir
     P: Sir
     P: Sir
     P: Sir
                 (
     T: It had its good things but it also
                                          (
     P: Sir
                                          (
     P: Sir
     T: had its bad side
     P: Sir (   )
                     (
     P: Sir
                       (
     P: Sir
                          (
     T: Just a minute hands down
     Pn: Augh: :
     T: Look at this side of the class what's the matter with them
     Pn: Sir   Sir
     T: Numbskulls c'mon
     Pn: Sir   Sir
     T: Wha–what–where d'you think a river can be a nuisance?
     P: Yes sir
     P: Sir
     T: If you lived in a village an' there was a river running
                 right past it, in what way would the river be a nuisance
     P: Sir   Sir
     T: a problem?
     Pn: Sir   Sir
     T: Now look, I can see you, I don't need to have a silly
                 chorus, y'sound like a lot of little sparrows bumbling
                 away in the hedgebottom
     Pn: ((Mimics of sparrows))
     T: It's somebody over this side I'd like to hear from. What
                 way could a river be said to be a nuisance yes? (D)

On such occasions, the teacher is attempting to maximize the attention of all members of the class by demonstrating the potential built into directly selective questions for the embarrassment of pupils who have not been 'following' the lesson. The problems of participation control that this kind of action causes point to a conflict of purpose facing the teacher: the more successful he is in generating pupil motivation to attend and participate, the greater may be his problems in controlling participation. However, this is not just a problem for teachers but one which also faces pupils. Pupils' 'failure' to conform fully to the participation rules is not to be explained in terms of their perversity or on the grounds that they are operating on the basis of values opposite to those of the school. If these explanations were correct, it could be expected that there would be a refusal to answer questions rather than the clamour that generally occurs.[4] The teachers demand participation and differentiate pupils on the basis of the 'quality' of that participation, yet the form which official participation must take is highly restricted and there are only limited opportunities, given the number of pupils in a class.[5] It is not surprising, therefore, that considerable unofficial participation occurs.[6]

However, there is no need to assume that clamour to answer the teachers' questions is simply the product of successful mobilization by the teachers. On many occasions, pupils seemed to be pursuing their own rather different purposes. They seemed to be using the teacher as a quizmaster, turning teacher questions into a contest. Acclaim from other pupils appeared to be desired as much as praise from the teacher, and the aim to be not the building of an academic career but the acquisition of a reputation for smartness.[7]

To be successful in demonstrating 'intelligence' to the teacher or in the quiz, a pupil must get his answers heard and if possible accepted by the teacher as 'the right answer'. But a pupil is only one among many, a good number of whom may be equally anxious to provide the answer. It is known that the teacher very rarely asks all those offering answers and sometimes does not ask any of them. Even if the teacher does start an answer-round, there is always the danger that another pupil will come up with 'the right answer' and thus stop the round (unless the question asked for the members of a list); that someone-else will suggest the answer which the pupil is seeking to present and thus make it difficult for him to claim it as his own; or that the teacher may stop the round to reformulate or drop the question before the pupil has had chance to get his answer in.

These contingencies explain why pupils are not content merely to put their hands up and wait to be selected. Pupils use two main strategies in trying to win the competition. They may try inserting 'answers' as soon as or just before the teacher has apparently finished the question. It is important to get in first for the reasons I have mentioned and because if the answer is 'right' the teacher may, or may be forced to, accept it despite the fact that it was 'shouted out'. The insertion of answers maximizes the possibility of success if the answer turns out to be adequate. Identifying the point of question completion, however, is no easy matter, since teachers often repeat, elaborate or reformulate questions before they actually begin to select answerers. Hence pupils often find themselves talking simultaneously with each other and with the teacher, and this reduces, even if it does not eliminate, the chances of getting an answer heard and accepted.

Instead of 'shouting out' his answer, a pupil may seek explicitly to summon the teacher by the use of 'sir'. 'Sir' has the obverse advantages to answer insertion, being of short duration and immediate impact; it is easily insertible into what turns out to have been a minor pause, and requires little work at understanding. Indeed 'sir' is often inserted into what must be recognized as non-terminal pauses in teacher or official pupil talk in the hope of turning them into terminal pauses and securing the floor – a strategy which trades on both the features mentioned above. 'Sir' works, if it works, like all summonses: if the teacher replies and replies with an invitation to speak not a deferral (with 'yes' not 'hold on a minute'), the pupil is then virtually guaranteed a hearing. The aim of a summons is not just to attract attention but to gain the floor and the deferential character of 'sir' is important in this. While something like 'Hey you' would be doubly effective in attracting the teachers' attention and quieting competitors, it would be unlikely to result in the speaker being able to present his answers. This highlights the problem pupils face in answering teachers' questions. To obey the rules by not 'shouting out', or even trying to summon the teacher with 'sir', involves the danger of losing the chance of the floor to other less conforming answerers. On the other hand, to be the most effective competitor opens a pupil up to charges of 'bad manners'. To the extent that pupils are quiz-motivated they will care little about being labelled 'bad mannered', but there is always the danger that the teacher may ignore or rule out an answer simply on the grounds that it was inappropriately presented or that he will not appoint an answerer who tries to summon him with 'sir'. Pupils have to make some trade-off between the two sources of possible failure on every answering occasion.

The point of the above analysis of pupil answering is to suggest that, first, there are reasons for pupil deviance built into the organization the teachers seek to impose on classroom interaction; and, secondly, that pupils' orientations are not usually simply for or against school but generally involve using or attempting to adapt its organization to make something 'valuable', 'bearable', 'enjoyable' and/or functional for certain purposes. There are of course limitations to pupils doing this, but then there are also limits to the teachers' power to prevent such 'making out'.

Pupils are not wholly restricted to offering answers to teacher questions; they do make initiatives, again sometimes inserting them in gaps they hope are adequate, sometimes trying to summon the teacher. In making initiatives pupils operate under the same constraints as in the presentation of answers. The teachers do not totally proscribe pupil initiatives but they frequently ignore 'shouted out' initiatives and 'sirs' and demand that pupils 'do not talk while I'm talking' and speak 'one at a time', though even raised hands are sometimes ignored or waved down by teachers.

The teachers insist on their control of pupil initiatives, as on their control of pupil answers, in order to control the setting and maintenance of topic. The teacher 'starts the lesson' by embarking on the topic he has decided to deal with in the lesson.

(d) ((Noise of class entering and talking))

P: Sir can we read those short stories?

((Movement noise and talking continues, apparently no answer from the teacher))

T: Right a'right close your books look this way. Now, you boys at the back, no reason why you shouldn't have books, are there any more left?

P: No sir

T: Right then eh will you share with him please, (   ) you share with him. All you need to do is . . . ((Much shuffling of chairs)) All you need to do is to sit . . . ((Noise continues)) Oh dear me can we have the noise stopped as soon as possible. Now look this way, close books and look this way. Anybody tell me, keep your feet still, and everything else, anybody tell me what a legend is?

P: It's a story

T: Sh: : what is a legend?

P: Sir it's a story that's been told thousands and thousands of years ago and people still believe in it. (W)

The teacher always starts the topic talk and his right to do so is never challenged, although the first utterance in (d) above seems to be an attempt to influence the lesson by suggestion. Note, however, that the suggestion is framed as a request, tagged with 'sir', and that the pupil does not insist on an answer. Not only are pupils given no rights in topic establishment, the teacher only rarely provides pupils with any initial indication of what the topic he has decided on is, or what he intends to teach them in this lesson. He launches straight into the lesson and they are required to pick up the pieces as he goes along. The expectation that they correctly construct 'what this lesson is about' from what he says as the lesson goes on may well be intended as, and certainly operates as, an attention-maintaining device, relying on the relevance of 'what this lesson is about' to the provision of answers to the teacher's questions.

Having set the topic by starting out on it, the teacher controls and develops it himself by speaking for extended periods and controlling pupil participation:

(e) T: A little while ago there was a general election, that is a time when everybody who can *vote* that's most people over the age of?

Pn: Eighteen

T: Over eighteen that's right when the people who can vote vote for the persons that they would like to represent them in parliament, and to *try an' make* people vote for them, the men who are trying to get into parliament often go and *visit* people whose votes they are trying to catch. Our MP did that, he came round in an open sports car with one of his helpers driving with himself

not sitting on the back seat but sitting on the back of the car with his feet on the back seat so that he was raised up a little bit, in shirt sleeves, it was a sunny evening and he
(

P: Blah blah blah

T: That's right, saying things like that through a mega-phone saying vote for me I am a good bloke I have been in parliament for umpteen years y'can't go far wrong with me. His name is Sir --- ---. What do we call someone who is allowed to put 'sir' before their name?

P: Knight

T: What?

P: (Lord)

T: He's a knight, that's right. Now there are lots of *knights about*, people called Sir something or other some of them become Sir 'cos their dads were called Sir and some of them are called Sir because the Queen decides to reward them for something that they've done. Can you think of any recent people who've been made a Sir for something that they've done?

P: Sir Alf Ramsey

P: Sir Alf Ramsey

T: Alf Ramsey. When England won the World Cup in sixty-six he was just plain Mr Alf Ramsey and he became Sir

P: Sir Stan Matthews

P: Francis Chichester

T: Francis Chichester because he was a lone yachtsman he sailed round the world

P: Stanley Matthews

T: Stanley Matthews is an earlier footballer

P: Sir Walter Raleigh

T: Sir Walter Raleigh, now there's one going back a bit isn't it, which Queen made him a knight?

P: Victoria

P: Elizabeth

T: The first Elizabeth that's right, all the others that we've mentioned were made knights by?

P: (   )

T: The present Elizabeth, Raleigh was made a knight by the first Elizabeth, well he was a knight in her reign.

P: Sir Francis Drake

T: Sir Francis Drake was another of the knights of the first Queen Elizabeth's reign

P: Alexander Fleming

T: Erh yes he was rewarded for his work on a famous drug

	which can cure people, can you see what it is by looking around?
P:	Penicillin
T:	Penicillin, oh there now, it used to be just there ((pointing to wall)) didn't it, Alexander Fleming one of those little people, it used to be there. Penicillin is a famous drug which is used in just about every hospital in the world to cure diseases and Alexander Fleming was a scientist who discovered what it could be used for, now that's obviously important and he was knighted for it. Now a little while ago when we were talking about the set-up in Norman England with the King at the top and the serfs the ordinary people down at the bottom we mentioned knights then. Now if you could imagine a ladder with four rungs on it the King was on the top of his own, the serfs were right at the bottom and the other groups were knights and lords and barons now which of those two groups would come higher up the ladder?
P:	Barons
T:	The barons. The knights were very often ordinary skilled fighting men who ended up being employed by a more important baron or lord. Remember also in Norman times each person *including* the barons and the knights each person *owed* his land to somebody else, he had his land thanks to somebody else above him (B)

Teacher questions form the major opportunity for pupils officially to participate in the lesson. But these questions differ from questions in other settings in two respects. First, the teacher demands and is accorded the right routinely to command, interpret and openly judge answers. Secondly, they are not usually requests for information, opinions, experiences, etc., unknown to the questioner. The teacher knows the answer he wants and although he may occasionally be surprised by an unanticipated answer which is 'right' in some respect, it is always *he* who decides the status of any 'answer'. These two features result in question rounds aimed at forcing 'clarification':

(f)	T:	In a *blast* furnace. Good. What type of temperature do we need, ahm Calder, what type of temperature do we need?
	P:	Sir very high temperature
	T:	Yes that's pretty obvious but what *type of range* are we talking about? Three candle power?
	Pn:	((Laughs))
	P:	A thousand degrees
	T:	A thousand degrees
	P:	Right

T: Any advance on a thousand?
                           (

P: Sir

P: Fo-fourteen hundred
                  (

P: Sir   fourteen hundred

T: Really

P: 'Bout eight 'undred
                      (

P: 'Bout fifteen 'undred sir, 'bout fifteen 'undred
                    (

T: Now let's get this straight we're not talking about the melting point of *iron* we're talking about the melting po-or the, the maximum needed or the minimum needed in a blast furnace to release the iron from the iron ore

P: About eight hundred sir

P: Eight thousand sir, eight hundred and fifty

P: Sixteen hundred sir
                    (

T: Now look we-we've really got confused with this. We need a *minimum* of
                    (

P: Seven thousand (   )

T: two thousand degrees *centigrade*. Once you've got the iron out then yer fourteen fifteen hundred degrees centigrade was about right (H)

(g) T: Anybody tell me what a legend is?

      P: It's a story

      T: Sh : :   what is a legend?

      P: Sir its a story that's been told thousands and thousands of years ago and people still believe in it

      T: A story that's been told thousands and thousands of years and people still believe in it. Can anyone improve on that answer?

      Pn: Sir   Sir

      P: Sir it's a story that's been made about something that's happened and er people—everybody knows about it (nearly everybody) sir

      T: Yes. Yes Campbell?

      P: Sir it's half-true and half not true sir

      T: It's?

      P: Sir sort of made up sir, half true

      T: It's half true, yes. The actual definition, that means the meaning, of a legend is a story that is, probably true but not absolutely true. Can anybody tell me a legend they know? (W)

The teacher knows the answer he wants because he knows the point he is trying to make; the question he asks is designed to get pupils to make that point. He asks questions to which he wants a particular answer and he will work until he gets that answer or some substitute or until he decides to provide it himself.

The teacher's framing of his questions and his treatment of pupil answers and initiatives are lesson-planning decisions – decisions about the topical organization of the lesson; what the topic is, what points will be made, in what order and detail, with what slant, in order to carry on from and lead on to what, etc. It is the teacher who makes all these decisions; he continuously organizes his talk as a lesson-long phenomenon and it is *his* talk which officially constitutes the lesson. Pupils are officialy limited to making or trying to make contributions to his talk, their participation is not on their own terms but on his; they are expected to listen to what he says and follow his development of the topic in order to 'learn'.

The underlying image is of the transmission of knowledge from teacher to pupils. What is to be learned is pre-ordained: pupil contributions must either reproduce something already known by the teacher or be judged correct in terms of his criteria. There is no question of pupils exploring or discovering in an open-ended kind of way; 'what has to be learned' would not be learned in that fashion. The teachers set out to teach a body of knowledge, but this knowledge is not seen as something which simply might be useful to pupils but rather as something anyone *should* know; it constitutes a definition of cultural competence. Hence, pupils are not accorded the ability to judge the education they are receiving, they must subordinate themselves to the teacher and be taught. The function of the teacher is not seen as to entertain them or to minister to their 'psychological needs' or 'social problems', but to render them 'culturally competent' up to the level of their 'capacities'. The teacher is the source of 'knowledge' and therefore his communications must dominate proceedings, he must be free to direct pupils so as to maximize their 'learning' and he must be allowed to present the curriculum in an 'orderly' fashion.

The teachers in this school seek to organize classroom interaction on a two-party basis, reserving for themselves the rights to extended speech, speaker selection, evaluation of pupil contributions, and thus the control of lesson-topic. There are reasons for pupils not to conform fully to the participation rules built into this organization itself, besides those deriving from particular pupil orientations to school activities. But, by one means or another, the teachers to a large extent successfully impose an order on classroom interaction which enables them to set the topic, expound at length on it, and make pupil answers and initiatives contribute to it.

In order consistently to display their 'intelligence' to the teachers and to their fellows, pupils must command the necessary cultural resources both to work out what the teacher is getting at in questions and to construct answers which meet his requirements. They must also, for one reason or another, be prepared to adopt the teacher's topical interests. Similarly with initiatives, since the teacher decides what the lesson-topic is to be and continuously defines its proper bounds and inner structure, to display 'intelligence' a pupil must orient to that topic and either add something 'valuable' or anticipate what the teacher is about to say. Thus, in order to 'learn', to develop the cultural resources required to answer questions or produce 'acceptable' initiatives in the future, pupils must have been attending to and 'correctly' processing teachers' talk in the past, and in the present must follow at the pace the teacher sets, covering the ground he deems relevant, and going by the route he decides is appropriate.

To demonstrate 'intelligence' also requires accepting the teacher's claims legitimately to speak for long periods, to ask questions to which he knows the answers, and to be the ultimate arbiter of candidate answers. This is true whether the pupil's aim is to impress the teacher or other pupils. Thus, an even more basic requirement for the display of 'intelligence' is 'recognition', at least for working purposes, of the teacher's 'right' to organize classroom interaction, of the authority the teacher claims.[8] Every time a pupil answers a teacher's questions, allows him to control the topic, or accepts his evaluations of answers or initiatives, even by default, that interaction can be seen by the pupil, other pupils and the teacher as symbolizing and reinforcing the teacher–pupil, superordinate–subordinate relationship. There were signs on many occasions in the lessons I observed that the interaction was being seen in that way by the participants.

These two conditions of 'intelligent' answering indicate the importance of the way in which the teachers organize classroom interaction. Furthermore, they apply not only to the pupils' oral contributions, with which I have been concerned here, but also to the written work that is set. The teachers stress the importance of 'proper presentation' of written work; they formulate the task, which usually derives from the oral lesson-topic; and they mark the work in relation to 'what was wanted'. The investigation of what constitutes 'school achievement' is essential both for sense to be made of pupils' actions and for the analysis of schools as socializing agencies.

Key to transcriptions

T:	Teacher speaks
P:	Pupil speaks
Pn:	Two or more pupils speaking at once
(( ))	Observer descriptions
( )	Uncertain/guessed materials
(H), (W), (B), (D)	The four teachers whose lessons have been quoted from
Sir Sir (Dear me	Speech overlap
need	Raised voice
Sh: :	Sound prolonged
All you . . .	Speech tails off

2 School Learning: The Cultural Resources Required by Pupils to Answer a Teacher's Question[1]

This second chapter deals with the other precondition of the successful answering of teachers' questions mentioned in Chapter 1: the ability to interpret the question to identify the answer that the teacher has in mind. The analysis deals with a single lesson, and the process by which the teacher organizes the interaction so that pupils provide 'the right answer' at the 'right' time. In key respects, this pattern of questioning represents the style of teaching that was dominant at Downtown.

Selection and socialization have for a long time been the terms in which the functioning of education systems in industrial societies has been conceptualized in the sociology of education.[2] By selection is meant the allocation of pupils to categories receiving differential treatment, whether within the same school class or by means of distribution to different classes or different schools. This process is seen as resulting in differential life chances via the award of credentials which determine school-leavers' positions on the labour market. By socialization I mean attempts to shape pupils in terms of certain cultural ideals, cognitive and moral, whether one set of ideals is seen as applicable to all pupils or different sets are regarded as appropriate to the different categories of pupils produced by selection.

It is only relatively recently, however, that any real investigation of the nature of selection and socialization processes in schools has occurred. The first move in this direction, represented by the work of Hargreaves and Lacey,[3] shifted the focus from the inputs and outputs of the education system to streaming and its consequences for pupil achievement. More recently still, attention has been given to social interaction between teachers and pupils in the classroom. The central concerns have been the assumptions about humanity, society, knowledge, learning and children built into particular forms of teaching, the complex interpretive practices involved in teacher–pupil interaction, the process by which teachers come to categorize pupils, teachers' construction of 'classroom order' and 'school knowledge', and the perspectives pupils develop to make sense of and adapt to school.

In this chapter I want to investigate the nature of learning in school by focusing on a teacher's question, albeit one which took up a whole lesson. Teacher-asks-a-question-pupils-answer is a central interactional form in classrooms, in both oral and written media. My interest in this question concerns what the pupils have to do to answer it.[4] The nature of the cultural resources required to answer teacher questions has implications both for what pupils must do in school in order to 'do well' in selection terms, and for what they might learn, for what 'world' they are being socialized into.

The transcript: Selected excerpts from a secondary school English lesson[5]

Key to transcription

T:	Teacher talks
P:	Pupil talks
Pn:	Two or more pupils speaking at once
(( ))	Observer descriptions
( )	Uncertain/guessed materials
Sir Sir	
(	Speech overlap
Dear me	
need	Raised voice
Sh : : :	Sound prolonged
All you . . .	Speech tails off
: : : :	Part of transcript omitted
long-it's–sir	Utterance reformulation

No. 1

1	T:	Last week we were talking about legends, and we read a
2		Greek legend about a king who wanted to kill his son
3		and as it happened he wasn't able to, in the end, his son
		took over the kingdom. Now we have modern legends
		of course today
4	P:	Sir there's one (on telly) tonight
5	T:	We have modern legends today but we're not going to
6		concern ourselves with legends this lesson. Would you
7		mind closing *the book*. ( ) We have different kinds of
8		story today, and a very interesting kind of story is a tall
		story, what does that mean a *tall* story?
9	P:	Sir
10	T:	(Put that back)
11	P:	(Yes)
12	T:	Well what does tall mean?
13	P:	Big

14	T:	Big a big story d'you think that's right? What do you mean by big story then?

          (

15	P:	Yeh
16	T:	What would you think a big story meant Dicey?
17	P:	Sir is it eh a long one sir?
18	T:	A *long* one, maybe anybody any other suggestion c'mon what's a tall story?

          ((

19	P:	/ Sir Sir

                                             (

20	P:	Sir
21	T:	( ) Can you give me any suggestions as to what a tall story is?

:   :   :   :

                         ((Interruption))

:   :   :   :

22	T:	Now we're trying to find out what a tall story is, Dicey
23		suggests a very long story, (could) be, anybody, c'mon you must have some suggestions, a tall story

                    (

24	P:	Sir

                                       (

25	P:	Sir
26	T:	What do you think it is Thompson?
27	P:	Sir it's half true.
28	T:	A story that is half true. All right, that's an attempt, anyway look at all these

                  (

29	P:	Sir
30	T:	people, no attempt.
31	P:	Sir
32	T:	I can think of a meaning
33	P:	Sir a lie sir
34	T:	A lie
35	P:	Yes sir
36	T:	A story that is a lie, could be
37	P:	Sir a stupid story
38	T:	A stupid story
39	P:	A story that did happen
40	T:	A story that did happen
41	P:	Yes sir
42	T:	Do you think it might be a story about a giant, a tall story, anybody think that?
43	P:	No sir
44	T:	Anybody think it might be a story written on a long piece of paper?

45	P:	Sir
46	T:	Instead of in a book, well there are plenty of suggestions
47		all I asked you for was for suggestions
48	P:	Sir, sir it could've been ( )
49	T:	It was yes, could be a tall story that the story's written on a long scroll of paper.
50		Y'think that's what it is? Anyway we've got several
51		suggestions. Half true, not true, true
52	P:	Stupid
53	T:	a lie, stupid, any of these, a tall story. Can anybody tell
54		me any story, a short story of any kind. Anybody tell me a short story that is a sort of joke
55	P:	Sir
56	T:	can tell me a joke. Nobody knows a joke
		(
57	P:	( )
58	T:	*Good heavens.* Who can tell me a joke yes, c'mon then tell us a joke, c'mon then
59	Pn:	( )
60	P:	Sir ( )
61	T:	tell us a joke
62	P:	Sir which bird goes down a coal mine, a minah bird
63	T:	That's a riddle not a joke (anyone have a joke) that's a riddle
		(
64	Pn:	((Laughs))
65	P:	Sir what was . . .
		(
66	T:	Ah ah I don't want a riddle I want a joke
:		: : : :
		((Three pupils provide jokes))
:		: : : :
67	T:	A'right that'll do fine. Now, those are *jokes*. Now we're
68		trying to find our what a tall story is so let's read one
69		example and then see if you can tell me what a tall story is. Turn to page one hundred and thirty five. Sh : : :
70		( ) Right, My name as all the world knows is Baron
71		Munchausen. I want to tell you about one of my exploits, exploits, give me another word for exploits
72	P:	Exploring
73	T:	No, another word for exploit
		(
74	Pn:	( )
75	P:	Journeys
76	P:	Journeys
77	P:	Journeys

78	T:	Journeys no
79	P:	Adventures
80	T:	Adventures good lad. It happened during the siege of Gibraltar, what's a *siege*?
81	P:	Sir
82	P:	Sir
83	T:	A siege, during the siege of Gibraltar, I can't get much
84		out of you people at the back can I?
85	P:	Yes sir
86	P:	Sir
87	T:	I don't think you ever pay attention to what's going on, the *siege* of Gibraltar

                                       (

88	P:	Sir
89	P:	Sir is it a sort of landscape?
90	T:	A landscape
91	P:	(The landscape of Gibraltar)
92	T:	No
93	P:	Sir when (ehm sir) when an army surrounds a town sir ( ) . . .

                                      (

94	T:	Very good when
95		a town is surrounded by an army and nothing can go in
96		and out then the town is said to be a-having a siege,
97		when Gibraltar was surrounded nobody could go in an' nobody could go out so it was the siege of Gibraltar.

No. 2

98	T:	Good thank you. Anybody doesn't know what a telescope is?
99	P:	Yes
100	T:	Who does *not* know?
101	P:	((Laugh))
102	T:	You all know what a telescope is?
103	P:	Yes sir
104	T:	Good tell me tell me what a telescope is then Dicey
105	P:	Sir it's a long glass sir
106	T:	A long?
107	P:	Glass
108	T:	A long glass
109	P:	Sir
110	P:	Sir
111	T:	When you take it can you pour a pint of beer in it then
112	P:	Sir
113	T:	If it's a long glass?
114	P:	Sir
115	Pn:	((Laughs))

116	Pn:	Sir sir
117	T:	Sh please give Dicey a chance he knows what it is I'm
118		trying to ask for it. Have another try
119	P:	Sir a long-it's-sir it's like a long glass it's got a eh
120	Pn:	((Noise))
121	T:	Can you keep quiet and give him a chance
122	P:	a magnifying glass at the end sir (one little at one end
123		and a big one at the other and you look through the little end)
124	T:	It's not a long glass it's a long tube, isn't it?
125	P:	Yes sir
126	T:	with er lenses each end correct a'right that was a very
127		good try after a bit when you got yourself sorted out

No. 3

128	T:	This writer says he ordered the cannonball to be fired
129		from Gibraltar from inside the garrison at the same time
130		as the enemy (over here) fired their cannonball. His
131		cannonball hit the other one at such a force that it drove
132		it back, it killed a man who fired it, went rushing
133		through the cavalry killed sixteen more an' went *straight*
134		on from Gibraltar over the Mediterranean, the little
135		channel there – you know where Gibraltar is do you? Yes I'm sure you do here we have Gibraltar something like this, coming out like that, and here you have the land just here like this, an' it flew across this coast
136	P:	Right across the straits
137	T:	right across the straits that narrow area of water, and
138		kept on going, destroyed the masts of some ships, finally landed in somebody's house in a room
139	P:	( )
140	T:	Do you believe that?
141	P:	(Yes) sir
142	P:	(No sir)
143	T:	Y'don't why not?
144	P:	Sir ( ) it could be true
145	P:	( ) could be true
146	P:	Sir
147	T:	Could be true
148	P:	Sir
149	P:	Sir sir (it'd blow up) . . .
		(
150	T:	One at a time
151	P:	Sir it'd blow up
152	T:	Wouldn't blow up if it were a cannonball
153	P:	Yes sir (with shock it'd blow up)

154	T:	May be may be
155	P:	Sir cannons didn't 'av' the power to send it that fast
156	P:	They did ( ) . . .
		(
157	T:	Didn't have the power to send it that fast or that far alright so you
		(
158	P:	( )
159	T:	don't believe it on the whole let's see what 'appens then

No. 4

160	T:	Good. So the cannonball by now very small I suppose, went into the lady's throat
161	P:	( )
162	P:	( )
163	T:	as she lay asleep with her mouth open snoring away
164	P:	((Imitation of snoring))
165	T:	knocked out a few teeth, when her husband came home
166		and tried to get it out, couldn't get it out, so he took a
167		ramrod, a long rod, an' he jammed it down her throat and into her stomach, d'believe that?
168	P:	Sir (he'd choke her sir) . . .
		(
169	T:	D'you believe that?
170	P:	Sir she would die
171	Pn:	( )
		(
172	T:	Is it possible?
173	Pn:	No sir
		(
174	Pn:	No sir
175	P:	Sir it'd get stuck
176	T:	Is it pòssible?
177	P:	Sir ( )
178	Pn:	No ( ) . . .
		(
179	T:	Have you ever
180		swallowed a whole pea?
181	P:	Sir ( )
182	P:	Yes ( )
		(
183	T:	You said it's not possible
184	Pn:	Sir
185	Pn:	( ) . . .
		(

186	T:	Have you ever swallowed a pill?
187	P:	Yes sir ( ) . . .
		(
188	P:	Sir I ( ) . . .
		(
189	T:	'Av' you ever swallowed a gob-stopper?
190	Pn:	No sir
191	Pn:	( )
		(
192	T:	Yes sir
193	P:	No
194	T:	Have you ever read stories of people going to hospital having swallowed marbles?
195	Pn:	(Yes, sir)
		(
196	Pn:	Yes sir
		(
197	Pn:	( )
		(
198	P:	No sir ( )
199	T:	Is it possible?
200	P:	Cannonball'd be as big as yer head
201	T:	But this is a *smaller* one now it's been worn out its been
202		worn away it's been travelling a long way it's been knocked about, it wouldn't be it couldn't be a
		(
203	P:	(Yes sir)
204	T:	big cannonball go in her mouth could it'd 'av' to be small
		(
205	P:	No
206	Pn:	( )
		(
207	T:	Didn't 'av' a mouth the size of a cage did she?
208	Pn:	((Laughs))
209	T:	Is it possible?
210	P:	Yes sir
		(
211	Pn:	Yes sir
212	T:	Is it probably not possible?
213	P:	No
214	Pn:	( )
		(
215	P:	Yes
216	P:	Yes sir
		(

217	T:	Which is it more possible than impossible who would say it's possible?
218	P:	Ahm
219	T:	Who says it's more possible than impossible? Who says
220		it's more impossible than possible? A'right so we have a divided opinion. Right let's carry on from there
221	P:	Sir (can I?)
222	T:	Remember we didn't say it was probably possible that
223		the two cannonballs could hit in the middle and the
224		other one would travel back so fast, we said that was not
225		probable didn't we? Many of you didn't believe that,
226		you wouldn't believe that a cannonball could travel all this distance which is quite a long way. Possible, but highly improbable. Agreed?
227	P:	(S'pose so) sir
228	T:	Y'sure?
229	P:	Yes
230	T:	Right let's go on.

No. 5

231	T:	Now he says that their cannonball having given the
232		other one a fourpenny one and sent it backwards
233	Pn:	((Laughs))
		(
234	T:	carried on, hit the gun that'd been fired, destroyed
235		that n'went straight down into the ship, made the ship sink with everybody on board
236	P:	( )
237	T:	D'you believe that?
238	P:	Yes sir
239	Pn:	Yes sir
		(
240	Pn:	No sir
		(
241	T:	Who believes that absolutely, who believes it
242		absolutely, who thinks it's probable, who thinks it could
243		happen, who thinks it's most unlikely to happen. Good,
244		that's another thing then, notice this. Right let's go on.
245		'This to be sure was a most extraordinary exploit. I will
246		not however take all the credit myself. My judgement
247		was indeed the chief cause of its success, but chance also
248		helped me a little for I found out afterwards that the
249		soldier who charged our forty-eight pounder put in by
250		mistake a double quantity of powder, without that we
251		could never have succeeded so much beyond our ex-
252		pectations, especially in driving back the enemy's

253		cannonball.' Now here he's saying that by having two
254		amounts of powder, they made their cannonball go even
		faster, explosion made it go faster. Now that's a tall story,
		the story is called a tall story. Thinking over what we've
		said, would you mind sitting still ((Name)), thinking over
		what we've said about this story and what happens in it,
		think carefully, can you now tell me what a tall story is.
		This is a tall story.
255	P:	Sir
256	T:	What we've just read, now we talked about it and we
257		talked about those happenings, can you now tell me
		what in your opinion
258	P:	Yes sir
259	T:	is a tall story ((11 sec. pause. T. presumably decides
260		there's not enough hands up)) (Now) let's go back to
261		the beginning. How many of you believe absolutely as
262		truth, the fact that these two cannonballs could be fired
263		in such a way that they would meet and hit each other.
		Who believes that, absolutely true? Is it possible?
264	P:	Yes
265	P:	Yes sir
266	T:	Yes?
267	P:	Sir
268	T:	Who believes that the cannonball that was hit could do
269		all those things that this writer said it could, travelled all
270		that way and do all these things? Who believes that
271		absolutely as true, absolutely? Who thinks that it's poss-
272		ible but *very* improbable, it could happen but you don't
273		think it would? Right, good. How many of you believe
274		that, s'absolutely true, absolutely true without a shadow
275		of a doubt, this cannonball went in this woman's throat,
		couldn't move it and her husband rammed it down into
		her stomach, who believes that's absolutely true,
		absolutely, you do?
276	P:	Yes sir
277	T:	Who believes that it's possible but highly improbable,
278		who believes that it could happen but it probably didn't
279		happen, what do *you* think? Nothing, what do you be-
		lieve ((Name)), what do you think?
280	P:	Impossible
281	T:	Not at all possible?
282	P:	Sir it's very (improbable)
283	T:	Absolutely impossible, *absolutely*?
284	P:	Sir
285	T:	without a shadow of a doubt?
286	P:	Yes sir

287	T:	Right. Who believes, that this cannonball, hitting the
288		other one, could carry on and destroy the gun that fired it.
289		Who thinks it *might*, who thinks that it probably *wouldn't*?
290	P:	Sir
291	T:	Right. Don't go any further.
292	P:	( )
293	T:	This is called a tall story, what does it mean by a tall story?
294	P:	Sir
295	P:	Sir
296	P:	Sir
297	T:	What do you think we mean by a tall story?
298	P:	Sir
299	T:	Any of the things we suggested before or something
300		new, can you now tell me having read this tall story what a tall story is? Yes ((Name))?
301	P:	Sir a joke
302	T:	A joke, no it's funny but it's not a joke, try again.
303	P:	( )
304	P:	Sir ehm a story that's untrue
305	T:	(A story that's on stilts?)
306	P:	Sir that's not true
307	T:	That's not true
308	P:	Yes sir
309	T:	No
310	P:	Sir
311	P:	Sir is it one that's ehm got a lot of possible and impossible (things in it)
312	T:	S'got a lot of possible and impossible things in it. Could be
313	P:	Sir
314	P:	Sir
315	T:	Yes?
316	P:	Sir
317	P:	Sir
318	P:	Sir a story that could happen
319	T:	A story that could happen but every story is probably a story that could happen but every story's not a tall story.
320	P:	Sir, something which happened.
321	T:	That's what he said. That's what he said, something that happened.
322	P:	Sir (wasn't)
323	T:	Something that could happen
324	P:	Sir
325	P:	Sir summat that something happened and some people believe

326	T:	Well, I don't believe this story, does anybody here be-
327		lieve this story, anybody here believe this story, really
328		believe it? Nobody believes it. I don't think anybody
		would believe it, this is a tall story.
329	P:	Sir
330	P:	Sir is it a story that that nobody believes in, or summat
		like that?
331	T:	Ah . . . ((Laughing))
332	P:	Sir (is it a stupid story)
333	P:	Sir ( )
		(
334	T:	One at a time yes Dicey
335	P:	Unbelievable
336	T:	*An Unbelievable story*
337	P:	(I said that anyway)
338	P:	(So did I)
339	P:	Sir made up story sir
340	T:	Made up story, most stories are made up, if they're not
341		actual facts. Dicey's got the nearest an unbelievable
		story, that's nearest
342	P:	Sir impossible
343	T:	Not impossible. A tall story is one that is, very very
344		much exaggerated, y'know what exaggerated means?
345	P:	Yes sir
346	P:	Yes sir
347	T:	Well a tall story then is a story that's very very much
		exaggerated. I'll give you another example from this
		man Baron von Munchausen, close your books.

Commentary

In the first excerpt the teacher starts the lesson by formulating 'what we talked about last week' and setting this lesson's topic via a question about a 'different kind of story' to the type looked at the previous week.[6] So the teacher asks:

Line 8   T: What does that mean a *tall* story?

On the grounds that not enough hands go up he then indicates a method for finding an answer.

Line 12   T: Well what does tall mean?

The teacher directs pupils to scan the possible meanings of 'tall' to see if any of them could be sensibly combined with 'story'. Breaking down a problem into steps is a common strategy adopted by anyone in searching for solutions. It is also a device often used by teachers to make questions 'easier', thereby hopefully raising the number of pupils offering candidate answers and increasing the chances of a pupil providing 'the answer'.[7] Of course, the pupils or some of the pupils may themselves have already tried this method and got nowhere with it, produced no 'likely answer' or 'likely sense', or it may be that the answer thus produced appeared to them to be too easy.[8] Indeed, some of the answerers he declines to appoint may well have used this method.

In asking the question the teacher necessarily implies that the pupils may know or even that they ought to know the answer on the basis of the information he has provided – that a tall story is another type of story different from a legend.[9] The stronger interpretation is suggested by the fact that, even though some answers are offered, the teacher reformulates the question so as to stimulate more offers of answers. This interpretation is reinforced further in lines 23, 'c'mon you must have some suggestions', and 28–30, 'all right, that's an attempt, anyway look at all these people, no attempt'.

His reformulation of the question amounts to an instruction to pupils to use a particular method to find the answer – if you know, and again you ought to know, what 'tall' means you can put it together with the meaning of 'story' which you also should know.

A pupil provides the answer 'big' to the reformulated step question and the teacher feeds it back into the original question and asks the pupils if they think that's the right answer. At least one pupil indicates that he believes that it is, or might be, and the teacher asks for clarification of 'big'. In response a pupil tentatively offers 'long' and the teacher accepts that in a provisional way and asks for alternatives.

It is usual for the teachers in this school to ask questions which require pupils to produce 'the right answer' and for teachers to openly and immediately judge the candidate answers in terms of their 'rightness'. In this first phase of the lesson, however, the teacher is suspending his judgement. This becomes clear with his use of the words 'suggestions' and 'attempts' and the absence of any evaluation of the pupils' answers, beyond letting them stand as possibilities. It may be that he started out to get the right answer but decided from the pupils' initial responses that he was not going to get it easily. However, it seems much more likely that he only expected and wanted suggestions right from the beginning, that the lesson was pre-pitched at this level.[10]

On the other hand, it is also clear that his judgement is only being postponed, not cancelled entirely, it is clearly indicated that there *is* an answer and that he knows it. The evidence for this is his use of the word 'attempt', and formulation of the task in line 22: 'Now we're trying to find out what a tall story is.' Also in line 32, he says, 'I can think of a meaning' and of course towards the end of the lesson the teacher curtails his suspension of judgement of answers and rejects answers, treating them simply as failures until he gets an answer that is 'near enough'.[11]

However, this suspension of evaluation does not mean that the teacher is exploring the pupils' experience or ways of thinking, he simply accepts candidate answers and lets them stand as possibilities. Only in one case in the first phase of the lesson does he ask for more and the more he stops at is 'long' as a specification of 'big' (lines 16–18).

To demonstrate that, as far as the whole lesson is concerned, the teacher is not exploring pupil experience, it is worth looking at Excerpt 2 where the teacher might seem to be exploring a pupil's understanding of the word 'telescope'. He certainly asks for 'more' rather than simply evaluating the pupil's answer as 'right' or 'wrong'. However, close attention to this exchange shows that the teacher is shaping the pupil's answer into 'the right answer' rather than exploring the pupil's thinking. The teacher seems to allow this pupil to develop the initially unacceptable answer because he thinks that the pupil will be able to, or because the pupil shows signs of being able to, produce 'the answer'.[12] Hence in justification to other pupils the teacher says, 'he knows what it is'. Furthermore, this is the only instance in the lesson where such extended clarification by a pupil is requested or allowed.[13] So over the lesson as a whole it should be clear that the teacher is still, despite some contrary appearances, trying to get pupils to provide him with the 'right answer'.

Returning to Excerpt 1, having prompted a number of suggestions, the teacher changes tack. He asks for examples of jokes, presumably as representing another kind of story to legends and tall stories, in relation to which the distinctiveness of 'tall stories' is to be seen, though he does not make this intention explicit nor indicate what pupils are to do with the jokes.

He then says

Lines 67–9 T: Now we're trying to find out what a tall story is so let's read one example and then see if you can tell me what a tall story is.

Now this presentation of an example would seem to be an indication of, and provision of the material necessary for the use of, another method pupils are to use to answer the original question. The teacher is saying: what we are about to read is a tall story, see if you can see what there is about it that makes it a *tall* story.

The teacher begins by reading the story himself and later appoints various pupils to read sections of it. He interrupts the telling of the story at various points, for instance:

Line 71   T: Give me another word for exploits.
Line 80   T: What's a siege?
Line 98   T: Anybody doesn't know what a telescope is?

These interruptions would seem to be checks that pupils have the knowledge to understand the story *as a story*.

There are other interruptions which, though not marked as different from the interruptions already mentioned, later turn out to have a quite diferent and more central significance, for instance:

Line 140   T: Do you believe that?
Line 169   T: Do you believe that?
Line 172   T: Is it possible?

It is made clear in line 254, where the teacher re-asks the original question, but adding that pupils should 'think over what we've said', and in lines 260–91 where he tries to get the pupils to formulate 'what we've said', that in *these* interruptions the teacher is providing the clues to 'tall' happenings, features of the story which indicate that it is a *tall* story. However, it should be noted in passing, that 'what we've said' is a highly problematic reference. In the final phase of the lesson (Excerpt 5), the teacher attempts to elicit a consensual formulation of 'what we've said' and then asks the original question again. After many 'wrong' answers an answer is finally presented which he judges to be 'near enough' to be accepted as 'the right answer'.

So the whole lesson is built around the question, 'What is a tall story?' I have proposed that this is a question which the pupils are not expected to be able to answer adequately even though he asks it at the beginning of the lesson. The whole lesson is premised on pupils not being able to answer the question. But, having confirmed that the pupils cannot provide the answer, the teacher does not just present it, offer illustrations and then ask them to remember it. Rather, the lesson is designed to make pupils get to the answer themselves, they are to *climb* the ladder of knowledge. The teacher first asks the question without providing any clues as to how they are to answer it, other than that they are to search their memories to see if they already know what a tall story is. Then he indicates a method that might be used to produce 'suggestions'. They are to see if they can work the answer out from what they know about the meaning of 'tall' and 'story'. Next, he recommends another method, induction, and provides them with some material with which to use that method: jokes (i.e. another form of story), and an example of a tall story (and in a previous lesson the class had talked about and provided examples of legends). It is implied that, by listening to the example of a tall story presented and comparing it with the examples of jokes and legends provided, pupils should be able to work out 'what a tall story is'.

One possible implication of the recommendation of this last method is that pupils are being set a problem and provided with the necessary evidence with which to think through to the correct conclusion. Under this interpretation the hints like 'do you believe it?' and 'is it possible?' are *just* hints, or prompts, they are not in principle essential to pupils finding what a tall story is from the evidence provided.

Another possible interpretation of what the teacher is intending to do is that he believes that to transmit 'what a tall story is' to 'this type of pupil', that is the 'less-able', it is necessary to adopt this indirect approach in order to maintain their attention and get them to remember it.

However, whether or not the teacher is attempting to teach a way of thinking, the pupils clearly have to engage in some kind of thinking and as a result may come to see thinking and knowledge in terms of the image of them embedded in this and other lessons. Similarly, it is in terms of their ability to think in these terms that the teacher will come to see some pupils as relatively 'bright' and others as 'thick'.[14]

It is reasonably clear from the transcript that the teacher's guiding plan is to get the pupils to produce the answer 'a tall story is an exaggerated story'. The fact that 'a tall story is an exaggerated story' is the main 'point' of the lesson would be understood by pupils paying sufficient attention, since the whole organization of the lesson is of the nature of a crescendo, with the ratification of the 'near enough' answer marking the peak of that crescendo (line 336).

There are two methods of finding the answer to the question suggested by the teacher. However, neither of them is sufficient in itself for pupils to produce the answer, as we shall see. The model of the nature of knowledge, thinking and learning underlying them both presents knowledge as a body of factual statements. Teacher questions relate to these statements in such a way that the correct answer completes the statement: What is a tall story? A tall story is an exaggerated story.

However, knowledge is not a collection of isolated factual statements; rather, 'tall story' is a category and its meaning is derived from its position within a particular category system. Now the teacher does refer to other categories which may be in the taxonomy he is using: legends and jokes. But there is no specification of the nature of the taxonomy as a whole, tall stories would seem to be presented as just another kind of story.[15] Furthermore, questions are *not* transformations of previously well-established statements. Rather, questions come first and statements are answers to particular questions. Another way of looking at this is to say that there are no statements about the world which do not themselves rest on a prior framework of assumptions built into the terms used.[16] To omit the questions or treat them as simply elicitation devices for facts is to neglect the fact that there are always a multitude of questions that could be asked about any aspect of the world but not all these questions are of equal significance. Hence without any indication of the relevant taxonomy it is difficult to know how to classify this story so as to find what makes it a tall story. A 'lie', an answer given by one of the pupils in the early part of the lesson, would be correct were the relevant taxonomy concerned with interpersonal acts rather than forms of story or literature. In this lesson, the particular questions asked are left unjustified, the implication being that the facts that they require to answer or complete them are their justification. Thus there is no presentation of the rationale for this particular typology of literature. A reasonable inference is that what are being presented are 'facts anyone should know'.

If the criticisms I have sketched here are correct, the implication is that the methods suggested by the teacher are not sufficient for pupils to be able to answer his question. As regards the pupils remembering 'what a tall story is' or working it out from what they already know, two conditions would need to be met for this to be possible. First, they would have to have sufficient background knowledge, for instance, of examples of 'tall' stories. However, such background knowledge would not provide 'the answer' in any immediate way unless this knowledge were derived from previous occasions on which the specifications of an appropriate answer to the question 'what is a tall story?' were similar to those involved here. Thus, and this is the second condition, the pupils must have sufficient knowledge of the official context to be able to produce an answer which meets the requirements enforced by the teacher. I shall argue in a moment that the meaning of questions and answers is always context-bound. This method, given that these two conditions are met, provides more likelihood of pupils reaching the answer than does the second one.

However, we have noted that the lesson seems to be premised on the assumption that the pupils only have sufficient resources to produce suggestions rather than 'the answer' by this first method.

Turning now to the second method suggested by the teacher, if one does not know what a tall story is it would seem to be impossible reasonably to infer what makes this particular story a tall story. There are many valid statements that could be made regarding this story.[17] But the teacher requires pupils to discover what makes it a *tall* story as defined by him. One of the difficulties involved in induction is that an infinite number of examples is required to logically *ensure* recognition of what are the *crucial* differences between different types of objects since any set of objects can be differentiated in an infinite number of ways. Of course, a learner *might* come to be able to discriminate correctly given a large number of examples perhaps constructed so as to involve critical differences and similarities. But in this case pupils are only provided with a few examples of legends (in a previous lesson), a few jokes (and one riddle) and an example of a tall story.[18]

To infer the characteristics of *tall* stories from this limited evidence is close to impossible. There is little chance of pupils narrowing down what the crucial dimension is on which this story *as a tall story* differs from other types of story. All the pupils can do is to suggest possible descriptions of this story and hope that they come across the crucial dimension, but this procedure is potentially endless.[19] If this analysis is correct, therefore, pupils must have to use other resources than those specified in the teacher's suggested methods to find the answer to his question. Before looking at what the pupils must do to get the answer it is necessary to say something more general about the nature of questions and answers.

Questions and answers

A question cannot be answered simply by scanning one's memory or one's perceptions for the statement to which it refers. As I said earlier, statements get their sense from the questions to which they are an answer. However, 'question' does not refer to a sequence of words which has a meaning specified by rules assigning meaning to those words; that sequence being independent of the context in which it occurs. It has for a long time been recognized that certain words, such as I, me, it, he, today, this, that, etc., are dependent for their meaning on the circumstances in which they occur. However, Garfinkel has recently argued that all meaning is produced by the attribution of a 'context' or 'background' to the utterance, though the ascription of 'background' in turn depends on the identification of the 'figure'.[20]

Thus even questions as a form are not immediately recognizable. There is no set of behavioural or linguistic features which defines a question such that their occurrence constitutes a necessary and sufficient condition for the attribution of questioning intent. There is, however, a set of linguistic and behavioural features whose presence can be taken as suggesting the possibility that what is occurring is questioning, such things as the use of interrogative words like 'when', 'which', 'how' at the beginning of utterances, tags like 'isn't it' at the end of utterances, reversed word order, interrogative intonation, questioning looks, etc. While the presence of any one of these features or of more than one of them suggests the likelihood that what is involved is a question, this is not guaranteed. The utterance still must be interpreted and continually interpreted in terms of some underlying intent, it may be a 'rhetorical' question or something else entirely. So to decide that an utterance is a question requires its location in a possible plan being followed by the 'questioner' which can be seen as motivating it. As further evidence comes in, this hypothesis may be rejected or confirmed.

However, what defines questions is simply that they normatively require answers such that failure to answer constitutes a noticeable absence.[21] Questions are not homogeneous in what kind of thing constitutes an answer or in how answers are to be produced to 'fit' questions. Hence, not only is deciding that an utterance is a question without also deciding just what it is asking for impossible, but any such identification, if it were possible, would also not provide any basis for answering.

There are three issues that have to be resolved whenever a question is asked: relevance, validity and elaborateness. Answers can be seen as not answering the question without the statement produced by the combination of question and answer being seen as invalid; there are usually innumerable valid statements that could be made from the terms of any question. I touched on the issue of relevance earlier. It refers to the question: what kind of 'what' is being referred to in 'What is a tall story?' There are different sets of 'whats' that could be being referred to, different category systems that can be related to 'tall story'. This is indicated by the following possible and compatible descriptions: a story like the ones told by Baron Munchausen, '*A tall story* is a colloquialism, originally American'[22] a lie or boast, etc.

Conversely, a statement produced from a question can be seen as invalid, while the answer is nevertheless seen as an answer to that question, a wrong answer. So validity refers to what is seen as good or adequate evidence, which is often a highly debatable issue. It is also one on which, as with relevance, the teacher legislates for the pupils.

Finally, even given the sense of the question, the elaborateness of the answer required has still to be decided. To what extent are clarification, explications, qualifications, etc., necessary, so that for instance whole books could be written in answer to the question: what is a tall story? I am thinking in part here of Husserl's notion of inner and outer horizons:

Let us for the sake of simplification restrict our examples to the so-called perceptions of corporeal things. What I am perceiving is only one aspect of the thing. Not only when I move around do other aspects appear. In addition, the aspect of the thing caught by my perceiving act suggests other possible aspects: the front side of the house suggests its back, the facade the interior, the roof the unseen foundation and so on. All these moments together may be called the 'inner horizon' of the perceived object. . . . But there is an outer horizon too. The tree refers to my garden, the garden to the street, to the city, to the country in which I am living, and finally to the whole universe. Every perception of a 'detail' refers to the 'thing' to which it pertains, the thing the other things over against which it stands out and which I call its background. There is not an isolated object as such, but a field of perceptions and cogitations with a halo, with a horizon or, to use a term of William James, with fringes relating it to other things.[23]

The crucial point in this discussion of questions and answers is that even when the same linguistic formulation is used on different occasions there are no algorithmic rules for resolving these issues: there may well be different relevance, validity and elaborateness requirements in force. A question is usually asked because the speaker has a problem – he requires certain information. The questioner usually frames the question so as to indicate the problem he or she has as clearly as possible. The limits on the speaker's formulation of a question can, however, vary in nature and degree. Usually, the limits consist of her or his understanding of the problem and knowledge of the other. But however clearly the speaker frames the question the answerer must still work out what the problem is by using her or his own resources. There is no way in which the problem can be spelt out in so many words – there is always reliance on the cultural resources of the hearer. Indeed, what is a clear question can only be determined in relation to these resources. A moment's thought will indicate that, however explicit the instructions are, there will usually, perhaps always, be possible alternative interpretations. Moreover, these instructions will require, to be understood, certain background knowledge which may well be of a very particular nature. The search for full explicitness is a wild goose chase. Furthermore, there are sanctionable limits on explicitness: to be too explicit is to insult the hearer's intelligence or perhaps to throw one's own into doubt.

The answerer's search for underlying relevances probably initially operates via the set of questions – *why* is *this person* asking *me this*? Hypotheses may be developed on one or more of these questions but a hypothesis on one question implies certain answers to the other questions. The 'this' refers to possible answers to the question, 'What could this combination of words mean?', a clue-source I have argued is inadequate alone in indicating what kind of answer is required. The other terms refer to motive.

Finding a motive for a question can be crucial in the attempt to assign sense to it. Motives are tied to identities so that those occupying particular 'positions' are seen as having certain typical concerns, or grounds for action. However, these concerns are not just defined by their typicality, they are also legislative in one way or another. To ask a question is to claim a right since in asking it one is claiming a certain identity. Questions make claims on people's time and energy. More importantly, they initiate or continue an interaction, thus enforcing a relationship which, however fleeting, may be used to reflect on the identity, status and character of those involved. Often, the status claimed by a questioner is 'an equal' – casual conversationalists, for instance, treat one another as equals for working purposes, whatever their views about each other.[24]

While even strangers will generally accord one another equal status by answering questions, there are limits to the kind of questions that strangers or acquaintances may legitimately and thus probably successfully ask.[25] One set of limits pertains to privacy or to what Goffman calls the individual's informational preserve.[26] Certain 'strangers'[27] claim and are usually routinely, if grudgingly, accorded the right to ask 'personal' questions, although they may be required to observe 'confidentiality'. Tax officials, police officers, doctors, lawyers, etc., claim and are usually accorded this licence. Conversely, knowing that a person is acting under the auspices of such an identity may, depending on the experience of the answerer, provide a set of likely relevances, associated with the collection of routine concerns considered as typical of and maybe normative to the particular public identity, with which to search for the kind of answer that is wanted. Such knowledge is also of course essential if any false front is to be presented, sustained or detected, or if the official's desires are to be subtly or even overtly countered.

Another set of limits concern having legitimate motivation in the sense of the question not being 'silly' or 'obvious' or not having an answer known to be known by the questioner. The asking of a question not having a legitimate motive may be seen by hearers as wasting their time and thus implying a conception of them as someone whose time is not worth much. Alternatively, it can be taken to imply that the target is a person who in some other way can be legitimately asked that kind of question, indicating his cultural incompetence, sub-human character, etc. If the answer to a question seems obvious, in other words if it involves what is assumed by the hearer to be 'common knowledge', what anyone would or should know, of if the speaker is seen as being able to look and see to find out, or if there is no apparent reason why anyone would want to know that, the person questioned is faced with a problem. He or she must either find some legitimate motive behind the question, for instance, the questioner is a foreigner or is 'mentally sub-normal', or must assume illegitimate motivation and in either case deal with the situation accordingly.

As I have indicated, what I referred to above as two sets of limits are not simply rules to be enforced to order interaction in a 'proper' manner but also provide a basis for deciding what an answer would be. Categorizing the other as a stranger or acquaintance for instance provides certain concerns and likely plans which can be used to make sense of what is said. If it becomes clear that the questioner knows the answer, both sets of limits can be seen as having been passed since the question has become a test. Questions having 'obvious' answers and questions having answers which the questioner clearly knows, so that the questioner is really asking whether *you* know, are routinely asked by teachers of pupils in this school and probably in most schools.[28] By doing this teachers are claiming a certain authority: they are claiming superior interactional rights, enforcing an asymmetrical relationship. But more than this, knowing the speaker is a teacher, given a certain conception of teaching, provides for the relevance of certain relatively specific resources for answering the question, or at least for producing an 'appropriate' answer, i.e. one which fits the relevances of the questioner.[29] And the teachers in this school claim the right to enforce their relevances by publicly and finally evaluating candidate answers, as does the teacher in the final phase of this lesson.

Knowing that the questioner is a teacher makes irrelevant certain normally usable strategies and makes other clue-sources relevant. There is no 'problem' that motivates the question in the sense that ideally an answer would provide a solution to the problem, so the attribution of possible 'problems' does not give any clue to the meaning of the question. On the other hand, the fact that the answer is known by the teacher, and that the question, and to a certain extent the whole situation facing the pupil, is structured so as to enable her or him to know or work out the answer,[30] makes available a whole range of other resources that are not normally present. Clues are embedded in the way in which the situation they face as pupils is organized. School knowledge is differentiated by subject and therefore the subject of the lesson may be a crucial consideration indicating what could be (or could not be) an answer to the question.

The pupil situation is also structured by the allocation of pupils in batches to classrooms in each of which a single encounter is the dominant mode of organization. The lesson as presented by the teacher is pitched at a certain level of 'difficulty' according to the co-ordinate position of the class in relation to age and ability. So the pitching of lessons is largely pre-set in relation to the division of pupils into classes on the basis of age and ability and the structuring of knowledge according to 'difficulty'. This pre-setting is designed not only to ensure that pupils are taught something 'new', that they 'keep moving', but also that they have the resources to understand what the teacher is to teach. However, despite this pre-setting, teachers have continually to check that the pupils do understand what is being taught. The teacher's control and development of lesson-topic constitutes probably the most important source of clues to what he is asking for.

I said earlier that in normal circumstances the questioner tries to frame questions so as to indicate the problem he or she has, in other words, what sort of thing would constitute an adequate answer. If the answer were known, he or she presumably would not ask the question. The teacher is faced with entirely the reverse problem: he or she usually knows the answer, not just possibly adequate answers, but the actual answer wanted from the pupils. Given this, the teacher has to decide how many and what type of clues to provide pupils with.

So the pupils can, and must, assume that they only have to search their world-within-reach for an adequate method of answering the question.[31] They can assume, at least as a working hypothesis, that everything they need to know to answer the question has been provided. The pupils must search their surroundings and their knowledge for possible methods of answering the question. If they find one, whatever its relevance or level of adequacy or validity in their eyes, what it produces could be the answer the teacher is looking for.[32] In other words, the very fact that a method is available is evidence that it might be the way to the answer. Conversely, the absence of the resources necessary to use a particular possible method can be taken to indicate that this is not the method to use to get the answer the teacher wants on this occasion.

However, the availability of a method is not fully determinate evidence of that method's 'appropriateness'. Nor is the availability of information a sure sign of its relevance, for instance the exchanges on 'exploits', 'siege' and 'telescope' in the lesson being analysed here do not give any clue to the meaning of 'tall story'. For one thing, the method intended by the teacher may not be available to pupils if, for instance, they have not 'correctly' processed previous lessons, or if the teacher has misjudged the availability of the method to these pupils in some other way. Secondly, there may well be more than one method available. One way in which pupils probably solve this second difficulty is by taking over the school's definition of levels of difficulty of knowledge and looking for a method of answering the teacher's question that lies at the appropriate level of difficulty. A method which appears too 'easy' or 'obvious' may not be used for the reason that the pupils assume that the teacher would not ask such an easy question of them.[33]

The management of learning

Certain methods of finding an answer to the question 'what is a tall story?' are ruled out by the rules operating in the lesson, indeed rules constitutive of oral work phases of lessons: you cannot look it up in a book, ask the teacher to tell you, or even ask the person sitting next to you, or at least not legitimately. The teacher recommends two methods for answering the question but neither in themselves make it possible for the pupils to provide the answer. Rather, there is a process of gradual provision of more and more clues to 'what the answer is' by the teacher which begins in the course of the reading of the story. Indeed, the teacher seems to pace the lesson in such a way as to get the answer to emerge towards the end of the lesson. As I said earlier, the structure of the lesson is a crescendo, and that structure would have been undermined and its attention potential destroyed if the question had been successfully answered early on.

In relation to the first phase of the lesson (up to line 53) I have commented on the way the teacher implies the pupils ought to be able to provide suggestions and suspends his evaluation of pupil 'answers'. This points to a peculiar characteristic of teacher questions which I mentioned earlier: that, unless specifically indicated otherwise, there is the implication that pupils ought to be able to answer. The teacher knows the answer and is pre-pitching the lesson and question. He 'knows' what they ought to know, and therefore any failure to provide the answer reflects on pupil knowledge and ability. Yet, even though it becomes plain later that the lesson is premised on the expectation that the pupils cannot answer it, the teacher sets out on the lesson by asking them 'what is a tall story?' This apparent inconsistency can be removed by taking the teacher's talk of 'attempts' and 'suggestions' and his suspension of evaluation as indicating that the usual levels of certainty regarding relevance and validity on which pupils are required to operate are being relaxed for the moment. He is asking them to provide *possible* answers, answers that could be right. However, there are no doubt still constraints even as far as the teacher is concerned, there still could be answers that he would treat as 'silly', and of course other pupils may well continue to use the old criteria in evaluating the offerings of their fellows. This relaxation of the usual levels of certainty regarding relevance and validity adds force to my argument about the nature of questions and answers. What is accepted and let stand as a possible answer in this first phase of the lesson is not acceptable and is rejected in the final phase.

The change 'back to normal' in the criteria for acceptable answers probably occurs after the teacher has finished reading the story when he re-asks the original question. In relation to these normal criteria, it is only possible for pupils to begin to work out 'what a tall story is' when the teacher begins to give hints like 'Do you believe that?', etc. These hints are not extras which help the pupils along to the answer, which speed up the process – they are essential.

The procedure required to work out the answer to the teacher's question is quite simple in this case, though the pupils have to recognize this method as the one to get them the answer. So at various points in the lesson the teacher asks: 'Do you believe that?' (e.g. line 140), 'Is it possible?' (e.g. line 172). These two questions indicate the dimension that in the teacher's estimation is relevant when one is deciding whether a story is a tall story: believability/ exaggeration, though he does not actually say that this dimension is related to 'tallness'. The teacher does not say which end of his dimension applies to this story and hence, given his prior categorization of this as a tall story, to tall stories. He simply asks the pupils whether parts of the story are 'believable'. Nevertheless, his asking the question constitutes a potential clue not just to the relevance of that dimension but also to the unbelievability of the story. We do not normally ask if something is possible unless there is some suspicion that it is not. In 'normal' circumstances we may be unsure and our asking, 'Is it possible?', simply indicates our unsureness. But in this classroom, where the fact that the teacher knows the answer but wants pupils to provide it is clearly and continually signalled, his asking this question *can* be taken to indicate that he thinks this story is unbelievable and that that is what makes it a tall story.

So the teacher's hints must be seen by pupils as hearing instructions – listen to this story for whether it is possible or plausible. Furthermore, the very asking of the question indicates that the story, or various parts of it, might be seen as implausible. In other words, he indicates a solution to the issues of relevance and elaborateness (what is the relevant dimension, how much elaboration is needed) and validity (see the story as containing unlikely or improbable happenings: 'I think they are improbable, don't you?')

Moreover, the teacher clearly indicates that the doubts raised at each point are to be seen as cumulative, so that while in relation to 'Do you believe it?', 'Is it possible?', 'Is it probably possible?' . . . etc., the teacher suspends his evaluation of answers, at each point he draws pupils' attention to what they decided at previous points and at the end he revises all the 'tall' happenings and again attempts to get the class to recognize their implausibility. Pupils are being required in other words to employ retrospective–prospective interpretation,[34] to find a certain underlying feature by seeing each point in relation to other aspects of the story already mentioned and to be mentioned. Thus, after reading the passage about the woman swallowing the cannonball, asking the pupils 'Is it possible?', and discovering that opinion is divided, the teacher (lines 222–6) tells them to remember that about one cannonball being fired so as to hit the other and knock it back: 'We didn't say it was probably possible . . . we said that was not probable didn't we? Many of you didn't believe that, you wouldn't believe that a cannonball could travel all this distance which is quite a long way. Possible but highly improbable', and he asks pupils if they agree, or rather to agree. So the doubts that the teacher raises at various points of the story about believability are to be seen as cumulative, so that the crucial feature of this story, for the purposes of this lesson, is made to stand out more and more as the lesson progresses. Each additional 'doubtful' feature reinforces the doubtfulness of the others. The teacher indicates the importance of this accumulation of doubt:

Line 243–4   T: Good, that's *another* thing then notice this.

Given the raising of the question, 'D'you believe that?', and the implications I pointed to as arising from it, 'another thing' can only be intended to mean another point of doubt, of possible disbelief.

So rather than the pupils being able to find the answer ready-made in their memories or being required to work out the answer from the evidence provided, their production of 'the answer' is dependent on the teacher's provision of clues. He manages the lesson so as to get pupils to provide 'the answer' and to provide it at the right point. While the teacher suspends his judgement of pupil 'answers' prior to and during the reading of the story, in the last phase of the lesson (from line 293 onwards) he reverts to immediately, publicly and, finally, evaluating pupil answers. His treatment of candidate answers in this phase provides further clues to the answer. While in general his evaluations do not display their grounds they do indicate which possible answers are ruled out and which are 'warmer'. Pupils can use these signs to work out in which direction the answer lies. One of the evaluations (lines 326–8) does elaborate and in fact gives the game away. The whole lesson can, and if the pupils are to get to the answer must, be seen as a process of increasing clarification by the teacher of what the question is asking for and what the answer might be. It begins with a question that pupils have no very adequate resources to answer, and proceeds via more and more indications by the teacher regarding what is relevant and valid, until a pupil finally produces an answer the teacher judges to be 'near enough' towards the end of the lesson. The teacher has managed it.[35]

Conclusion

Selection is usually assumed to proceed on the basis of pupil ability, or at least it is thought to approximate to the distribution of 'general ability' among pupils. What is suggested by the analysis here, however, is that the knowledge and skills required by pupils to show 'intelligence' in this lesson may be specific to the school setting. Being able to produce 'the answer' to the teacher's question requires knowledge of the conventions governing a particular kind of teaching and the ability to 'read the signs' in the teacher's structuring of the lesson. Together these are both a necessary and a sufficient condition of answering the question. It is not clear that this 'knowledge' and 'ability' have any 'general' application.

There are two other important consequences of the structure of this lesson. First, it is premised on the pupils' ignorance of the answer to the teacher's question and involves the constant reinforcement of that 'ignorance'. This may have long-term effects on the pupils' confidence and on their assessment of their own 'ability' and thereby on their 'achievement' in school. Secondly, in order to display 'ability', the pupils must conform to the teacher's definition of the situation, a definition which legislates an asymmetrical distribution of inter-actional rights. They must 'pay attention' and 'follow' the teacher's con-struction and management of the lesson. In other words, they must act in such a way as to indicate recognition of his authority, though they may also use various means to display distance from the pupil role.[36] Recognition of teacher authority is therefore a determinant of 'intelligence'.

The socialization consequences are rather more difficult to establish. What is clear is that the pupils, or at least most of them, have learned a form of interaction in which authority and knowledge are bound together. The lesson is so constructed as to produce a world in this classroom in which the pupils are ignorant of 'the answer' and cannot work it out until the teacher provides them with the necessary clues. They are being socialized into a world in which knowledge is something known by those 'in authority' and which can be learned only by taking heed of 'authorities'. However, knowing that world, in the sense of being able to perform competently in it, does not *necessarily* mean believing in its value, generality or inevitability. What pupils actually learn from this lesson and others like it is likely to be very much more complex. Furthermore, it may well be that the form of society embedded in this lesson is at odds, and perhaps increasingly so, with the forms implicit in interaction in the other settings in which these pupils engage.

So the extent to which the structure exemplified in this lesson performs social control functions beyond the school is a matter that has yet to be determined. That it performs such a function within the classroom, however, is fairly clear from the analysis here. The theory of knowledge and society embedded in the teacher's explicit recommendations of methods for finding 'the answer' and in the method the pupils have to use to answer his question both reinforce the teacher's control. The former legitimates his power, since it presents the teacher as having the knowledge and pupils as having to climb the ladder of knowledge held by him. Given the structure of interaction in this classroom, their differential success in doing this reflects on their individual abilities, not on the validity of the criteria involved. The method the pupils must use if they are to answer the teacher's question sustains his claim to legitimately control classroom events by making pupils almost totally dependent on him if they are to 'learn'. It turns his authority into a 'fact'.[37]

Explanation of the structure of this lesson, like the issue of its consequences beyond school, can only be speculated upon at the moment, given the paucity of research on the social production of teaching. What is clear is that it must be seen as a collective rather than a purely idiosyncratic phenomenon.[38] The sociocultural forces operating on this teacher and on others in similar social structural locations need to be explored. It is in this complex of forces that the explanation will lie, though whether these forces can be simply traced back to the nature of capitalism or industrialism remains to be seen.[39]

3 Pupil Culture and Classroom Order at Downtown

This chapter was written some 10 years after the data were collected, and after I had finished the original research report. As a result, it reflects some of the changes in my point of view that had occurred in the interim, as well as developments in the field of the sociology of education during that time. This chapter examines the viability of culture conflict theory. It documents what, from the point of view of that theory, is the unexpectedly low level of overt conflict between teachers and pupils to be found in Downtown classrooms; and it considers the reasons for this. In the process I challenge some other accounts of the perspectives of working-class boys towards schools, notably that of Paul Willis.

A common perspective used in examining teacher–pupil relations in secondary schools is the idea of conflict between dominant and subordinate cultures, of a clash between white, middle-class teachers on the one hand, and working-class and/or ethnic minority pupils on the other. In the case of some writers, this view is wedded to the idea, in the spirit of 1968, that some school pupils are a proto-revolutionary force.[1] From this point of view, it is precisely in inner-city boys' schools like Downtown that major confrontations between teachers and pupils would be expected. Here, if anywhere, we could expect the analogy with guerrilla warfare[2] to be most apposite. And, indeed, the Downtown teachers' staffroom comments serve to reinforce this expectation, with pupils being described as 'little buggers', 'bastards', 'louts', 'savages', etc., who are 'immature', 'aggressive', 'vicious', 'unstable' and 'nasty'.[3] These views mirror those of the anti-school, working-class boys studied by Corrigan:[4] 'Teachers are fucking crap', 'Bastards', 'Fucking mad', 'A load of shit'. Moreover, on occasions, Downtown teachers themselves appealed to the analogy of warfare, albeit in the course of jocular griping:[5]

(Staffroom conversation)
Webster: I don't know what'll happen this term, it'll be a matter of containment, it's the last two days I'm worried about.

Dixon: We'll be issued with guns for the last two days, Thompson
              sub-machine guns mounted on our desks!

There is more than a hint here of a potential for classroom disorder at Downtown. However, the concept of classroom order is highly problematic, it needs
clarification before any judgement can be made about the state of relations
between teachers and pupils.

Classroom order and pupil deviance

Like the concept of *social* order, 'classroom order' is often used in ways which
conflate description with normative evaluation. As used by teachers, it generally refers not to the orderliness of classroom interaction in a purely descriptive
sense,[6] but rather to the extent to which classroom process approximates the
teachers' requirements. It contrasts, then, not with chaos, but with all forms of
interaction which do not meet those requirements.[7]

Downtown classrooms were not chaotic in the sense of participants experiencing almost complete uncertainty as to what might happen next.[8] Indeed, in
the main, classroom interaction there followed the utterly familiar and now
well-documented form of 'chalk and talk',[9] and the equally commonplace
pattern of 'written work'.

'Chalk and talk' involves the pre-allocation of interactional rights on a two-
party basis with the teacher exercising the bulk of those rights. He[10] starts the
lesson, sets the topic and speaks for extended periods with pupils being expected to request permission when they wish to initiate contributions to the
lesson. Indeed, their major opportunity for participation is in answering the
teacher's questions. Moreover, as I showed in Chapter 1, these contributions,
whether in the form of initiatives or answers, are subject both to possible
interruption and to definitive evaluation by the teacher.[11]

In written work phases of lessons the teacher sets work for the pupils which
is to be performed at their desks, and they are expected to work alone and with
a minimum of noise. The teacher seeks to enforce a certain pace and quality of
work through monitoring activity in the classroom and intervening where
necessary, and through marking pupils' work, both during the lesson and later.

While the specific requirements placed on pupils in 'chalk and talk' and
'written work' lesson phases are clearly different in the sense that different kinds
of pupil activity are proscribed and prescribed,[12] at a more abstract level the
structure of the two formats is similar: the distribution of activity rights is much
the same. In both pupils work individually on standard tasks and the teacher
exercises the right to control what is done, when and how.[13] Undoubtedly,
this represents a sharply hierarchical form of social relations.

However, while classroom interaction at Downtown broadly matched the
chalk and talk and written work formats, pupil deviance was much in evidence:
'mucking about' and 'having a laugh' were rife.[14] And we might be tempted to
view this as evidence of pupil resistance to the authority claims of teachers and
thus of culture conflict.[15] However, most of this deviance was 'routine': a

stream of common and minor breaches of the rules expected by the teacher and dealt with by him in routinized ways.[16] Lessons were rarely brought to a standstill by the inability or unwillingness of pupils to participate. Certainly, the kind of showstopping disorder portrayed by books and films of the Blackboard Jungle genre, or reported in NAS pamphlets, was not to be found at Downtown. Despite the teachers' fears of being physically attacked in the classroom, I neither witnessed nor heard of any example during my stay in the school.[17]

For the most part, pupils took care to disguise their deviance: hiding what they were doing from the teacher by making sure he was not looking, or doing it under cover of some legitimate activity; though they were by no means entirely successful in this. Moreover, in general, they accepted teacher censure and punishment without challenge. On those rare occasions when pupils did offer a challenge, it did not develop into outright confrontation.

(Walker: Reading lesson. Merrick and partner are reading in funny voices, looking for double meanings, etc.)
T:　　　　　I wish you'd stop it Merrick, you're getting sillier every day
Merrick:　　I didn't do anything
T:　　　　　You are, you're getting silly
(No response from Merrick)

(Baldwin: History)
T:　　　　　Don't hit lads with rulers
Walters:　　He was talking about me
T:　　　　　No need to hit somebody for talking about you is there? Cut it out Walters, I don't like bullying
Walters:　　(　　　　　　　　　　　　　)
T:　　　　　Yuh what?
(No response from Walters)

(Baldwin: Written work lesson dealing with Scotland. Otley is looking at a map on the wall)
T:　　　　　That's Localtown, not Scotland Otley
Otley:　　　I'm looking at something
T:　　　　　You can look at break if you're that keen, I don't suppose you will be

Moreover, the response of other pupils when someone was punished, more often than not, was to laugh:

(Holton: Science. Pupils, especially Walters, laugh at the teacher saying to Jones: 'You're going to get clouted, go and stand in the corner', and Jones struggling to get out of his seat to avoid getting hit)

(Holton: Science. The teacher hits Walters, Barker laughs)

(Holton: Science. Many pupils laugh at Johnson holding his fingers after being caned)

Little of the classroom interaction observed at Downtown matches the 'guerrilla warfare' described by Willis:

> The lads' specialise in a caged resentment which always stops just short of outright confrontation. Settled in class, as near a group as they can manage, there is a continuous scraping of chairs, a bad tempered 'tut-tutting' at the simplest request, and a continuous fidgeting about which explores every permutation of sitting or lying on a chair. During private study, some openly show disdain by apparently trying to go to sleep with their head sideways down on the desk, some have their backs to the desk gazing out of the window, or even vacantly at the wall. There is an aimless air of insubordination ready with spurious justification and impossible to nail down.[18]

Classroom deviance at Downtown rarely seemed to involve any sustained, explicit element of resentment and insubordination. For the most part, it was apparently aimed primarily at counteracting boredom: daydreaming; reading comics, magazines and wall-charts; looking out of the window; writing on desks and rulers; playing with cards, coins, etc.; talking; having mock fights; etc. And indeed disputes among pupils were much more common than disputes with the teacher.

Only a small number of incidents match the account provided by Willis, and all of these centred on two white third-year pupils: Wilson and Todd. The threat posed by Wilson was well recognized by the teachers:

(Staffroom)
Webster: Wilson, he's going to kill someone one day, he's got the killer instinct. How he's changed, you can see the mentality breaking up, he's unstable
Denison: You should have seen him loping across the road at four-o-clock yesterday, like a prehistoric animal

(Baldwin talking to the researcher about class 3t after a lesson)
Baldwin: They're really immature, childish aren't they, can't get on with work when you give them it. Wilson, he's becoming just a yobo. He could have been in the city team for a number of sports. When he was younger there were great hopes for him as a boxer. Mr Vaughan took the trouble to introduce him to T----- youth club (. . .) They said he could have been Olympic standard if he'd stuck to it. He went a couple of times, then stopped. It's the same with all his sports. But he's got a record as long as yer arm, keeps getting those fines. His mother's quite concerned, his brother was a nice lad, but soft, not good at sports like this one. He's a bright lad. He might change when he gets to a new school but his reputation will probably go ahead of him and he'll probably be in there for status. When you face him his chin's up here (about nose level) and I'm fairly tall. It's quite alarming in a physical sense. I wouldn't like to have to control him for another two years.

Below are fieldnotes describing Wilson's and Todd's classroom deviance in the three lessons I observed at which they were present (all with Baldwin as teacher):

(Lesson 1)
T: Eh Wilson will you come up nearer the front please
(Wilson makes no move)
T: Eh you two will you just sit there please
(Still no move)
T: Come on lad, these lot've just moved up to the front
(Wilson moves to the front. A little later he flicks something at the teacher, who either doesn't see or pretends not to)

:   :   :   :   :   :   :   :

(Wilson pinches a comic from another pupil)
T: Would you like to give him that back
(Wilson gives the pupil part of the comic back)
T: All of it, don't mess me about

:   :   :   :   :   :   :   :

Wilson: Sir, Dalbir wants to move forward
T: He is moving forward
(Wilson has been teasing Dalbir, he was the one who had the comic stolen)

:   :   :   :   :   :   :   :

The teacher asks a pupil to go to the shop to get him some innersoles. Wilson says 'I'll go'. The pupil asked says he doesn't know where the shop is. (That seems unlikely, is he afraid of Wilson?) The teacher says to Wilson 'Okay, you go'. The teacher leaves the classroom to go and get changed for Games. Later Wilson returns to report that 'they only have size nines not size tens'. The teacher sends him back for the nines. (On the way out Wilson moves the teacher's pumps from his desk and puts them on top of the cupboard)

(Lesson 2. There are only 10 pupils. Wilson and Todd sit at the back, initially. The teacher tells them to move forward, they do so, but only after a delay and reluctantly. Wilson is chewing without any attempt to hide it. Wilson gets the teacher to give him another book by pretending the relevant pages aren't in the one he has)
T: (to Wilson and Todd) Are you gonna go on much longer
      with that?
Wilson: What?
T: The chat
Todd: (   )
(The teacher picks up on something that one of them says and offers a solution to the difficulty)

:   :   :   :   :   :   :   :

Wilson: This fuckin' ruler's bent
Todd: You're bent. You wanna get some straight rulers sir
(No response from the teacher)

(Lesson 3: Written work. Wilson is openly chewing but the teacher says nothing to him. Nrinda asks the teacher for a rubber).

T: Who's got a rubber?

Wilson: I've got one

T: Let Nrinda borrow it please

(Wilson turns round and gets on with his work without giving Nrinda the rubber. Nrinda asks him for it twice)

T: Oh stroll on, 'ere you are then (feels in his pocket and throws a rubber to Nrinda). It's very dirty

:   :   :   :   :   :   :   :

(A pupil is reading a magazine)

T: Fold it up, put it in yer pocket then you've got it at home and then when yer sittin' on the lavatory you can read it from top to bottom

Wilson: When yer sittin' on the shit-box

(Roberts repeats this, laughing, teacher ignores)

:   :   :   :   :   :   :   :

(As the teacher and the researcher are talking after the lesson, about Wilson and co., Wilson and some other pupils run down the corridor)

T: Hey stop. (They don't, the teacher starts to walk after them) WILSON. (They still take no notice, Baldwin turns to me as he leaves): A case in point!

(Having caught up with them, the teacher sends Wilson back to his room, tells him to do a side of writing, and gives him a sheet of paper and a book)

Wilson: I'm not carrying a book around

T: A side of writing by tomorrow morning

Wilson: Huh!

(As he walks out he screws up the sheet of paper)

T: I'd prefer it on that piece of paper

Here we have something close to the behaviour described by Willis. However, Wilson and Todd were the exception even among the third- and fourth-year pupils observed.[19] For the most part, the pupils at Downtown did not display opposition to teacher authority, even when they were breaking the rules. Indeed, many, if not most, participated enthusiastically in lessons, especially in 'chalk and talk' phases. While some, *including* Wilson, rarely answered teachers' questions, there was scarcely ever a shortage of pupils offering answers, and answerers were not restricted to those of low status in the informal pupil culture. Thus, for example, in 2n, where Harris was 'top dog', he was also, from the teachers' point of view, 'one of the brightest lads in the class' and an active participant in lessons.[20]

Many pupils were also apparently committed to being seen as successful at school, or at least to not appearing 'stupid'. This is the obvious explanation for the amount of 'copying' and 'cheating' that went on. In 'chalk and talk' lessons pupils sometimes looked up the answers to teacher questions in textbooks or whispered answers to one another. In written work lesson phases there was much comparing of work.

(Holton: Science. The teacher has set written work. When he leaves the room for a moment there is considerable checking up on one another's work. Leach holds up his book and shouts to Harris 'Is that right?'. Jerry Coard and Harper are talking and playing around. Leach goes to see what Richardson is doing. Morton carries on with his work. Jerry comes over to Dunn saying 'It's not like that'. Harper comes over and has a look)

Leach: That's how it goes

(Richardson shakes his head)

Leach: Bet you it does Richardson

(Richardson carries on with his work)

:   :   :   :   :   :   :   :

Harris: (to Richardson) What you copying for?

(Harris moves away to the next set of desks)

Richardson: I'm not copying off you I put (   ) I'm not copying off you (shows Harris his book, Harris laughs at it, Jerry joins in the laughing)

Harris: Shut up Jerry or I'll bang you

Jerry: You won't

(Harris gets up)

Jerry: You will, you will (gets up and moves rapidly in the opposite direction, Harris goes over and looks at Richardson's work and laughs. Richardson tries to get a look at someone else's).

There was also cheating in tests:

(Holton: Science. The class has just done a test, have swapped papers and marked them. The teacher scrutinizes a pupil's paper. Leach says that the marker of Jerry's paper has been filling in the answers. The teacher checks the handwriting and finds this is the case)

Harris: They're both in Blue House, that's why he did it (merits are awarded to houses in tests)

(The teacher sends the marker, a small Sikh lad, for the stick and book. This looks to me like a set-up, but I have no evidence)

Commitment to school success was also evidenced in some comments elicited in a brief interview with some of the most influential pupils in 2n:[21]

(Interview with Leach, Harris, Harper and Richardson. In response to a question about what's wrong with the school, they say that there should be more discipline)

Leach: There'll be more discipline at the new school. (As a result of comprehensivization these pupils will be moving to another school the following year)

R: Is that a good thing?

Leach: Yes

P: We'll learn more at the new school, we ought to do
            homework

(In response to a question about examinations they say they'd feel great if
they came top in the exams. All but Harris think that the school-leaving
age ought to be raised, all think they ought to 'stay on at school to learn
about things', though they are not clear about what they are learning)

In summary, then, most Downtown pupils did not display 'an entrenched
general and personalised opposition to "authority" '.[22] While classroom
deviance was endemic, in general it did not seem to involve any intended
challenge to teacher authority. Such challenges were rare, and would seem to
have been limited to a very small minority of pupils and occurred only occasionally. Moreover, many pupils, including some of those apparently playing a
dominant role in the informal culture, displayed a commitment to 'doing well',
or at least to not doing badly, at school.[23]

Now these findings are not entirely incompatible with Willis's account. Applying the latter, the few who were 'troublemakers' from the point of view of the
teachers, such as Wilson and Todd, would correspond to 'the lads', with the
remainder being the conformists or 'ear 'oles'. Moreover, the fact that my data
comes largely from second- and third-, rather than fourth-year classes, may have
had the effect of minimizing the number of 'lads' in my sample; though Willis's
'lads' report having 'gone astray' in the second and third years.[24]

However, this interpretation involves a number of problems. First, as already
mentioned, it is not at all clear why 'the lads' should be taken as representing
the archetypal working-class pupil; even Willis does not claim that they are in a
majority among working-class youth.[25] Moreover, there is nothing in Willis's
theory which explains why fourth-year pupils should be *more* oppositional than
second- and third-year pupils; though one can think of possible supplementary
explanations. Furthermore, it seems that at Downtown it was the third-year
pupils that the teachers found to be the most troublesome. It was that year
group which had been 'streamed' into 'troublemakers' and 'those who want to
work'. Moreover, many of the second-year pupils whom I observed were
hardly stereotypical 'conformist' pupils in the eyes of the teachers:

(Phillipson and Baldwin talking about 2n)
Baldwin: There's seven good lads but there's some little buggers:
             Short, Cook, Mills, Dunn's top of the list. Arnold's vicious,
             aggressive, resentful . . .
Phillipson: Is that all? (laughing)
Baldwin: Richardson, I can get along with him, he's just a bit loud
             that's all
Phillipson: Gary's not so bad
Baldwin: He's easily led that's his trouble. I get no pleasure at all, I get
             more pleasure out of teaching third year classes

(The researcher and Denison talking after a lesson about a second-year pupil)
R: Richardson is a big nuisance

Denison: Yes but he's bright
          (
R: He's intelligent though, I can't understand it
Denison: Well he's off his head I think, partly at least, what some
          people would call a behaviour problem. He goes wild,
          berserk, if you cross him, that's true of many of these West
          Indians

Nor were the out-of-school activities of second-year pupils what one might expect from 'ear 'oles'. During one lesson a teacher asked 2n how many of them have ever 'got into trouble with the police', saying 'this is off the record, I won't report anybody'. Nearly half of the class put up their hands. The offences reported included breaking into factories, stealing lead and stealing money.

On this evidence it seems unlikely that the discrepancy between Willis's account and the Downtown findings can be explained as merely the product of sampling different year groups. Indeed, it may be that 'the lads' were in a minority among working-class pupils at Hammertown (the school that Willis studied) too; though Willis provides no basis for assessing this. However, whether or not they were a minority, the fact that some working-class pupils were 'conformists' clearly raises a serious problem for Willis's analysis. Once it becomes clear that the lad/ear 'ole distinction does not simply reflect a clash between middle- and working-class cultures, the culture conflict model begins to break down.

In large part, the problem stems from Willis's adoption of 'the lads'' own typology of pupil orientations as an analytic description. It is a characterstic feature of folk typologies that they often take an us/them form, where 'them' consists simply of all those who are not 'one of us', whatever other differences there may be among them. There are of course precedents for the conformist/ non-conformist distinction in the literature, notably in the work of Hargreaves and Lacey,[26] where it is grounded much more effectively through interviews with a wider range of pupils and by means of sociometric data. And perhaps these studies provide us with a basis for understanding the relatively low level of pupil opposition at Downtown in that there was virtually no streaming in the school. However, as a secondary modern the school represented the 'bottom stream' of the English education system, and we might expect some polarization as a result of that. Furthermore, differentiation-polarization theory does not help us to explain the range of orientations between pupils like Wilson and Todd, on the one hand, and the majority of pupils on the other. And, in general, it seems that the culture conflict model fails to account for the subtle variation to be found in pupil orientations towards school.[27] What is required is a model which recognizes a wide range of pupil adaptations rather than operating simply with pro and anti categories.

Woods provides one such model, distinguishing between a range of adaptations: conformity, retreatism, colonization, intransigence and rebellion.[28] In terms of this typology, most Downtown pupils would seem to be close to the colonization mode:

The colonizer accepts that the school is to provide his basic social environment during term-time for five years and attempts to establish a relatively contented existence within it by maximising what he perceives as the available gratifications, whether they are officially permitted or proscribed.[29]

However, much classroom deviance at Downtown could also be read as a sign of retreatism. For retreatists life at school is very empty and boring:

the immediate problem is how to pass the time, and they do this by 'doing nothing', 'mucking about', 'having a laugh'. They might also practise 'being away'; a kind of mental removal from the scene, like daydreaming during lessons, and indulge much more than others in 'removal activities' which are 'voluntary unserious pursuits which are sufficiently engrossing and exciting to lift the participant out of himself, making him oblivious for the time being to his actual situation' (Goffman 1968:67). Such activities in schools would include unofficial games, playing cards, group smoking, listening to the radio, contra-school conversations (i.e. 'talking' as an undercover activity) and reading 'illicit' literature.[30]

'Lads' like Wilson and Todd, on the other hand, might be regarded as approximating 'intransigence' in Woods' terms:

The pupil adopting this mode is indifferent to the school's ends and rejects its means. He may not care about the future and is characterized mainly by persistent and powerful detestation of rules, rituals and regulations and much of his 'front' and presentation of self is based on that simple fact. He replaces the school's means with his own antipathy to them. He is 'agin the government', 'bolshie'. He is bored by the school's normal procedure and outraged by attempts to interest or discipline him. He is very awkward to handle. His rejection of the school's methods involves lesson disruption, hidden and open, verbal, non-verbal and sometimes physical assaults on staff, open and disguised truancy, destruction of school property, pronounced misbehaviour in public while in school uniform or on school business. His opposition is frequently symbolised by his appearance, taking on the style of dress, hair and demeanour of whichever youth sub-cultural group he identifies with – teds, skin 'eads, greasers and so on.[31]

However, this crude application of Woods' categories to Downtown pupils reveals one of the problems with the adaptation model as currently formulated: some of the categories – notably retreatism and intransigence – seem more applicable at the level of particular pupil actions than to that of general orientations towards school. Even intransigent pupils such as Wilson and Todd are not intransigent all the time; indeed, for the most part their behaviour seems closest to the retreatist mode. Woods' typology spans these two levels uncomfortably. And he recognizes that his modes of pupil adaptation are generalizations:

A pupil might adopt one mode through his school life, though it is more likely he will move through a series. . . . He might employ one mode for one section of the school, one subject or one teacher, and another for another. He might have a dominant mode, or a mixture of them. Though I have talked of the 'ritualist' and the 'retreatist' I have talked of them as abstracted people. It is really the *modes* that we have been discussing. There are bits of all of them in most people.[32]

Once this is accepted, there seems limited scope for types of general orientation towards school.

One of the major problems with work focused at the level of the school is that it is content to identify correlations between school features and fails to build up from analysis of the concrete contexts in which pupil activity takes place and pupil orientations are shaped.[33] There is a considerable literature documenting the contextual variability of pupil orientations;[34] pointing in particular to the significance of teachers' behaviour as a factor in producing that variability. What this suggests is that, initially at least, we should seek an explanation for the character of pupil behaviour at Downtown in the nature of the teachers' classroom practices. And indeed I shall argue that the strategies they use to enforce the two major interactional formats operating in the classrooms are of central significance in this respect.

The teachers' enforcement strategies

There has been a considerable amount of research on teacher strategies,[35] but unfortunately little of this has linked them to pupil orientations.[36] What I want to do here is to consider the strategies Downtown teachers use to establish and maintain classroom order and to consider what role these may have played in producing the relatively low levels of pupil resistance to be found there.

Corrigan[37] argues that the coercive power resources teachers are able to wield against pupils is the major factor in shaping the school behaviour of working-class pupils. And, indeed, coercion or domination[38] is one major control strategy to be found at Downtown. At the limit, teachers may refer pupils to the headmaster for suspension or expulsion, they may cane pupils or detain them after school. Of these, the cane seemed much the most frequently used and threatened:

(Holton: Science. The teacher sends Jerry Coard for 'the stick and the book' for 'writing gibberish' in his book and tearing a page out of it. When he returns Holton canes him. There is a hush in the class, though also a few laughs. The teacher complains about the cane, which is a ragged piece of wood, he shouts across to R: 'What a ghastly implement!' The teacher and Jerry go away to get a better stick)

(Walker: English)
T: 　　　　If I have any more stupid remarks I'll cane you for being stupid

These sanctions were resorted to relatively rarely, and apparently much more by some teachers than by others.[39] Rather more common was the 'clouting' or 'slapping' of pupils or its threat:

> (Holton: Science. The teacher has been out of the room getting a better cane to hit Jerry Coard with. On his return he points to Dalton to come out, ineffectually clouts him and tells him to 'put it in there')
> Dalton: What sir?
> T: Don't come that with me, you've been chewing like an old cow, I was watching
> Dalton: Swallowed it sir
> T: Get back to your seat
> (I'm not at all sure Dalton had anything in his mouth: he had asked Harris for a sweet when the latter had been handing them out, but Harris had not given him one. Could Dalton have thought the teacher wouldn't believe him if he'd said he hadn't anything in his mouth?)

> (Holton: Science. Written work lesson. The teacher leaves the room for five minutes. While he is out Jerry Coard ousts Dunn from his seat and sits there himself. When the teacher returns he hits Jerry for getting out of his place. Later he hits Richardson for talking (Harris laughs) and hits Jerry again, this time for talking)

> (Baldwin: History)
> T: You're going to look silly with that (a ball) stuck up yer nose aren't you?

> (Holton: Science. A test is in progress)
> T: If you turn round again I'll leap over this desk and hit you very hard, get yer eyes glued to that paper

> (Holton: Science. The teacher hits Leach)
> T: You should know me by now, I won't tolerate constant chattering. If I have to come from this desk again I shan't be just straightening flies out of your hair

There were also less severe punishments of course: for example, seat reassignment, making pupils stand through the remainder of a lesson, and confiscation of pupil property such as cards, balls, etc. These were common and more evenly distributed across the teachers. Even so, only a small proportion of censures were accompanied by such sanctions or even the threat of them; in most cases a telling off or a straightforward deviance imputation were judged sufficient.

Punishment certainly played an important role in Downtown classrooms, though clearly more so in some than in others. However, domination relies more on pupils' belief that teachers have access to powerful measures, and that they are willing and able to use them, than on the actual use of punishment. Indeed, to punish every offence would not only seriously disrupt lessons but might also prove counterproductive. For one thing, the pupils might become inured to the pain and shame involved. And indeed the teachers believed that the coercive measures at their disposal were pretty ineffective:

(Denison talks to the researcher about 'the brutality of the pupils')
Denison: All they're interested in is fighting
R: If they don't have any interest in learning anything it must be difficult to control them
Denison: All we have is second- or rather tenth-rate measures, some of those kids give each other worse beatings than that. I think the only way to control them would be to really beat them up, they'd respect you for six months then

Moreover, the use of punishments involved dangers for the teachers. Even apart from the threat of pupil retaliation, 'clouting' was officially proscribed, though informally tolerated, and there was an ever-present fear of parents taking legal action:

(Larson and Walker talking in the staffroom in the presence of the researcher)
Larson: You ought to be the official NUT convenor
Walker: I'm only in the NUT for one reason
Larson: (looking significantly at R) In case you get prosecuted for hitting someone
Walker: That's right

Similarly, those measures which involved recourse to the head endangered the teacher's reputation; too much use of them and it might be thought that he was incapable of keeping discipline.

At least as important as the use and threat of punishment, then, seems to be the creation of an aura of power to persuade pupils that the teacher has effective punishments available to him, that he is only too prepared to use them, and that he can execute them effectively. Paradoxically, the creation and maintenance of such an aura of power may require that the actual use of punishment be minimized, otherwise pupils may not only become used to the punishment but also discover the limits to the teachers' employment of it. Even explicit *threats* to use coercion may have to be minimized, since they always carry the danger that they will have to be backed up with action, if the impression is not to be given that the teacher is unwilling or unable to carry them through.

Of course, the teachers' use of punishment cannot be separated from their authority. What is involved is not simply the domination of one person by another, or even of children by an adult. Teachers and pupils operate in the context of institutionalized conceptions of their rights and obligations. And in their dealings with pupils Downtown teachers treat their authority, and the associated obligations placed on pupils, as fact, as something normal, natural and unchangeable which must be simply taken account of and not questioned. For the most part, it goes unmentioned, and where it is made explicit it is treated in ways which trade on its institutionalized character:

(Denison: Geography. It is nearing the end of the lesson, the teacher is still talking. A pupil starts to clear up and then brings his pencils out to the front)

T: I'm only the teacher here, if you lot feel like getting up and going you might as well go

(The pupil returns to his desk. The teacher demands that he stand up)

T: Aren't you ashamed?

(The teacher demands that he apologize, and after the pupil had done so, says 'Louder, say you won't do it again')[40]

No justifications are presented, either for teacher authority *or* for the particular demands made. Indeed, pupil demands for justification are rejected out of hand:

(Walker: English. A pupil asks to go to the toilet)

T: You're a scrounger, you're always scrounging

P: I'm not, is wanting to go to the toilet scrounging?

T: Don't shout at me. Stand up straight when you're being talked to. Ten minutes, if you're any longer I'll keep you in playtime or dinnertime

This is an example of the authority maintenance device which Goffman found operating in mental hospitals and which he calls 'looping'.[41] Instead of following on from the topic raised by the pupil and offering a justification, the teacher treats the demand for an account as itself an accountable matter, and as further grounds for negative character definition.

While the institutionalization of teacher authority does not lead to absolute, routine compliance on the part of the pupils, it is a major cultural resource which teachers rely on in classroom interaction. It provides the basis for what is undoubtedly the most common punishment in Downtown classrooms: 'showing them up'.[42] Deviance attributions have the potential for embarrassing pupils by spotlighting them as individuals in the relatively public setting of the classroom, and highlighting their deviance from 'appropriate classroom behaviour'. But, of course, the pupils' conceptions of 'appropriate classroom behaviour' are unlikely to be identical to those of the staff. Perhaps for this reason the teachers seek to enforce their definition of the situation by drawing on a number of legitimizing rhetorics[43] in their formulation of deviance attributions. These rhetorics heighten the latter's capacity to 'show up' pupils through the identity implications they project. One such rhetoric appeals to 'civility':

(Holton: Science)

T: May I have a conversation with Arnold without you interrupting?

(Baldwin: History)

T: A lad bad-mannered enough not to be giving me his attention

(Walker: English)

T: Next time, anyone who can't sit still, I'll chuck him out. You've no manners at all, it's rude to speak when someone else is talking

(Baldwin: History)

T: I know you'll think I'm rude Morton, put yer pen down, stop drawing while I'm talking

Here the teachers appeal to general conventions of polite behaviour rather than to their particular rights as teachers.[44] The effect of this is that teacher authority is clothed in a more general conception of morality, and pupil deviance is portrayed not just as the infringement of classroom rules but as reflecting a character defect.

Often appealed to are the rules of conversation: don't talk when someone else is talking, listen to what is being said, etc.[45] Of course, in conversation, interactional rights are symmetrically distributed, and this no doubt provides some of the force of the rhetoric. Indeed, symmetry of rights is sometimes appealed to explicitly:

(Walker: English)

T: Could I just remind you again I'd like you to sit properly, it'll be better for you, it'll make your back straight. If you see me lolling about you can do the same

(Baldwin: History. On arrival at the film room one boy asks permission to go to the toilet and is given it. The teacher goes to get the key for the room. When he returns several pupils are coming out of the toilet and he complains that he only gave permission for one of them to go: 'I don't go down to the Eldon Arms every time I feel like a pint')

The other legitimization rhetorics by means of which the teachers seek to 'show up' pupils work not so much in terms of morality as through appeals to cultural competence. One of the most common is age rhetoric:

(Walker: English)

T: Don't be silly, try an' grow a little bit

(Baldwin: History)

T: I'm sick of child-like bad manners repeatedly from the same people. You behave like little children and yet you expect to be treated as young adults

(Holton: Science)

T: (to Richardson) You're growing up now, let's try'n use some precision rather than just this (he points to a diagram in Richardson's exercise book. Then he starts speaking to the whole class). Let's try'n act like schoolboys in a secondary school, not someone on their first day at school. During the holidays I have been looking at the work of five-year-olds and I'm not jesting the presentation of that work was better than ninety-five per cent of yours. You'll be going to work soon, you'll have to grow up instead of acting like five-year-old children. You're now doing an *adult diagram*, an *adult diagram* not a pretty child's picture. You're so childish. We need an *adult* approach.

(Baldwin: History)
T: There was a lad in 4s this morning who said 'Sir he's pulling my hair'. You'll be skipping in the yard next, having sand-pits in your form room

Here offenders are shown up as childish or immature. Similar appeals can be made in terms of gender and intelligence.

(Holton: Science.)
T: Now WILL YOU STOP BEING SO SILLY, the next boy who laughs in that stupid maner like a little girl I shall drop on quickly

Here silliness, stupidity, childishness and girlishness are all used to characterize the same piece of behaviour. They seem to be used as synonyms, reinforcing the imputed character of anyone who engages in that behaviour. Hints of homosexuality are also employed to similar effect:

(Denison: Geography)
T: Can you two control yourselves now you're out of arm's reach?

(Baldwin: History)
T: I understand they have double seats at the Rialto. C'mon take no notice of each other it's embarrassing to watch

A common feature of these rhetorics is that pupil behaviour is formulated not as something specifically intended and motivated but as the product of in-capacities of one kind or another. This is a feature of other strategies for showing up also:

(Baldwin: History. Harris, Leach and Mills are standing up looking out of the window watching a football game in the yard. The teacher tells them to sit down, Harris does, the other two don't)
T: Which words are you having difficulty with Leach and Mills?
Leach: Don't know sir

(Walker: English)
T: I don't know, some afternoons you come in here and you'd think there's something wrong with you, no self control at all

(Holton: Science. The teacher has the class 'sitting up straight')
T: Let's just get a bit of self-discipline, the first thing we've got to learn to control is our own bodies, some of you don't know what it's doing

By means of showing-up strategies, the teachers legislate a definition of male adult competence which includes 'appropriate' behaviour in the classroom and is designed to discourage pupil deviance. Offenders are shown up as 'ill-mannered', 'childish', 'sissy' and/or 'stupid'. Deviance is deprived of possible rationales: indeed, the very possibility of a rationale is undercut and the 'naturalness' of teacher authority reinforced.

Above and beyond such explicit attempts at legitimization through 'showing up' pupils, the maintenance of classroom control by the teachers has a curiously reflexive and self-confirming character. To the extent that the teacher successfully imposes an asymmetrical 'order' on classroom interaction, he turns his claimed authority into a fact to be reckoned with. By successfully demanding attention and disciplined participation, the teachers actually 'demonstrate' their competence as teachers, that they *are* teachers, and therefore their 'superiority' to pupils. Similarly, the acceptance of physical punishment by pupils not only involves recognition of teacher authority but also displays the impotence of the punished. Moreover, pupils know what 'good discipline' is, and seem to judge a teacher at least partially in terms of how well he is able to achieve what is presumed to be his goal. Any 'failure' to maintain 'discipline', whatever the motive, is in danger of being seen as weakness, and thus lack of 'authority', and of being exploited by pupils.[46]

Clearly, the effectiveness of 'showing up' relies on pupil commitment to the values of civility, adulthood, manhood and intelligence. It seems that, for the most part, the teachers can safely trade on these values. I have already documented the pupils' desire not to appear stupid, and their commitment to male adult status, at least, can be taken for granted.[47]

A major strategy employed by teachers at Downtown, then, is what has been termed 'domination', comprising a subtle blend of coercion, bluff, legitimizing rhetorics and sheer gamesmanship. However, the term 'strategy' is potentially misleading in this context. While commonly used in the literature, it is rarely defined. It has a range of usages in which such features as unofficial status, adaptation to circumstances, deception, innovation and unpredictability of outcome take turns in acting as the criterion.[48] Certainly, some of these seem at least partially applicable to the case in point. Thus 'clouting' is 'unofficial', and bluff obviously trades on deception. However, these features do not apply to the whole corpus of techniques we have included under the heading of 'domination'. In many respects, the key element of the meaning of 'strategy' is adaptation to circumstance, and this does indeed seem to be a central feature of domination. However, adaptation to circumstance is often thought of as necessarily involving deviation from ideals.[49] This does not seem to be the case here. Domination closely matches the paradigmatic assumptions of the traditional teaching to which Downtown teachers are committed:[50] it maintains distance between teachers and pupils; it is compatible with the view of pupils as recalcitrant, apprentice adults; it relies on an individualistic vocabulary of motives, etc. Domination, then, is not just a pragmatic strategy, adopted to deal with adverse circumstances, it forms part of the 'traditional' conception of teaching to which Downtown teachers are committed.

It is a mistake, then, to treat strategies as separate from teaching, parasitic upon it, and as the product of pragmatic adaptation or false consciousness.[51] Strategies vary in the degree to which they are compatible with particular teaching paradigms, and in their origins. In this respect, domination stands in sharp contrast to the other major control strategy used by Downtown teachers: avoidance of provocation.[52] Here the teacher relaxes his requirements and tempers his responses on the basis of the anticipated consequences of his actions, particularly in relation to likely 'trouble' involving costs in terms of time consumption, loss of face and physical danger. This strategy, too, is not *necessarily* purely pragmatic, but it runs counter to the traditional paradigm of Downtown teaching. Indeed, Downtown teachers spent a considerable amount of time in the staffroom complaining about 'progressive' teachers who did not face up to their responsibilities.[53]

There are serious problems in identifying the use of this second strategy since it operates through what is *not* done as much as through what *is* done: who is not asked, who is not told off, whose possessions are not confiscated, who is not 'clouted', who is not 'caned', etc. Moreover, since what is involved is probably a matter of degree, of how far various pupils can go before the teacher feels that he must intervene, the problem of identification is compounded.

However, there is strong evidence that such a strategy is used by Downtown teachers; though it is difficult to assess its scale:

(Staffroom conversation)
Greaves: Has the younger Harris been up to anything recently? He used to be fine but he's become all sulky recently?
Walker: Just ignore him, he gets on with his work okay
Greaves: Oh yes I know

(Staffroom)
Denison: You've got to try and avoid confrontations, although they sometimes force confrontations on you (he later explained how he'd spent twenty minutes telling a class off that day), you could spend all your time trying to persuade or force the reluctant to work, if there's some who are willing to work it's better to concentrate on them

Identification of this strategy in operation was more difficult, but the following seem fairly clear examples:

(Baldwin: History)
T: Harris will you shut up
(Harris starts talking again. The teacher sees but ignores)

(Holton: Science. When Richardson and Harris return from doing an errand for the teacher, Richardson moves Harris's books and Harris moves the rest of his things back to his original place next to Richardson, from which the teacher had originally moved him. The teacher sees but says nothing)

(Baldwin: History. Chalk and talk. The teacher sees two pupils looking out of the window. One pupil realizes the teacher has seen him and stops, the other continues looking out. The teacher pauses a moment and then continues without dealing with the deviance)

(Baldwin: History. Written work lesson. Arnold is writing on a ruler)
T: Try not to do that Arnold if you can help it
(Arnold looks up and indicates that it is a ruler he is writing on and not a book)
Arnold: S'mine
(The teacher watches as Arnold continues writing on the ruler; and then he turns away)

(Baldwin: History. The teacher tells the pupils to clear away by rows. Arnold and Johns get up straight away and bring out their equipment)
T: Arnold and Johns sit down
(They are about half way to the front and keep coming)
T: Oh come on then, it's a waste of time

Avoidance-of-provocation seems likely to have been an important strategy that Downtown teachers used to maintain 'order' in their classrooms, complementing (but also in a sense in conflict with) domination.

Conclusion

I have argued in this chapter that, despite the implications of culture conflict theory and of the teachers' own staffroom comments, Downtown classrooms were not characterized by major conflict. While there was considerable deviance, most of it was 'routine' and did not involve any direct challenge to teacher authority. Thus, only a small minority of the pupils fitted Willis's description of 'the lads'. A much more subtle model of pupil adaptations is required than those which portray them as simply pro- or anti-school. Moreover, it must begin at the level of pupils' classroom activities, since there is good evidence that these are affected by teachers' practices, and are not simply the product of features of school organization or class background.

I have suggested that the relatively low level of conflict in Downtown classrooms stems, in part at least, from the strategies used by the teachers to enforce the major interactional formats of 'chalk and talk' and 'written work'. However, contra Corrigan and Willis,[54] it does not seem that coercion is the all-important element in these strategies. To one degree or another legitimizing rhetorics play a major role, trading on the fact that most of the pupils are concerned not to appear 'stupid', 'childish' and 'sissy'. While it is easy to over-estimate the significance of teacher labelling of pupils,[55] under the influence of subculture theory one can equally forget the influence that the teacher can have over pupils.

Clearly, then, the situation at Downtown is far more complex than would be predicted by culture conflict theory. At the very least, it is clear that what is meant by 'conflict' requires clarification, and different levels and types of conflict must be distinguished. While there may have been a clash between the conceptions of classroom order held by teachers and pupils,[56] this by no means amounts to a rejection of teacher authority by pupils, nor does it lead to major battles. In part, this stems from the teachers' use of domination and avoidance-of-provocation strategies. But this latter point itself carries an important lesson: that intra-school factors may play a major role in defusing and deflecting, or on the contrary, exacerbating conflict.[57] Indeed, even this formulation may be misleading. It may be that we should view class or ethnic cultures and the interests around which they are focused as no more than latent factors,[58] having their influence and being drawn on in ways which reflect the characteristics of the situation in which pupils find themselves. Indeed, we should subject the notion of distinct class cultures to close analysis,[59] and it is a mistake to assume that each social class generates a single distinct adaptation to school. In the same way, ethnic cultures cannot be assumed to map straight on to school adaptations. At Downtown there did not seem to be consistent, clear-cut differences in adaptations between different ethnic groups.

The danger with the view that in schools social forces exert pressure on pupils to behave in characteristic ways which can only be suppressed, deflected or allowed to play themselves out, is that it amounts to a mere qualification of culture conflict theory, when a complete revision may be required. Moreover, it is a qualification whose implications are often largely ignored even as they are being voiced. Indeed, the 'relative autonomy' involved in mediation may be celebrated as showing 'the cunning of the system', as functioning to disguise what is 'really' happening.[60] The question must be raised as to in what sense Downtown pupils, or those elsewhere, can be usefully viewed, first and foremost, as representatives of 'the working class' or of 'black culture'. Is that their primary self-conception? If it is not, in what sense and to what degree are their activities best explained in class or ethnic terms? Are intra-school factors simply mediators of wider social forces or do they generate conflicts and consensus themselves, drawing on latent identities and cultures? Perhaps the most serious problem with culture conflict theory is the danger that, through its starting assumptions, it prevents such questions being asked. Behind everything that happens in school is assumed to lie, at however 'deep' a level, the demons of class and ethnicity.

Fieldnote and transcript conventions

( )	Stretch of talk that could not be deciphered
Speech presented in capitals	Words that are shouted
R	The researcher
T: He's intelligent R: He's not stupid	talk that overlaps

4 Examinations and Teaching: An Exploratory Study

(written with JOHN SCARTH)

The final chapter in this first part of the book is very different in character to the previous three; though it reflects my continuing concern with 'transmission teaching'. This article comes from my later research in which I collaborated with John Scarth and Sue Webb to study the effects of public examinations on teaching style. Whereas the Downtown research was guided by a fairly traditional concept of ethnographic method aimed at producing a theoretical description of various aspects of social interaction within the school, this later research was explicitly concerned with developing and testing a theory. And, as part of this, there was an attempt to measure variations in transmission teaching. As a result, much of the emphasis came to be placed on quantitative data.

The introduction of the General Certificate of Secondary Education (GCSE) in England and Wales has highlighted, once again, concern over the effects of public examinations upon secondary schools.[1] Given the many claims made about how the new examinations will affect teachers,[2] now is a good time to re-assess the nature of the claims made about the influence of examinations on schooling. In this chapter we focus upon those claims which relate to the effects of examinations on *teaching*, and specifically the charge that examinations encourage teachers to concentrate upon *fact-transmission* and the memorization of information by pupils.[3] We shall begin by reviewing these claims and the small amount of empirical work in the area, before reporting some recent research of our own.[4]

Claims and evidence

It is often suggested that success in examinations requires detailed factual knowledge of subject content, and that in order for their pupils to achieve good examination results teachers adopt didactic forms of teaching and 'cramming'. Such criticism has been common ever since public examinations for secondary school pupils were introduced in the middle of the last century. Roach, for example, cites James Bryce, an Inspector for the School's Inquiry Commission in the late nineteenth century, describing what he observed during a visit to a private school in Lancashire as an instance of how a school teacher could achieve success by training pupils for the examination:

> I examined one class minutely on some of the subjects in which they had last been trained. The training proved to be no sham; the boys knew a great deal about many things; in English history, for instance, it was difficult to puzzle them; but they had been not taught, but crammed. They answered hurriedly, not stopping to think what the question meant, but pouring out stores of information which they did not understand. Every reply witnessed to large knowledge, but then it was not a reply to the question put. Their minds, to use a familiar illustration, were like a full sack of corn, which if you press it down at one point, rises and runs over at some other. It was noticeable that they usually answered in the words of their text-book; and that while knowing English history minutely, they were wholly ignorant of the course of events in other European countries. In English grammar and analysis, as it is called, they did not, as I had first expected, answer by rote, but seemed to have mastered the principles sufficiently to take any ordinary sentence to pieces, and describe correctly the relation of its parts. Something in their manner showed that this was a forced capacity, the result not perhaps of cramming, but of overteaching, and that it did not witness to any natural and healthy growth. But such as it was, the capacity was there. These boys looked jaded and overworked, and the whole aspect of the school was one of discomfort. The assistant masters were numerous in proportion to the numbers of the pupils, and seemed to be employed manipulating them in small classes, with a view to individual preparation.[5]

Mackenzie makes much the same claim about teaching in twentieth-century secondary schools:

> Throughout Britain (and indeed the western world), teachers are busy dictating to pupils the acceptable, mark-earning answers that will gain them high grades in the certificates.[6]

HM Inspectors, too, have pointed to the consequences for teaching of an over-concern with examination success:

> the effect of the dominating pursuit of examination results was to narrow learning opportunities, especially when work was concentrated on topics thought to be favoured by examiners. Sustained exposition and excessive note-taking by the pupil tended to limit oral work. . . . Even preparation for oral examinations became too dependent on the formal requirements of the examination. . . . In many schools writing tended to be stereotyped and voluminous – the result of the widespread practice of dictated or copied notes, instead of encouragement to engage in a variety of kinds of writing for different purposes.[7]

While the claim that examinations produce high levels of fact-transmission teaching is a recurrent one, there has been very little systematic research upon the subject. There is a considerable amount of research on examinations in general, but most of this has been concerned with such things as the validity and reliability of examination questions and the comparability of examination results across different syllabi.[8] There has also been some research on the effects of examination boards on curriculum planning, but this has not focused on classroom practice.[9] There are few studies which look specifically at the effects of examinations upon teaching. We shall look at the two most substantial ones, those of Turner and Lewin.[10]

Turner studied the impact of one Integrated Humanities course on secondary school teaching. This was a course which gave teachers a great deal of flexibility and freedom of choice over both content and assessment. There was no body of material which all schools had to cover. The syllabus presented ten topics, and any candidate's work had to cover five, though one of these could be of the centre's or the candidate's own choice. While the syllabus sketches in the content of these topics, the Board made it clear that this detail was not binding. Schools could determine for themselves how to handle the material. There was no externally set and marked examination paper. Instead, the Board listed a range of types of assessment from which schools could choose. The only constraint on the choice of assessment was the range of qualities that had to be assessed, for which the marks (out of a total of 150) were awarded as follows:

Qualities	*Range of total marks available*
Knowledge	55–75
Ability to locate and select evidence	20–30
Interpretation of evidence and evaluation of argument	25–45
Presentation of explanations, ideas and/or arguments	20–30

Schools could use an examination to test any or all of these qualities; but, equally, the entire assessment could be based upon candidates' coursework.

Turner sent a detailed questionnaire about the philosophy and practice of the Integrated Humanities course to all schools which entered candidates for the 1981 examination (there was an 82% response rate). He also collected case-study data from two schools. On the basis of the questionnaire returns, Turner claims that teachers of Integrated Humanities still relied on traditional forms of assessment:

> None of the more radical assessment techniques sugested by the syllabus proved very popular. The ubiquitous essay, objective testing and comprehension exercises appeared alongside the project in about eight out of ten schools. Oral assessment, discussion work, reviews, surveys and the

like were rarely mentioned. The flexibility of the content list was little used. It would seem that student freedom to choose ways of working through themes or of pursuing research were severely restricted in most schools.[11]

Turner argues that the move to less traditional syllabuses, with the development of courses like JMB Integrated Humanities, represented an attempt by teachers to gain control of the curriculum by controlling the assessment, with the intention of reducing the domination of teaching by assessment requirements. However, this had not in fact been the outcome: 'Teachers have tended to devise assessments which had the same effect upon their teaching as the [more traditional syllabi] did earlier.'[12] In the case studies Turner explored why this should be so. He reports that the teachers he studied, even on a course like Integrated Humanities, still felt constrained by the regulations of the examination board, which they perceived as requiring 'too many written assignments' and 'a formal system of testing'.[13] He reports one teacher, who set an examination as part of the assessment, as summing up the course in the following terms:

The influence of the assessment upon the teaching staff is covert but it passes on the message about what is really important: formal knowledge backed up by the examination. Overtly, it created an unresolved tension between doing what we want, and the last minute flurry of paper before each test. It is tempting to decide what the test wants and do just that.[14]

On this basis, it seems that even in the absence of external examinations, teaching is still heavily influenced by traditional assessment techniques which are perceived as a major determinant of pedagogy.

Turner's results are interesting and suggestive. However, there are some weaknesses in his study that make it difficult to accept his findings with confidence. In particular, he did not carry out a systematic study of classroom teaching on the Integrated Humanities course. He makes a judgement on the basis of the (primarily interview) data available to him that no radical change had occurred. But, by its very nature, this judgement is unspecific and questionable. The comparative standard remains implicit, so that no rigorous assessment of variation in pedagogy is possible. Furthermore, Turner's claims about the role of the Examination Board's syllabus and regulations in determining the types of assessment selected by teachers are not well-established.

One of the few investigations that have systematically investigated the effects of examinations on classroom practice is Lewin's study of an innovative integrated science course in Malaysia.[15] The Malaysian Integrated Science programme is modelled upon the Scottish Integrated Sciences Course,[16] and places great emphasis upon discovery learning, rather than the transmission of scientific facts.

The course is examined by means of a 75-item multiple-choice paper. However, Lewin's analysis of the examination papers for 1972–5 suggested that over half the multiple choice items required the recall of information. Moreover, there was no practical assessment involved in the examination.

Lewin used a number of sources of evidence to assess whether the course was being implemented in line with its aims. Teachers were sent a free-response questionnaire about the form and effects of the examination, and a smaller sample were interviewed. In general, the teachers were very critical of the examination, claiming, for example, that it discouraged understanding by rewarding powers of recognition and recall. Lewin also reports that a quarter of the teachers interviewed:

> referred unprompted to examination orientation dominating teaching in their schools, saying, for example, that 'teachers only teach for examinations', 'the headmaster, parents and pupils are only interested in examination results'; 'good teachers are those who give good notes for examination revision'. One teacher pithily observed: 'the purpose of the integrated science course is to develop the ability to observe and reason; the purpose of the school is to get as many examination passes as possible'.[17]

Lewin also looked at methods of internal assessment, noting that few teachers tested practical skills despite the fact that this was the only other form of assessment explicitly recommended in the course materials apart from multiple-choice objective questions. He sent a questionnaire to a sample of pupils, from which it emerged that they saw multiple-choice questions in internal and the external examinations as primarily dependent upon recall, and a majority felt that 'there were too many facts to remember in integrated science'.[18]

Finally, Lewin observed 22 classes in 40 lessons (18 double periods, 4 single periods) in 15 of the schools. He used an observation schedule to record the frequency of various types of activity:[19]

Classroom interactions by percentage of time spent

1. Settling the class/administration	4.5
2. General class discussion	32.2
3. Group–teacher discussion	8.3
4. Individual–teacher discussion	0.9
5. Teacher draws/writes/reads	7.0
6. Pupils draw/write	2.9
7. Pupils use text/reference books	2.1
8. Pupils use worksheets, reading/writing	16.6
9. Teacher explains experimental procedure	5.6
10. Teacher demonstrates experiment	4.2
11. Class experiments	15.7

Less than 16% of time was spent in experimentation. Moreover, in a further breakdown of the category 'general class discussion', over half this time was spent in introducing facts and principles and in requiring recall of facts and principles:[20]

*Classroom interactions: General class discussion
by percentage of time spent*

Introduce facts/principles	21
Recall facts/principles	35
Apply facts/principles	6
Hypothesise	1
Observe	28
Interpret data	7
Infer from data	1

Lewin adds that:

> Further analysis of other observation data indicated that the 'guided dis-
> covery' approach recommended in the course materials was used by very
> few teachers. For example, on no occasion were pupils observed contrib-
> uting to the design of experiments, and they were rarely asked to hypoth-
> esise, predict, interpret or infer.

And he concludes:

> The observed pattern of teaching described very briefly here is consistent
> with an interpretation which holds that the lack of emphasis on practical
> work and related skills is at least partly attributable to patterns of examin-
> ing. In so far as these encourage the acquisition of factual knowledge they
> inhibit teachers from devoting more time to experimentation and the use
> of 'guided discovery' methods.[21]

While certainly an advance upon criticisms of examinations based on impressionistic evidence, there are none the less some serious problems with
Lewin's research which make it unwise to accept his conclusions as following
from the evidence he presents. First, questions can be raised about the effectiveness with which he has measured both the degree to which the examination required recall and the features of teachers' practice which he reports. It is
difficult accurately to read off from questions in an examination either the
cognitive capacities which the examiner intended the questions to assess or the
capacities which candidates actually used in answering the questions; and of
course these two things may be quite different. Similarly, measuring the
amount of classroom time taken up by different types of activity, and in
particular distinguishing between class time involving recall of facts, application
of facts, observation, etc., is extremely difficult to achieve with a reasonable
level of validity.[22] And Lewin provides no evidence about how successfully he
achieved this. There is also the problem that Lewin's sample of each teacher's
teaching is very small, at most one double lesson. Teachers' patterns of teaching, even on examination courses, do vary between lessons, and 60 minutes of
teaching on one day is a weak basis for generalization to a whole course.[23]

However, even if the measurement problems had been resolved effectively,
there would still be considerable doubt about whether the evidence Lewin

presents supports his claim that the examination encouraged the transmission of facts rather than discovery learning. This is because there are many other factors which might equally plausibly explain the presence of fact-transmission teaching in the classrooms observed. We could try to deal with this problem by controlled comparison. We might compare the same course taught under different forms of assessment to discover whether it is indeed the case that when the course has an examination which emphasizes recall the teacher adopts a more didactic pedagogy than when the assessment gives less emphasis to recall. On the basis of such a comparison, assuming Lewin's conclusion was confirmed, we would be in a stronger position to claim that it was the examination which produced the effects rather than other factors. Of course, such a comparison may not have been available to Lewin, but some comparison which controls for other factors that might encourage fact-transmission teaching is necessary if we are to be able to draw conclusions from the study with any confidence.

Measuring fact-transmission on examination courses

There is, then, little solid empirical evidence about the effects of assessment regime on teaching, despite more than a century of claims and counter-claims. In our research, we set out to investigate whether courses assessed only by examination have a higher level of fact-transmission teaching as compared with other types of publicly assessed courses (examination versus other-assessed courses). We also compared courses having *any kind* of qualification-dispensing assessment with courses having no such assessment, that is first-, second-, third-year courses and a non-assessed fourth-year course (assessed versus non-assessed courses).

We decided to compare the *same teacher* teaching different courses rather than making comparisons *among* teachers, on the grounds that this would provide some control over the stable characteristics of individual teachers. We also focused our attention on humanities courses, since in the schools we were studying these provided the widest range of types of assessment.

In order to make comparisons between courses taught by the same teacher, we relied upon a single set of interrelated measures of fact-transmission teaching: the proportion of public classroom talk allocated to pupils, and the number and length of pupil contributions to such talk.[24] We focused only on public talk because that was a central element of the teaching we observed and because practical difficulties prevented us from obtaining data about private conversations between the teachers and individual pupils. Calculating the number and length of pupil contributions gave us data on how the differences between courses in terms of the proportion of public talk allocated to pupils were produced.

We studied 11 teachers in five schools. All lessons were tape-recorded and for each lesson teacher and pupil contributions to public classroom talk were timed. The teachers, their courses and the number of lessons that we observed of each are summarized in Table 4.1.

Table 4.1   Number of lessons and amount of classroom discussion per course

Teacher course (with type of assessment)	Number of lessons	Public classroom talk (in mins)
1 Social and economic history 'O' level 5th year (examination only)	9	130
Schools Council 13–16 history 'O' level 4th year (examination and coursework)	27	364
Schools Council 13–16 history 'O' level 5th year (examination and coursework)	11	131
2nd-year history (non-assessed)	16	248
2 Social and economic history CSE 4th year (examination only)	9	86
Schools Council 13–16 history 'O' level 5th year (examination and coursework)	12	304
3 Social and economic history CSE 4th year (examination only)	6	81
3rd-year history (non-assessed)	6	81
4 Social and economic history CSE 4th year (examination only)	3	69
3rd-year history (non-assessed)	3	59
5 Religious education 'O' level/CSE 4th year (examination only)	31	308
Philosophy and biblical studies 'A' level L6th (examination only)	33	881
Personal relations 4th year (non-assessed)	12	351
2nd-year religious education (non-assessed)	21	314
3rd-year religious education (non-assessed)	14	308
6 Sociology GCE 'O'/'A' level L6th (examination only)	4	90
Integrated humanities 'O' level/CSE 5th year (coursework only)	16	62
Integrated humanities 'O' level/CSE 4th year (coursework only)	12	87
7 Geography 'O' level 5th year (examination only)	14	197
Integrated humanities 'O' level/CSE 5th year (coursework only)	14	92
8 Geography 'O' level 5th year (examination only)	6	68
Integrated humanities 'O' level/CSE 5th year (coursework only)	14	57

Table 4.1   cont.

Teacher course (with type of assessment)	Number of lessons	Public classroom talk (in mins)
9 Schools Council 13–16 history 'O' level/CSE 5th year (examination and coursework	16	199
Schools Council 13–16 'O' level/CSE 4th year (examination and coursework)	12	70
3rd-year history (non-assessed)	6	68
2nd-year history (non-assessed)	10	146
10 History 'A' level L6th (examination only)	9	243
Schools Council history 'O' level 5th year (examination and coursework)	6	100
Schools Council history 'O' level 4th year (examination and coursework)	14	191
3rd-year history (non-assessed)	5	77
11 Integrated humanities 'O' level L6th (coursework only)	10	10
Schools Council 13–16 history 'O' level/CSE 5th year (examination and coursework)	16	267
3rd-year humanities (non-assessed)	7	129
2nd-year humanities (non-assessed)	11	120
1st-year humanities (non-assessed)	16	341
Mean =	12	185
Standard Deviation =	7.01	154.71

Results

The first comparison we wish to make on the basis of our research is between teaching on examination and other-assessed courses. That is a comparison between, on the one hand, teaching on courses assessed *only* by examination and, on the other, teaching on courses assessed either by course-work alone or by both course-work and examination. The proportions of public talk allocated to pupils in the lessons are summarized in Table 4.2.

In only three cases (Teachers 7, 8 and 10) are there clear differences between these two types of course. Correlation ratios[25] are shown in Table 4.3. The correlations are, with one exception, weak, and, apart from the case of Teacher 1, the differences are in the opposite direction to that we might have expected: for this measure, the level of fact-transmission teaching appears to be lower on examination courses than on the other-assessed courses.

Table 4.2   Proportion of pupil talk for examination and other-assessed courses

	Examination courses			Other-assessed courses		
Teacher	Number of lessons	Amount of public talk (mins)	Overall proportion of pupil talk (%)	Number of lessons	Amount of public talk (mins)	Overall proportion of pupil talk (%)
1	9	130	2	38	495	3
6	4	90	23	28	149	22
7	14	197	18	14	92	15
8	6	68	15	14	57	7
10	9	243	15	20	291	12

Table 4.3   Correlation ratios for the comparison of proportion of pupil talk on examination and other-assessed courses

Teacher	Correlation ratio
1	0.06
6	0.00
7	0.02
8	0.71
10	0.11

Of course, our category 'other-assessed courses' involves considerable internalvariation, with the Schools Council History 13–16 GCE and CSE course having a balance of marks for examination work and course work of 60/40, while the JMB Integrated Humanities course is assessed entirely on the basis of course work.[26] It could be that no difference would be found between Schools Council History courses and examination courses because the shift in balance is not great enough. However, it is, in fact, one of the teachers teaching the Schools Council course (Teacher 1) who shows a higher score on the other-assessed course than on the examination course he teaches, though the

Table 4.4   Number of pupil contributions per 1000-second period[27] for examination and other-assessed courses

	Examination courses		Other-assessed courses		
Teacher	Overall number of contributions	Mean per 1000 seconds	Overall number of contributions	Mean per 1000 seconds	Correlation ratios
1	50	6.6	52	6.3	0.05
6	262	48.2	523	57.8	0.06
7	681	57.9	300	56.8	0.00
8	229	56.3	106	30.0	0.74
10	387	21.5	349	18.8	0.31

Table 4.5 Length of pupil contributions per 1000-second period for examination and other-assessed courses

Teacher	Examination courses		Other-assessed courses		Correlation ratios
	Overall number of contributions	Mean length per 1000 seconds	Overall number of contributions	Mean length per 1000 seconds	
1	50	2.1	52	2.2	0.01
6	262	4.5	523	3.8	0.06
7	681	3.0	300	2.8	0.06
8	229	2.7	106	2.1	0.50
10	387	5.9	349	5.7	0.00

difference is very small. The Integrated Humanities teachers consistently show higher levels of pupil talk in their examination courses than on this other-assessed course. The same pattern of results was found when we examined the number and length of pupil contributions (see Tables 4.4 and 4.5).

In terms of the proportion of public talk allocated to pupils and the number and length of pupil contributions, there seems to be little difference between examination and other-assessed courses. There is little support here, then, for the argument that examinations, as compared with other forms of pupil assessment, lead to more fact-transmission orientated teaching.

We turn now to a comparison of *assessed* courses (that is both Examination and other-assessed courses combined) and *non-assessed* courses (i.e. first-, second- and third-year courses and a fourth-year non-assessed course). The aggregate scores for each of these types of course for the proportion of classroom talk allocated to pupils are summarized in Table 4.6.

For all but one teacher (Teacher 10) there is a clear difference in the overall proportion of pupil talk between assessed and non-assessed courses. However, the correlation ratios are, with one exception, low (see Table 4.7).

Once again, we must be cautious when interpreting these data. The high correlation ratio for Teacher 4 cannot be relied upon since the sample of public talk for these courses is very small. Of course, the low correlation ratios for

Table 4.6 Proportion of pupil talk for assessed and non-assessed courses

Teacher	Assessed courses			Non-assessed courses		
	Number of lessons	Amount of public talk (mins)	Overall proportion of pupil talk (%)	Number of lessons	Amount of public talk (mins)	Overall proportion of pupil talk (%)
1	47	625	2	16	248	5
3	6	81	7	6	81	10
4	3	69	2	3	59	14
5	64	189	5	47	973	11
9	28	269	9	16	214	14
10	29	534	13	5	77	13
11	26	438	11	34	590	18

some of the other teachers (especially Teachers 3 and 10) could also be a feature of small samples. However, the low correlation ratios for Teachers 1 and 5, for whom we have fairly large lesson samples, does suggest that in aggregate terms there is no strong evidence for a difference in the proportion of public talk allocated to pupils between assessed and non-assessed courses.

If one looks at comparisons between *particular* courses, there are some stronger correlations. For example, the correlation ratio for Teacher 10's second-year and fifth-year history is 0.72, that for Teacher 5's fourth-year RE and PR courses is 0.55. Despite these particular scores, though, if we examine

Table 4.7 Correlation ratios for the comparison of proportion of pupil talk on assessed and non-assessed courses

Teacher	Correlation ratio
1	0.29
3	0.00
4	0.81
5	0.12
9	0.37
10	0.01
11	0.02

Table 4.8 Correlation ratios for non-assessed and assessed courses: proportion of pupil talk

Teacher	Courses	Correlation ratio
1	2nd: 5 soc. and econ.	0.34
	2nd: 4 SCP	0.25
	2nd: 5 SCP	0.26
3	3rd: 4 soc. and econ.	0.00
4	3rd: 4 history	0.81
5	2nd: 4 RE	0.19
	2nd: L6 philosophy	0.02
	3rd: 4 RE	0.05
	3rd: L6 philosophy	0.00
	4 PR: 4 RE	0.56
	4 PR: L6 philosophy	0.32
9	2nd: 4 SCP	0.68
	2nd: 5 SCP	0.72
	3rd: 4 SCP	0.00
	3rd: 5 SCP	0.01
10	3rd: 4 SCP	0.00
	3rd: 5 SCP	0.02
	3rd: L6 history	0.10

Table 4.8 cont.

Teacher	Courses	Correlation ratio
11	1st: 5 SCP	0.54
	1st: L6 int. hum.	0.31
	2nd: 5 SCP	0.25
	2nd: L6 int. hum.	0.05
	3rd: 5 SCP	0.00
	3rd: L6 int. hum.	0.04

all the correlations between assessed and non-assessed courses for each teacher, we find that most of these are weak (see Table 4.8).

Only a small proportion (21%) of the correlation ratios show a strong relationship between assessed and non-assessed courses. In other words, in only five out of 24 courses could we feel confident in claiming that the assessed and non-assessed courses showed different levels of fact-transmission.

The pattern of differences between assessed and non-assessed courses is a complicated one, then, and is not easy to interpret. In some cases there may be a correlation between the presence of qualification-dispensing assessment and the proportion of pupil talk. But for the most part the correlations are weak. It is not possible at present to come to any sound decision on the basis of these data about whether, and under what conditions, qualification-dispensing assessment does affect the proportion of pupil talk in class instruction, though there are hints that it might under certain circumstances.

Much the same conclusion must be drawn for number of pupil contributions (see Table 4.9). The pattern for length of pupil contributions shows weak correlations, apart from the case of Teacher 4 (see Table 4.10).

Once again, rather than looking at the comparison in aggregate terms, we can look at the correlations between individual assessed and non-assessed courses for each teacher. Here we find that the results for number of contributions is similar to those for proportion of pupil talk, while those for length of pupil contributions show only one strong correlation (see Table 4.11).

Table 4.9 Number of contributions per thousand seconds for assessed and non-assessed courses

	Assessed courses			Non-assessed courses			
Teacher	Number of 1000-second periods	Overall number of contributions	Mean number per 1000 seconds	Number of 1000-second periods	Overall number of contributions	Mean number per 1000 seconds	Correlation ratios
1	35	343	8.1	14	269	18.6	0.24
3	4	128	21.3	4	162	27.0	0.00
4	4	49	12.2	3	115	38.0	0.71
5	86	1533	17.3	56	1898	32.2	0.12
9	15	598	28.9	12	611	43.6	0.32
10	30	701	23.4	5	131	26.2	0.01
11	26	527	20.3	34	1507	44.3	0.37

Table 4.10   Length of contributions per 1000-second period for assessed and non-assessed courses

	Assessed courses			Non-assessed courses			
Teacher	Number of 1000-second periods	Overall number of contributions	Mean of 1000-second means	Number of 1000-second periods	Overall number of contributions	Mean of 1000-second means	Correlation ratios
1	35	343	2.2	14	269	2.8	0.06
3	4	128	2.7	4	162	2.7	0.00
4	4	49	1.6	3	114	4.3	0.64
5	86	1533	2.7	56	1898	3.5	0.03
9	15	598	3.2	12	611	3.2	0.00
10	30	701	5.9	5	131	4.7	0.05
11	26	527	5.2	34	1507	4.9	0.00

Table 4.11   Correlation ratios for non-assessed and assessed courses: Number and length of pupil contributions

		Correlation ratios	
Teacher	Courses	Number	Length
1	2nd: 5 soc. and econ.	0.33	0.12
	2nd: 4 SCP	0.17	0.06
	2nd: 5 SCP	0.33	0.13
3	3rd: 4 soc. and econ.	0.00	0.00
4	3rd: 4 history	0.71	0.64
5	2nd: 4 RE	0.03	0.19
	2nd: L6 phil.	0.00	0.07
	3rd: 4 RE	0.01	0.16
	3rd: L6 phil.	0.00	0.00
	4 PR: 4 RE	0.40	0.20
	4 PR: L6 phil.	0.37	0.00
9	2nd: 4 SCP	0.57	0.01
	2nd: 5 SCP	0.66	0.03
	3rd: 4 SCP	0.00	0.02
	3rd: 5 SCP	0.01	0.00
10	3rd: 4 SCP	0.13	0.10
	3rd: 5 SCP	0.17	0.06
	3rd: L6 history	0.00	0.13
11	1st: 5 SCP	0.78	0.33
	1st: L6 int. hum.	0.83	0.35
	2nd: 5 SCP	0.52	0.23
	2nd: L6 int. hum.	0.65	0.32
	3rd: 5 SCP	0.06	0.16
	3rd: L6 int. hum.	0.20	0.40

Discussion

Our results suggest that examination courses may not exhibit higher levels of fact-transmission teaching than courses which involve course-work assessment. The findings are less clear-cut when we compare courses leading to and those not leading to qualifications. While, for all but one of the teachers we studied, the non-assessed courses showed higher proportions of pupil talk and more pupil contributions than the assessed courses, the correlation ratios suggested that in general this was not a strong relationship.

There are, of course, a number of respects in which our findings, and our interpretations of them, might be challenged. First, there is the question of measurement. As regards the independent variables (examination/non-examination courses; assessed/non-assessed courses) classification of courses is unlikely to be a major source of error. There is only one serious issue here, it seems to us. This arises from the fact that all but one of our non-assessed courses were effectively pre-assessment courses taking place in the first, second or third year of secondary school. While they did not themselves lead to qualification-dispensing assessment, for many pupils they did lead to other courses which *were* assessed. Given this, we might expect a backwash effect, with teachers using a higher level of fact-transmission teaching on them than might otherwise be expected, in preparation for the subsequent assessed course. And, indeed, there is some evidence for such a backwash effect, in that differences between fourth/fifth- and third-year courses are in general much smaller than those between fourth/fifth- and first-year or second-year courses. The argument might be, then, that if one were to compare assessed with truly non-assessed courses, striking differences would be found. The comparison between Teacher 5's teaching on the fourth-year RE course and the fourth-year non-assessed (personal relations) course does provide some evidence for this interpretation. However, even then the correlation ratio is only 0.55 for proportion of pupil talk and 0.58 for number of pupil contributions. Clearly, this invites further investigation.

Our measurement of fact-transmission teaching is much more questionable. We focused upon a small set of interrelated indicators which looked like good measures of fact-transmission teaching and which could be measured reasonably accurately. While inter- and intra-coder agreement was of an acceptable level on these measures,[28] the question of whether these measures capture variation in the level of fact-transmission remains open. Relying upon one set of interrelated measures rules out the possibility of assessing the measurements produced against scores for the same courses on other indicators, which is the main strategy for assessing construct validity.

Another measurement problem arises from our concentration upon public classroom talk. Fact-transmission need not rely upon lecturing, it could take the form of large amounts of written work involving the copying out of material from textbooks or other sources. It is quite conceivable that this might occur even while pupils are allocated a relatively large proportion of what public classroom talk does occur. In order to take account of this we would need to find a way of classifying types of written work and measuring their frequency and/or duration.

An additional problem is the size of our samples of the teachers' behaviour. While in some cases (and in particular Teachers 5 and 11) these are quite large, in others they are relatively small. Given the levels of intra-teacher variation, results based on small samples could be misleading. Future work will need to ensure large samples.

Finally, there are sampling problems concerning the number of teachers whose classroom behaviour we have studied. Eleven teachers is not as large a sample as we would have liked, though the total number of lessons observed, when compared to other classroom observation studies, is quite large. Moreover, when it comes to comparing examination versus other-assessed and assessed versus non-assessed courses, the number of teachers is down to five and seven, respectively. It may be that our findings arise from an unrepresentative set of teachers.

Over and above measurement and sampling issues, there are other research design questions. An experimental, or quasi-experimental, design might have enabled us to control for more factors, but in doing so we would have increased the risk of ecological invalidity. Faced with this dilemma, we chose to observe teaching in ordinary classrooms. As a result, we were faced with the problem of comparing groups of pupils of different ages and courses of different levels and types. Any differences we did find could have been produced, it might be argued, by maturation – or some other factors – and not by assessment regime. This, of course, is the problem facing all natural observational studies involving comparison. The comparisons available are limited, and as a result one cannot control for all relevant extraneous variables.

In order to make the research practicable, we focused upon humanities lessons. It might be argued that results obtained for this area of the curriculum are not generalizable to other areas. We might claim in response that it is in humanities that one would most expect to find a large contribution to classroom discussion by pupils in the absence of pressure from either public examination or other types of assessment regime. Clearly, this issue cannot be resolved other than by research on other areas of the curriculum.

Even within the sphere of humanities teaching, we have also been unable to control other factors that might well have an impact upon the level of transmission teaching, such as class size, pupil motivation, age of pupils, and the social class backgrounds of pupils. Differences between courses could be produced, or counterbalanced, by variations in these factors. Future research will need to investigate the effects of these factors and control for them where necessary.

A more general question that might be raised is whether a comparison of examination versus other-assessed, or assessed versus non-assessed, courses running simultaneously is an effective test of the claim that examinations produce fact-transmission teaching. It might be argued that the effect of public examinations would be felt throughout a school, not just on those courses which lead to a qualification-dispensing assessment of some kind. (Though we might argue that even if this were true there would still be differences in *level* of fact-transmission teaching between courses near to and those further away from the point of assessment.) To investigate this issue we would need to compare teaching before and after the introduction, or withdrawal, of public examinations for a school or an education system. This would certainly be worth studying, but it was not possible for us.

Conclusion

There are, then, some problems with our research and associated doubts about the validity of the findings. In particular, our measurements of the level of fact-transmission must remain questionable, until they can be compared with results using other indicators. Certainly, we do not want to make any very strong claims about the effects of examinations, or of qualification-dispensing assessment generally, upon teaching on the basis of our data. Our work does none the less raise questions about what seems to be an orthodoxy among educational commentators, and to a lesser extent among teachers: that the reason why much secondary school teaching still takes the form of fact-transmission, involving large amounts of teacher talk, despite many attempts to change it, can be blamed upon the examination system. It is certainly a striking feature of virtually all the courses we studied that the level of teacher talk is high, generally much higher than the two-thirds level claimed by Flanders.[29]

On a more tentative note, our work raises interesting questions about the impact of the new GCSE examination system on how teachers teach. Though it is claimed that the GCSE will lead to significant changes in teacher classroom practices, these claims are based on the largely untested assumption that examinations are a controlling factor in pedagogy. The results of our research suggest that examinations, and credential-dispensing assessment in general, may not be responsible for producing fact-transmision teaching. If so, this raises doubts about the likely success of any attempts to refom pedagogy simply by changing assessment procedures.

Acknowledgements

We would like to thank the many teachers and pupils who welcomed us into their classrooms and who made this research possible. We are also grateful to the Research Committee of the Open University and the Research and Higher Degrees Committee of the School of Education, Open University, for supplying the funds for this research.

PART 2

Theoretical and Methodological Reflections

5 Putting Competence into Action: Some Sociological Notes on a Model of Classroom Interaction

In the 1970s, research on classrooms blossomed, and there were several variants. In particular, there were approaches, such as those deriving from linguistics and from ethnomethodology, which were concerned with specifying the cultural resources used by teachers and pupils in constructing their interactions with one another. On the other hand, there was work influenced by symbolic interactionism that set out to document diverse perspectives and strategies on the part of teachers and pupils, and change in these over time. My own approach was influenced by both types of work, and in this chapter I try to identify their respective weaknesses and how these could be overcome by integrating what I called the 'competence' and 'action' models. (A response to this paper by David Brazil, defending the linguistic version of the competence model, appears in the volume in which my article was originally published.)

The study of classroom interaction has a quite surprisingly long history, and one of its distinctive features is a baffling array of approaches with different purposes, foci and terminologies. Despite this diversity, however, much of the most recent work in the field shares a fundamental idea which contrasts with the older 'classroom observation' tradition.[1] Crudely put, it is non-behaviourist: it has not sought to restrict itself to the description and explanation of 'observable behaviour'. Rather, the central aim has been to discover the assumptions, rules, strategies, etc., which underlie and produce classroom interaction. Nevertheless, within the boundaries of that common theme, there are still some major differences of approach and it is on one of these that I want to focus here.

Now, of course, the nature of the approach one adopts depends on one's purposes, and in the case of classroom interaction we are faced with several different disciplines as well as different schools of thought within those disciplines. My criticisms in this chapter are not meant to suggest that there is only one set of proper purposes, or that classroom interaction is the 'territory' of one discipline. However, I do think that we should work towards the situation where the purposes, theories and findings of neighbouring disciplines are at least compatible and preferably complementary. It is certainly true that much sociology ignores linguistics, indeed much sociology ignores language, and that is a target for justifiable criticism. However, in this chapter I want to point to some sociologically troubling aspects of some recent work in linguistics, sociolinguistics and the philosophy of language,[2] though I shall focus specifically on some recent work in the first discipline. I want to try to show that this work, while in many respects instructive, predicates a kind of sociological theory which is unsatisfactory in a number of different ways.[3]

I want to contrast what I shall call competence and action models of social interaction.[4] In the competence approach, particular instances or recurring patterns of human activity are treated as competent displays of culture membership, and the discovery of the rules or procedures by which that activity was, or could have been, produced is taken as the exclusive goal. I would count the following as examples of such an approach: 'the ethnography of speaking',[5] speech act analysis,[6] conversational analysis[7] and discourse analysis.[8]

Action theory, on the other hand, while similarly anti-behaviourist, treats patterns of activity as the product of interaction between groups with different concerns and interests, who define situations in distinctive ways and develop strategies for furthering those interests, often by means of negotiation and bargaining with one another. In relation to any particular action, the action theorist asks what intentions and motives underlie it and how these relate to the actor's perspective or definition of the situation. Examples of an action approach can be found in interactionist ethnography,[9] transactional anthropology[10] and social phenomenology.[11] Some work seems uneasily to span the divide between the competence and action approaches, that of Goffman being the most obvious example.[12]

At the risk of disclosing something of what is to come, I could say, baldly, that competence theories are concerned with explaining social order, action theories with detecting and accounting for patterns of social control.[13] However, for me this indicates the deficiencies of both, rather than the superiority of one over the other.

My argument is that, as an overall framework, the action approach is the more promising. However, this framework is underdeveloped; in part, I think, because of a kind of empiricism whereby more emphasis has been placed on investigating the content of perspectives and strategies employed by particular groups of actors in particular settings than on developing the underlying theory. The result has been that the concepts which are central to the action model, 'perspective' and 'strategy', have an inadequate and usually implicit theoretical context which takes the form of a vague pluralism in which different groups simply have different interests and different views of, and strategies for dealing with, the world.

There are two implications of this implicit theory relevant here. The first is that definitions of the situation tend to be treated as though they are produced out of nothing. This ignores both the cultural resources which are used to produce them and the fact that perspectives often become institutionalized. The second relevant feature of this implicit theory is that it fails to recognize the problem of mutual understanding which arises if different groups have different perspectives. Unlike Mead, the founder of interactionism, latter-day interactionists have not tended to address the question of how communication and the co-ordination of action are possible.[14] Those working within competence approaches, on the other hand, have addressed both these problems and made some progress in dealing with them. I am not suggesting, therefore, that work done by those operating within a competence framework is simply mistaken and should be discarded, but rather that it must be recast into an action-based approach, a process which will transform the latter.

Having briefly sketched what I regard as the deficiencies of the action model, I want to turn now to the failings of the competence approach. To illustrate my arguments I shall focus on the work of Sinclair and Coulthard, since this is the best-developed treatment of classroom interaction employing a competence approach.[15] However, I think my arguments apply equally to the other variants of competence theory.[16]

What I want to suggest is that the competence model amounts to a kind of cognitive functionalism sharing similar virtues and vices to normative functionalism.[17] The virtues are a disciplined search for systematic interrelation between the apparently unconnected, a concern with describing whole systems, and a willingness to seek explanations for the 'obvious'. Its vices are a reification of patterns of interaction as they exist at one socio-historical location into universal structures fulfilling universal functions;[18] an assumption of widespread consensus about rules and a neglect of the complex patterning of interests involved in social interaction; and an inability to explain change except as the result of the impact of external events. In this chapter I shall try to show that these criticisms are also applicable to the competence model of classroom interaction.

Where normative functionalism, at least in its Parsonian form, is concerned with the norms and values that must be internalized by members of a society if that society is to function, those researchers working within the competence framework set out to specify the rules or procedures that underlie the competent performance of various kinds of social activity. In both cases the nature of the product – a properly functioning society and the performance of a particular activity – are treated as consensually defined and/or as analytically identifiable. Thus, in their introduction, Sinclair and Coulthard explain their choice of classroom interaction as a focus in terms of its characteristic structure:

> we decided it would be . . . productive to begin . . . with a more simple type of spoken discourse, one which has much more overt structure than 'desultory' conversation, where one participant has acknowledged responsibility for the direction of the discourse, for deciding who shall speak when, and for introducing and ending topics.[19]

Here we have the distribution of conversational rights as it typically occurs in the classroom proposed as a feature of a type of discourse. With this reformulation an element of necessity is added. Certain features of classroom interaction are 'fixed' as constitutive of that discourse type. Furthermore, these features seem to be thought of as in some sense functional:

> Verbal interaction inside the classroom differs markedly from desultory conversation in that its main purpose is to instruct and inform and this difference is reflected in the structure of the discourse. In conversation, topic changes are unpredictable and uncontrollable, for as Sacks has shown, a speaker can even talk 'on topic' without talking on the topic intended by the previous speaker. Inside the classroom it is one of the functions of the teacher to choose the topic, decide how it will be subdivided into smaller units and cope with digressions and misunderstandings.[20]

One of the implications of the treatment of these features of classroom interaction as constitutive of a type of discourse is that any deviation from this pattern is conceived as resulting in meaninglessness:

> It is deviant to withhold feedback continually, and we have a tape of one lesson where a teacher, new to a class, and trying to suggest to them that there aren't always right answers, does withhold feedback and eventually reduces the children to silence – they cannot see the point of his questions.[21]

As a result, there are no rational grounds for deviance, it is the product of whim:

> This category (teacher direct) covers all exchanges designed to get the pupil to do but not say something. Because of the nature of the classroom, the Response is a compulsory element of structure. This is not to suggest that children always do what they are told, but it does imply that the teacher has a right to expect the pupil to do so. Just as anyone can produce an ungrammatical sentence when he feels like it, so a pupil can break the rules of discourse.[22]

Yet we have evidence that pupils often have different conceptions of how one should behave in the classroom from teachers, and this, in part, is because they have diferent patterns of interest.[23] And even if we did not have such evidence it would be cavalier to dismiss pupil deviance in this way. Now I do not want to deny that, in many senses, classroom interaction is a collaborative product, with teachers and pupils operating on the basis of similar working definitions of 'proper classroom behaviour'. I am not suggesting that the classroom is inevitably, or even typically, a setting in which there is an implacable conflict of interests between teachers and pupils: the relationship between the parties is much more subtle and complex; indeed, it is a mistake to assume that there are only two parties to classroom interaction and that these parties are stable.[24] However, conflicts do arise and these cannot be accounted for by the competence model except in terms of inappropriateness and irrationality.

But not only does this approach not provide us with any room for a satisfactory explanation of deviance, it also involves an implicit and quite inadequate account of conformity: participants conform because any other behaviour is 'inappropriate'. And yet, in many lessons, much teacher talk is expended in getting pupils to conform to the rules and even to respond to directives. Thus there arise what one might call disciplinary digressions, which can amount to anything from a look to a half-hour lecture. Furthermore, these often involve promises and threats of various kinds, which indicates that teachers recognize the possibility of rational alternative lines of pupil action even if rhetorically they often deny such a possibility.

In the same way, presenting the teacher's behaviour in terms of following the rules of discourse is unsatisfactory. We must investigate why these rules seem appropriate and, in part, the explanation is likely to be that such patterns seem to the teacher to facilitate her or his goals; though sometimes they may not, as in the example quoted above of the teacher who seeks to avoid giving feedback.

As a result of its failure to deal with motivation, the competence approach is unable to account for the possibility of change in patterns of classroom interaction, or even for the processes of socio-historical development which have produced those patterns which currently exist. The rules of discourse are presented as static and somehow given. Furthermore, the status of the rules documented by Sinclair and Coulthard is unclear: is the evidence for their existence statistical regularity or is it that these are oriented-to features of interaction? If the former, the problem arises that statistical regularities are not always normative. If the latter, the authors certainly do not provide evidence that all the rules are oriented to, and even where they do provide such evidence they appeal to their own and their readers' knowledge of classrooms rather than establishing that these particular participants orient to them.

Now I think I can anticipate two kinds of response to these arguments. The first is that competence theorists do, of course, recognize the breaking of rules for strategic purposes. Thus, immediately prior to the extract from page 51 quoted earlier, Sinclair and Coulthard comment: 'So important is feedback that if it does not occur we feel confident in saying that the teacher has deliberately withheld it for some strategic purpose'. The second response is that the competence model is being criticized for not doing something which it was never intended to do. According to this argument, its goal is the specification of the rules which define classroom actions and thereby make it possible for teachers and pupils to understand one another's actions. It is not intended to be a full account of what is actually done by teachers and pupils.

I want to reply to both these points simultaneously. It is perfectly possible for a competence theorist to recognize the strategic breaking of rules, so long as that strategy is not intended to modify, and does not result in modification of, those rules. Once this is admitted as a possibility, rules are no longer a sufficient basis for the explanation of action, nor can a useful distinction be drawn between rule-related and strategic considerations as bases for action. This is, I suspect, why Sinclair and Coulthard, after making the comment quoted above about the teacher's strategic withholding of feedback, then go on to say that, if this is done continually, the pupils are reduced to silence.

What I am arguing, then, is that the distinction between discourse rules, on the one hand, and the strategies employed by teachers (and presumably also pupils), on the other, is not viable. Sinclair and Coulthard do not provide us with any strong grounds for accepting a distinction between discourse and pedagogy. They base this distinction on the notion of 'linguistic patterning': thus 'a year's work' has no linguistic structure, whereas 'a lesson' does.[25] But we are not told what 'linguistic patterning' is, or what the other forms of patterning are from which it is being distinguished. From what little is said about the pedagogic level it is quite unclear how the patterning there is similar to and different from that at the other levels. Indeed, the meaning of the term 'linguistic' is obscure. Sometimes it seems to mean speech, as when they talk about 'linguistic introductions'[26] and linguistic and non-linguistic responses in distinguishing between elicitations and directives. Now this interpretation of 'linguistic' does not necessarily rule out linguistic order beyond the level of the lesson, though one would have to study the talk of the parties to lessons separately given their frequent dispersion before and after such occasions. And, indeed, it would allow us to deal with the important issue of topical coherence between lessons. However, it would rule out what the authors call 'reacts', since these are neither verbal nor 'non-verbal surrogates' for the verbal. Despite their inclusion of reacts, however, by the very nature of their data, and perhaps because of their disciplinary affiliations, the authors generally tend to restrict themselves to 'the linguistic' in this sense.[27]

This definition of 'linguistic' as 'the verbal' leads to a number of problems, one of which concerns the distinction between directives and elicitations. Elicitations are defined as requiring verbal responses, directives non-verbal responses. Here, it seems to me, the authors take what for them is an important consideration – the verbal/non-verbal contrast – to be a central feature of the orientations of participants. I think they are mistaken, and offer the following examples to suggest this:

(a) T: Now, who can tell me where Israel is? Go on then, Jackson
         (Pupil walks out to the front of the classroom and points to a place on
         the map drawn on the board)
(b) T: Do you think that's clever?
     P: No
     T: No what?
     P: No sir

While the teacher's utterance in (a) would presumably be classified by Sinclair and Coulthard as a directive, I suggest that it has more in common with elicitations. Conversely, 'No what?' seems best described as a directive even though it requires a verbal response. I suggest that the verbal/non-verbal distinction is not a satisfactory basis for distinguishing between directives and elicitations.[28]

There is, however, another way in which 'linguistic patterning' can be interpreted. It may be taken to mean the application of the notion of structure developed at the level of grammar to the analysis of social interaction. The goal here is the specification of rules of choice and chain. While linguistic patterning in grammatical terms is based on form, at the level of discourse it is to be based on function. Here again, though, we are faced with problems of interpretation: what kind of function is this and how are we to identify functions? The authors seem to identify function with teacher intention: 'Grammar is concerned with the *formal* properties of an item, discourse with the *functional* properties, with what the speaker is using the item for'.[29] Yet, clearly, only some kinds of teacher intention are to be included; much of what the teacher does in the classroom is left to the pedagogical level, but the basis for this allocation is not made explicit. So, for example, why is teacher direct-pupil react included while pupil deviance-teacher direct is excluded? In both cases the connection is complex because decision making, and not just rule following, is involved, though this is perhaps most obvious in the case of the latter connection.[30]

One final methodological point. Sinclair and Coulthard, quite rightly in my view, ground their functions in actor intentions, though there are times when they seem a little ambivalent about this, for example when they talk of 'discourse value'. However, the nature of the evidence at their disposal – transcripts – is an inadequate base for the identification of intentions, and the authors seem to place considerable tacit reliance on their knowledge of why teachers typically do what they do without testing it. An example occurs where they discuss 'starters':

> Starters are acts of which the function is to provide information about, or direct attention or thought towards, an area in order to make a correct response to the initiation more likely, even though this function is often only impromptu, when the teacher realizes that the intended elicitation was not adequate. What he has said can, however, serve as a starter to get the children thinking in the right area, and then the more explicit elicitation has more chance of success.

> 1. T: *What about this one? This I think is a super one.* Isobel, can you think what it means?[31]

While this is quite a plausible interpretation, it is not the only one. I think one could equally argue that here we have an attempt to mobilize pupil participation *per se*, and there are, no doubt, other candidate descriptions. Which is correct has to be tested, but it may not be possible to do this by relying on transcripts alone.

Conversational analysts, of course, would criticize the authors for attempting to ascribe intentions and motives in the first place (as would many sociological structuralists and functionalists). My point is a less severe one: simply that I believe the identification of intention and motive is more difficult than the authors seem to take it to be and that the use of other data sources, such as participant observation and interviewing, is necessary. All data sources are imperfect, but in different ways, and that means that, through their combination, we may be able to counter the major validity threats.[32]

In conclusion, let me repeat what I said at the start. I am not suggesting that the work of Sinclair and Coulthard be discarded as worthless. It is a very useful analysis, pointing to a number of important features of classroom interaction and indicating some of the requirements, hitherto ignored, which such analyses must meet. But it seems to me to restrict its focus to a subset of classroom interactional phenomena which is not a viable object of study. Furthermore, and for associated reasons, it conceptualizes classroom interaction in terms of the following of constitutive rules, a conceptualization which opens it up to the standard, and I think effective, criticisms which can be directed against normative functionalism. To escape such criticisms it is necessary to abandon the distinction between discourse and pedagogy and to treat classroom interaction as composed of interrelated actions which are the product not just of rule following, but also of decision making. What any particular action is, what its function is, should be assessed, in the first place, on the basis of some investigation of the patterns of intention and motivation which produced it, and this requires the use of a wider range of methods than just the analysis of transcripts of classroom talk.[33] This is not to deny that much classroom interaction is heavily institutionalized, and thus does amount to rule following. The point is, however, that these rules have become established through strategic thinking and actions and, at any point, may be suspended, modified or transformed as a result of strategic considerations. Only an action approach can take account of these features of classroom rules. However, as I remarked earlier, for it to become in any reasonable sense adequate, action theory requires considerable development, and this process of development must draw on the work already done within the competence framework.

6 From Ethnography to Theory: A Programme and Paradigm in the Sociology of Education[1]

My colleagues and I began our research on the effects of examinations with an explicit concern to develop theory, since we felt that this had been neglected by ethnographers, and was essential if further progress was to be made. We started by trying to apply grounded theorizing, but we came increasingly to question what 'theory' meant and what was involved in its development. One effort at clarification involved looking for an exemplar of theory development in ethnographic reseach. The most promising, we decided, was the work of Hargreaves, Lacey and Ball on differentiation-polarization theory. The following chapter outlines their work and why I believe it to be exemplary.

We have a wealth of theoretical ideas in sociology but a paucity of theories. The theoretical ideas we employ are rarely developed into an explicit and coherent form, and even more rarely are they subjected to systematic testing. This neglect of the development and testing of theory stems in large part from what in my view has been an over-reaction to 'positivism.[2] The consequences have been serious. Without well-developed and tested theories our explanations for social events cannot be more than speculative, however much we might dress them up in rhetoric.[3]

In recent years, British sociology of education has been polarized between neo-Marxist macro-analysis of one variety or another and ethnographic studies of school processes inspired by symbolic interactionism. The first has specialized for the most part in vague, though sometimes illuminating, ideas about the functions of schools in capitalist societies. The second has produced a considerable amount of empirical research, but its orientation has been primarily descriptive. Though interesting theoretical ideas have often emerged, they have rarely been developed very far. Neither of these traditions has seriously addressed the problem of testing theory and, as a result, neither has produced much cumulation of theoretical knowledge.[4]

My concern in this chapter is with how we might improve this dismal performance, and in particular with how ethnographic research could contribute to the development and testing of theory in the sociology of education. Though there has been a large amount of ethnographic work on schools since the beginning of the 1970s,[5] I shall argue that if we want a model for theory-focused ethnography we must look back to the early studies of Lacey and Hargreaves.[6] With the striking exception of Ball, more recent ethnographic research on schooling has not built directly on these studies.[7] Moreover, it has been shaped by a very different set of methodological principles. Under the influence of symbolic interactionism, social phenomenology and ethno-methodology, the primary aim of ethnographic research on schools became description of the diversity and complexity of the perspectives and activities of teachers and pupils, with only sketches being provided of explanations for the patterns discovered.[8] Concomitantly, there was widespread rejection of traditional measurement issues. Instead, reliance was placed primarily upon the provision of qualitative descriptions of behaviour, supported by extracts from field notes and transcripts; these were regarded as closer to reality than data produced by systematic observation, structured interviews or questionnaires.

I am not suggesting that the influence of interpretive sociology has been wholly bad. It has provided theoretical insights into the process of schooling. It has also produced a sensitive awareness of some previously underestimated problems involved in interpreting sociological data. Nevertheless, I believe that through its discouragement of explicit theorizing and formal hypothesis-testing, and its dismissal and/or neglect of traditional measurement concerns, it has hampered the development of theory in the sociology of education. As a result, interpretive ethnography is condemned to rely upon theoretical ideas which are vague and untested.

The work of Hargreaves, Lacey and Ball

Hargreaves' and Lacey's studies arose from a commitment on the part of what was then a combined department of Sociology and Anthropology at Manchester University to apply anthropological techniques to the investigation of urban industrial societies.[9] The original proposal for research in the field of education led to the study of two grammar schools in the same town, Colin Lacey investigating a boys' grammar school (Hightown), Audrey Lambart a girls' grammar school (Mereside). Later, David Hargreaves joined the research team to study a boys' secondary modern school (Lumley).

Despite a broad concern to analyse schools as social systems, Lacey and Hargreaves came to focus primarily on the polarization of pupils into groups with contrasting attitudes to school values.[10] They set about documenting this polarization, showing that pupils in the top streams, and those treated as the best academically within each stream, were more strongly committed to school values than those in bottom streams, and/or those at the bottom of each stream. To one degree or another, the latter rejected school values and behaved accordingly.

While some of the characteristics of the anti-school cultures that Lacey and Hargreaves describe are different, reflecting diferences between the schools, the explanations they propose to account for the emergence of these cultures are broadly the same: they appeal to a combination of home factors and features of school organization, especially streaming. Lacey, in particular, argues that streaming reinforces the effects of differences in cultural resources between middle-class and working-class families. At the same time, though, he provides examples of anomalous cases where working-class pupils have succeeded and middle-class pupils have failed academically, claiming that this demonstrates the partial autonomy of schools from wider social forces.

Despite some differences in strategy, the basic methodological approaches of Hargreaves and Lacey were also similar.[11] Both relied heavily on participant observation. They worked part-time as teachers within the schools they were studying for at least some of the fieldwork period, as well as observing other teachers' classes, and interacting informally with teachers and pupils inside, and to a lesser extent outside, the schools. Both also used interviews and questionnaires to supplement the data from participant observation.

Ball's study arose out of a rather different intellectual (and geographical) context, though there was an important link since Colin Lacey was his Ph.D. supervisor at the University of Sussex. Ball has stated that symbolic interactionism was his guiding theoretical framework, and his approach to fieldwork was shaped by that perspective.[12] Moreover, it seems quite clear that he did not set out simply to replicate Hargreaves' and Lacey's studies at a comprehensive school.[13] Nevertheless, a substantial part of Ball's study is concerned with the effects of school organization on pupils, and his account has much in common with those of Hargreaves and Lacey, both at the level of theory and of methodology.

Beachside Comprehensive, the school which Ball studied, had changed from streaming to banding before he began his fieldwork. However, Ball argued that banding would probably have much the same effect as streaming, that it would polarize the attitudes of pupils towards school values within and between bands, and that this would amplify social class inequalities in educational achievement. And, indeed, Ball documents the polarization he found at Beachside and the differential social class composition of the bands. In addition, during the course of his fieldwork the school introduced mixed-ability grouping and Ball looked at the effects of this on pupils' attitudes and behaviour. He found that it reduced polarization but had less effect upon social class differences.

To a considerable extent, then, the work of these three authors focuses on the same set of theoretical ideas, developing and testing these ideas in different settings. It provides a cumulative research programme, and as such is virtually unique in the sociology of education.

What is theory?

Up to now I have used the term 'theory' without defining it. However, it is a word which is employed in such a variety of ways that I must make clear what I mean by it. The first point to be made is that for me theory is not something restricted to science. We all use theoretical ideas in everyday life in order to develop explanations for events. Faced with some set of events, we draw on and develop ideas about what causes such events and why. This, in a more systematic and rigorous way, is also what historians do. Of course, the theoretical ideas on which we draw, in everyday life or in historiography, are rarely spelled out very clearly, nor do we usually have information about the conditions under which they hold. Nevertheless, what is important to recognize about them is that they are *general* ideas, they make claims about how one type of phenomenon produces another, whether this be unemployment causing riots or certain types of home causing criminality. Some methodologists prefer not to call these general ideas 'theories', reserving that term for more refined and developed versions of them.[14] Nevertheless, I think it is important to recognize that in broad terms theory is not something unique to science, it has its origins in commonsense knowledge; and, of course, like other types of theory, social theory also reacts back upon common sense.

This said, though, it *is* necessary to distinguish the type of theorizing I am recommending in this chapter from the ways in which we set about explaining events in everyday life, in historiography, and, for that matter, in much sociology. For the latter, the primary focus is a particular event, or set of events, and the aim is to explain, if not every aspect of those events, many aspects of them. In order to do this, resort will often be made to several different theoretical ideas, identifying multiple causes. Effectively, what is involved is the application (and perhaps also elaboration) of theoretical ideas in order to produce an explanation for some particular phenomenon which is of interest to us.[15]

Developing and testing theory in the sense I intend it here, on the other hand, involves a quite different orientation. Here, the focus is not on given events, but rather on a particular theoretical idea, and those aspects of *any* events whose investigation might facilitate the development and testing of that idea. The central concern is the clarification of the variables and relations intrinsic to the idea; the identification of indicators for those variables; and the testing of predictions derived from the theoretical idea. The goal of such theorizing is a set of conditionally universal (and clearly specified) claims of the basic form: given certain conditions, if such and such a type of event (A) occurs, it will be followed (or accompanied) by an event of type B. On this model, theories do not *describe* the world; they are not accounts of the relations between events in a particular setting, or descriptions of the interrelation of social structures in a society, or models of the causes of a phenomenon. They are not empirical generalizations of any kind. Rather, they are statements of some of the general principles which generate socio-historical events.[16]

I can illustrate this conception of theory by sketching the theoretical idea which lies at the heart of the work of Hargreaves, Lacey and Ball. I shall call it differentiation-polarization theory.[17] This theory claims that if pupils are differentiated according to an academic-behavioural standard, for example by being streamed or banded, their attitudes to that standard will become polarized. In particular, those given the lowest rankings will reject it and the values it embodies. This theory tells us what will happen *wherever* pupils are differentiated academically/behaviourally, given certain (unspecified) conditions (on which more below). It is important to recognize that this theory does not offer a complete explanation for pupils' behaviour, or even a complete account of the determinants of school achievement or of 'disruptive' behaviour in classrooms. It claims no more than that, under certain conditions, differentiation will lead to polarization.

Hargreaves, Lacey and Ball did not employ the kind of theorizing I have sketched here. Theirs was a more descriptive approach, identifying streaming/banding as one among a number of factors producing a polarization in values on the part of pupils. Nevertheless, as we have seen, a theory, in the sense I am using the term, can be extracted from their research relatively easily. Moreover, there are other respects in which their work can be usefully reinterpreted within this framework. In order to demonstrate this I shall begin by sketching the research programme which can be built on the basis of differentiation-polarization theory.[18]

Differentiation-polarization theory as a research programme

A first requirement for a research programme, of course, is that the theory on which it centres promises to be true. While the truth of differentiation-polarization theory has not been established beyond reasonable doubt, in my view there is more and better empirical support for this theory than for most others, not just in the sociology of education but in sociology generally. Furthermore, while there are those who have claimed to offer evidence against it, at best this evidence simply shows that there are conditions under which the theory does not apply.[19] This is true of any theory, however, and one of the main topics for the research programme is precisely the specification of those conditions.[20]

An equally important requirement for a research programme, in my view, is that it promises to produce consequential findings, whether for policy or for theory. There is little point in research which, while systematically, rigorously and even intelligently pursued, addresses a problem of little importance. Though one must be very careful in judging a research problem trivial – what at first sight seems banal may in another light become very important – the distinction between important and trivial topics for research is significant. Charles Peirce long ago pointed out the implications of the economics of research,[21] and recent cuts in the funding of social research only reinforce the point.

Differentiation-polarization theory has a number of interesting potential implications. The most immediate ones are that both pupil deviance and achievement will be affected by changes in the degree of differentiation at the level of the school and the classroom. It suggests that the more effective we are at motivating pupils to aim for academic success, the more strongly will those who come to perceive themselves as failing to achieve this goal react against school authority. At the same time, it indicates how we can avoid the development of a strong counterculture within schools, but suggests that his may have to be bought at the expense of lower levels of academic motivation on the part of the 'more able' pupils, and perhaps also lower levels of school achievement.[22] I am not suggesting that there is an inevitable dilemma here, simply that under some conditions, those under which the theory holds, this dilemma may arise. Taking a different stance, the theory also suggests one way, albeit a rather paradoxical one, in which we might stimulate a strong school counterculture should we wish to engender pupil resistance.

Lacey and Ball, in particular, were also concerned with a further possible implication of the theory: that differentiation within school amplifies the effects of the social class distribution of cultural resources, thereby increasing inequalities in school performance and life-chances. We might also consider whether differentiation has a similar effect on sexual and racial differences. How much change any reduction in the level of differentiation within the education system would have on social class structure or on the sexual and racial divisions of labour within British society remains to be seen. Currently available evidence regarding social class suggests that it might have very little effect, but conclusions can only be tentative given the complexity of this issue and the small amount of evidence available.[23]

In my view, then, differentiation-polarization theory provides the basis for a viable research programme. It is reasonably well-established and carries important implications. Moreover, there are many aspects of the theory which require further development. For example, Hargreaves, Lacey and Ball suggest a number of different mechanisms by which differentiation might produce polarization, but their data do not allow us to assess the validity of these alternatives with any confidence. Here are three of the alternatives:

1. *Reaction Formation.* Drawing on Albert Cohen's work on delinquency, it is argued that all pupils are committed to academic success and other school values when they enter school and that, as a result, pupils allocated to low streams (and/or to low positions within each stream) experience status frustration. To cope with this they invert school values and pursue those inverted values, values in terms of which they *can* succeed compared to other pupils in the school.[24]
2. *Substitution of Alternative Cultures.* Here it is argued that pupils cope with the experience of failure not by inverting school values, but by adopting an alternative set of values available within their communities (Lacey provides the examples of working-class culture and Jewish culture from Hightown).[25]
3. *Labelling Theory.* All three authors, but especially Ball, sometimes present labelling theory as offering a link between differentiation and polarization. Here the idea is that low stream pupils adopt and become committed to stereotypes which teachers and other pupils hold of them, and thus come to act in ways that confirm those stereotypes.

Clearly, further research is needed to assess the viability of these and other alternatives.

Identifying the psychological mechanism which enables differentiation to produce polarization provides a partial specification of the conditions under which the causal relationship between differentiation and polarization will be found. For example, if we adopt the reaction formation model then differentiation will lead to polarization only where pupils are initially strongly committed to school values. If we adopt Lacey's idea of pupils drawing on available alternative cultures, polarization might not occur if there were no such alternatives, as would be the case within certain closed religious communities or within tightly controlled families which share the same culture as the school.

However, the psychological mechanisms used to explain the links between differentiation and polarization are not the only source of conditions determining the applicability of the theory. For status frustration or negative stereotypes to generate a counterculture, pupils experiencing these must be able to communicate and co-ordinate their actions with one another. The easier this is, the more likely it is that an anti-school subculture will develop. Thus, presumably, there are conditions of the theory relating to ease of communication among pupils.

Similarly, the strength of the relationship between differentiation and polarization is probably affected by whether there is a single coherent set of school values leading to a single status hierarchy, reflecting a teacher consensus, or whether there are several status hierarchies on which individual pupils' positions are sharply discrepant. In the former situation, the relationship between differentiation and polarization would presumably be strong, whereas in the latter it would probably be weak or non-existent.

Another area requiring research concerns anomalies in the data which the theory, as currently developed, cannot explain. For instance, while the theory predicts that the bottom stream or band in a school will display the strongest reaction against school values, this was not what happened in the case of Beachside. In the bottom groups, one of which was a remedial class, pupils did not reject school values as strongly as those in the band immediately above them.[26] Assuming this evidence is valid, either the theory needs modifying to account for these results or the scope conditions must be specified in such a way as to exclude cases of this type. Either way, it is necessary to investigate why the effects predicted by the theory did not occur in these groups. Of course if all attempts at modification were to fail, one would have to consider rejecting the whole theory.

Further research is also required to discover whether the field of application of the theory can be enlarged. Does the theory relate only to schools and pupils, or does it apply to all institutions and people where the scope conditions are met? Does it apply to differentiation in terms of *any* standards, or only in terms of what Lacey calls an 'academic-behavioural' standard? In Glaser and Strauss's terms, can we transform this substantive theory into a formal one?[27] This, of course, opens up a considerable area for further research, from small group experimental investigations of differentiation to comparative analysis of differentiation processes in large organizations and perhaps even whole societies.

A paradigm

I have tried to show that differentiation-polarization theory provides the basis for an extensive research programme, and one that is well worth pursuing. In the remainder of this chapter I want to go further. I shall argue that, suitably reconstructed, Hargreaves', Lacey's and Ball's work provides us with a paradigm[28] for case-study research concerned with developing and testing theory.

The vindication of theory

Perhaps the most important respect in which this research provides a model is the very fact that it centres on a theory made up of conditionally universal claims, and that it provides powerful support for that theory. The strongest argument against the application of the covering law model of explanation to the social sciences has always been the claim, conceded even by many of its advocates, that no examples of well-established theories making conditionally universal claims are available. Moreover, the case for such theories has not always been furthered by the examples offered by proponents of the model (notably Homans),[29] since these have often been banal, vague and circular. Differentiation-polarization theory, on the other hand, is an example of a theory in line with this model whose validity is reasonably well-established and whose implications are far from vague or banal.[30] While we may be tempted to regard differentiation as the obvious explanation for polarization (in other words to treat the theory as a 'quasi-law' in Scriven's terms),[31] in fact it has at least one strong competitor: class sub-culture theory.[32] Nor, conversely, is it obvious that differentiation necessarily leads to polarization. Indeed, as already indicated, there will be circumstances where the relationship does *not* hold, and these need to be specified in the conditions which define the scope of the theory.

Above all else, then, in my view, differentiation-polarization theory represents a paradigm because it shows the feasibility of the positivist model of theory, the model which, as far as I can see, gives us the best hope of producing effective explanations for social phenomena, and thereby a sound basis for policy.[33]

A narrow focus

The work of Hargreaves, Lacey and Ball has sometimes been criticized for its relatively narrow focus: on the one hand for not explaining the contextual variability of pupils' behaviour,[34] on the other for not looking at the role that schooling plays in capitalist societies.[35] Yet in my view (now!) this narrowness of focus is one of its great strengths. If the development and testing of theory is to be pursued effectively, the research focus has to be narrow. Attempts to provide a rounded and detailed description of the institution or behaviour under study, or to integrate macro and micro levels of analysis, are, it seems to me, counterproductive as far as theorizing is concerned.[36] One cannot gather data on the broad front necessary to do either of these things while at the same time collecting the depth of data necessary to develop a theory and then test a wide range of specific hypotheses deriving from it.[37] Indeed, in my view, even the work of Hargreaves, Lacey and Ball suffers from a failure to restrict their focus to the theory.

None of the three studies is exclusively concerned with developing and testing this theory. Lacey spends his first two chapters providing an account of the historical development of Hightown Grammar School. While this is of great interest and value as a contribution to understanding the development of the English educational system, it is only indirectly relevant to the theory, providing an explanation for why differentiation was so strong at Hightown. Much the same can be said of Lacey's discussion of staff culture in the school. In the same way Ball's analyses of the subject-choice scheme, and of the processes which led to the abolition of banding in favour of mixed-ability grouping, describe the context in which differentiation and polarization occurred at Beachside, rather than being critical for the development of the theory. Hargreaves' study is rather more narrowly focused than the other two. Even so, it is much more concerned with describing the differences between the attitudes and behaviour of pupils in different streams, and in different positions within each stream, than it is with theorizing. This failure single-mindedly to adopt the development and testing of differentiation-polarization theory as the major goal almost certainly reduced the cumulative impact of the three studies, leaving such important issues as the nature of the mechanism producing the link between differentiation and polarization unresolved.[38]

Nevertheless, despite their expressed desire to 'provide an analysis of the school as a dynamic system of social relations',[39] Hargreaves', Lacey's and Ball's studies employ a narrower and more theory-oriented focus than subsequent ethnographic work in the sociology of education. As a result they provide a much better model for future research than does that more recent work.[40]

Research design

An important aspect of the development and testing of theories in non-experimental research is the selection of cases for study. We can usefully reconstruct the process of theoretical inquiry in terms of three stages, following Peirce.[41] The starting point is a doubt or puzzle which pinpoints some phenomenon as requiring explanation. The first step is the development of plausible explanatory ideas, a process which Peirce calls retroduction or abduction. Most case study research does not get beyond this first stage.[42] It is concerned, almost exclusively, with displaying as doubtful or puzzling what we previously took for granted, and with the generation of plausible explanations for these puzzling phenomena. Now I am not suggesting that every piece of research should traverse all three phases of inquiry; to demand that would be to commit the single study fallacy.[43] But I do think that sociologists have a collective duty to attempt the production of well-established social theory, and so it is important that some research does develop and test theory by pressing on into the second and third stages.

In the second stage of inquiry, one of the plausible explanations generated in stage one is clarified and developed into a theory having implications for other cases. Rationally reconstructed in these terms, the work of Hargreaves, Lacey and Ball begins from a concern to explain the increasing divergence in academic performance and behaviour between top and bottom stream/band pupils over the course of their school lives. And it focuses on a plausible explanation for this divergence which appeals to the effects of differentiation on pupils' attitudes to school values. In this research programme, the second, deductive, stage of inquiry involves the clarification of the concepts of differentiation and polarization and the derivation of hypotheses about what one would expect to occur under various conditions if the theory were correct. This provides the basis for the third stage of inquiry, the selection and investigation of cases in which these various hypotheses can be tested.

Ethnographic research is often criticized for its failure to use statistical sampling techniques in selecting cases for study. However, such techniques cannot provide a representative sample of the universe to which conditionally universal claims apply, since that universe is infinite.[44] Given this, a much more effective selection strategy is to choose cases which are in some sense crucial for the theory. Initially, for example, one might choose a case for investigation where one would expect the empirical relationships postulated by the theory to be discovered. Subsequently, having tested the plausibility of the theory in this relatively weak way, one might employ falsifying selection strategies, choosing critical cases in which the factors embedded in alternative explanations for the phenomenon are controlled.

It is in these terms that we can understand the peculiar appropriateness of the cases Hargreaves, Lacey and Ball selected for investigation. Lumley School, Hargreaves' secondary modern, would be the obvious first case to choose in assessing the validity of the theory, since it is attended by pupils who have, in effect, already been declared failures. If we are to find anti-school values emerging anywhere in the school system it is in such a school that we would expect to find them, and experience tells us that we are unlikely to be disappointed. But it is not just the emergence of anti-school values among pupils that is important. If the theory is correct we would expect to find these values at their strongest among those pupils in the bottom streams, whose failure is doubly stamped by the streaming system. And, indeed, Hargreaves shows how polarization of values parallels the differentiation of pupils, both among streams and within each stream.

In terms of our rational reconstruction, Lacey's study builds on Hargreaves' work in a very important way.[45] Whereas the case Hargreaves investigated was that where one would most expect polarization to occur, Hightown Grammar is, in many ways, a place where one would least expect it. Given that the pupils entering this school have been strongly committed to school values in their primary schools, we have partial control over those factors outside school shaping pupils' attitudes. This contrasts with the case of Lumley, where we have little defence against the argument that polarization was simply a reflection of the pupils' pre-existing attitudes.

The fact that polarization occurs concomitantly with differentiation at Hightown Grammar is, then, particularly strong evidence in support of the theory. Of course, in no sense does it provide proof, and indeed there are plausible alternative explanations we can suggest. We might, for example, question Lacey's evidence that all the pupils were committed to school values prior to entering Hightown Grammar. Or we might argue that it is precisely at around the age of 12 and 13 that neighbourhood peer group values start to have an influence on working-class pupils, and that the polarization in pupil attitudes at Hightown reflects *this* rather than the effects of differentiation. Although neither of these alternatives fits the data provided by Lacey better than differentiation-polarization theory, they cannot be ruled out. Nevertheless, the point remains that the selection of Hightown Grammar was a valuable strategy for testing this theory.

In a similar way, Ball's study of Beachside Comprehensive provides a further test of the theory. Ball shows that banding in a large, mixed, comprehensive school has similar effects to streaming in single-sex secondary modern and grammar schools. Perhaps the most important feature of Ball's study, though, is that he investigated the effects on the polarization of values among pupils of the reduction in differentiation involved in the introduction of mixed-ability grouping. In other words, he made use of a 'natural experiment'. As the theory would suggest, the result of this innovation was a significant decline in polarization. While, once again, this in no sense provides conclusive proof, it offers further evidence in support of the theory which, taken together with that provided by Hargreaves and Lacey, makes the case for the theory even stronger.

What we have here, then, are three pieces of ethnographic work which, in a limited way at least, build upon one another, developing and testing a particular theory. We look in vain for other examples of such complementarity in the sociology of education, and there are not many in sociology generally. The tendency has been for studies to investigate a diverse range of phenomena, their authors moving from one topic to another, with few attempts to capitalize upon earlier work. Yet unless researchers work collectively on particular theories, investigating cases which are critical for those theories, there will be no cumulative development of knowledge.

Sampling

Another important feature of the work of Hargreaves, Lacey and Ball is the attention they give to sampling within the cases studied.[46] This is one of the weakest aspects of more recent ethnographic research.[47] This weakness is, in part, one aspect of the over-reaction to positivism, within which representative sampling has sometimes been treated as the methodologist's stone. In this respect, Hargreaves, Lacey and Ball display a refreshing sense of proportion. Where appropriate, they seek representative samples. Faced with the problem of generalizing across six different forms at Beachside, Ball selects a single form to represent each of the two bands on which his study focuses. He does this on the basis of 'convenience and availability', but he makes systematic checks on the representativeness of his data from these forms, both by comparing it with data available from other forms and by means of significance tests.[48]

But Hargreaves, Lacey and Ball also show how effective systematic theoretical sampling can be. Thus, Lacey takes the top stream at Hightown Grammar to demonstrate the process of differentiation-polarization within school classes. It is precisely in this elite form, destined to take 'O' levels at the end of the fourth year, that one would least expect to find a polarization in values. The fact that such polarization does occur provides powerful evidence in support of the theory. Hargreaves, on the other hand, studied all the fourth-year forms at Lumley (apart from the remedial form) in depth, on the grounds that this is the point in the lives of pupils at which polarization will have its strongest impact, and in an exploratory study assessing the promise of a theoretical idea such a strategy is probably the most useful. Finally, theoretical sampling also underpins what is undoubtedly the most effective set of pupil case-studies in the literature, those presented in chapter 7 of Hightown Grammar.

In the area of sampling too, then, Hargreaves, Lacey and Ball set an excellent example; one which, in general, has not been followed.

Selection of indicators

Ethnographers have been reluctant to employ the language of concepts and indicators in thinking about the process of analysis.[49] Partly, no doubt, this is because they tend to see themselves as engaged in description rather than abstract theorizing. But even the kind of theorized description which is often the aim in ethnography involves making linkages between concepts and data. Unless this is done in a rigorous fashion, the value of the research is limited.[50]

Here too the work of Hargreaves, Lacey and Ball stands out. While only occasionally do they employ systematic triangulation of indicators, they frequently use several different measures for the same concept: sociometric data and observation of informal interaction to document friendships; absence, lateness and detention figures as well as behaviour in lessons to measure the effects of pro- and anti-school attitudes on pupils' behaviour; court appearances and self-reported vandalism to measure delinquency, etc. Perhaps even more significant is their willingness to use quantitative data. This includes not only 'official statistics' of various kinds, but also quantitative data they have generated themselves such as teachers' rankings of pupils, and sociometric data. The use of quantitative indices may be one reason why some commentators are reluctant to count Hargreaves, Lacey and Ball's work as ethnographic. But while it may be true that the authors do not always make as much use of qualitative data as they might,[51] they do use a considerable amount of qualitative data, and often to great effect. One could cite Hargreaves' material on the attitudes of the friendship groups in fourth year form, and his account of the rise and fall of leaders of the delinquescent group; Lacey's use of pupil case-studies, notably the contrast between Cready and Priestly;[52] and Ball's use of observational, diary and interview data to document the friendship patterns and values of banded and mixed ability forms.

It seems to me of great importance not to confuse the distinction between survey and case-study research designs with that between qualitative and quantitative data. To insist that only qualitative data be used in case-study research is just as misguided as the rejection of qualitative data as unscientific sometimes voiced by survey researchers. One should use any data that are available, of whatever type, if they allow one to develop and test one's theory effectively. While quantitative data must not be used *simply because they are quantitative*, especially when their relation to the relevant theoretical concepts is weak, the fact that quantitative data have certain advantages from the point of view of analysis, not least that they may allow the use of powerful statistical techniques, should not be overlooked. In their use of multiple indicators and their willingness to employ quantitative data and statistical techniques, where appropriate, Hargreaves, Lacey and Ball once again offer a lead.

Conclusion

In this chapter I have advocated a particular view of the proper nature of theory in sociology, and illustrated it by reference to the work of Hargreaves, Lacey and Ball. I have argued that this work, suitably reconstructed, offers a powerful research programme. Much more important, though, it provides a paradigm for case study research concerned with developing and testing theory. Elsewhere, I and others have sugested that ethnographers should give high priority to theorizing, of the kind recommended here.[53] But there is, of course, a gap between knowing what is required and knowing how to do it. The work of Hargreaves, Lacey and Ball provides us with a model of the research process which begins to close that gap.

7 Measurement in Ethnography: The Case of Pollard on Teaching Style

One of the areas of weakness in ethnographic research mentioned in the previous chapter is the relationship between concepts and indicators, in other words the problem of measuement. In this chapter I look at this issue in greater depth, taking an article by Andrew Pollard on teachers' coping strategies as an example. I examine the various ways that ethnographers offer evidence in support of their claims and the problems associated with these.

Measurement is not a term generally used by ethnographers. Indeed, many might argue that measurement is central to the experimental and survey research traditions, but not relevant to ethnography. Whether this is so, of course, depends upon what is intended by the term *measurement*.

If what is meant is the development of explicit measurement schemes which produce quantitative indices, such as intelligence tests, attitude inventories or systematic observation schedules, then it is true that ethnographers are not generally concerned with measurement (though there are exceptions, among both anthropologists and sociologists). Such schemes involve the establishment of a set of categories which are exhaustive and mutually exclusive, and ideally these should represent points on an ordinal or interval scale. In addition, the rules for assigning data to the categories should be explicitly stated, should specify concrete indicators, should be unambiguous, and should be applied in the same way to all of the data. For the purposes of this chapter, I shall call this conception of measurement the 'standard model'.[1]

However, while ethnographers rarely adopt this model, the fundamental issue with which measurement is concerned is the linking of abstract concepts to particular data; and this problem faces ethnographers as much as it does any other social researcher. Given that they are concerned with describing and explaining events in the settings they study, ethnographers are inevitably concerned with the relationship between their accounts and the data they have collected, and between these data and the events described.

Indeed, the issue of the proper relation between concepts and data is an area where ethnographers have often been critical of survey and experimental research. They have argued that the indicators used in such research often have only a highly problematic connection with the concepts presented and that, as a result, the validity of the findings is doubtful. For example, Douglas has criticized quantitative research on suicide, from Durkheim onwards, on the grounds that the indicators used to measure such concepts as 'social integration' are weak, if not entirely spurious.[2] Similarly, Mehan has challenged the findings of achievement tests by demonstrating the different ways in which children may interpret test questions.[3]

However, when we turn to ethnographic research itself, there is some vagueness about how concepts and data are linked. Sometimes the model adopted seems to be virtually identical to that of survey and experimental research.[4] On other occasions, an alternative approach seems to be recommended.[5] However, the precise nature of such alternatives is elusive.[6] And in my opinion no convincing alternative model has yet been provided. I believe that much the same problems face researchers in relating concepts to data whatever research strategy they adopt. In this chapter I want to examine these problems as they arise in ethnographic work.

As an illustration, I shall draw on an article on teaching styles and social differentiation by Andrew Pollard.[7] I have selected Pollard's article for discussion because, in many respects, it is an exemplary piece of ethnographic research; and it explicitly presents a theory and uses a wide range of data to examine that theory. The author recognizes 'the limited nature of the sample and the interpretative nature of the analysis' (p. 47) and thus by implication the need for further research. What I want to do in this chapter is to outline the ways in which Pollard's study, and ethnographic work in general, needs to be developed if we are to be reasonably confident that the links between concepts and data are sound.

The theory which Pollard presents is a complex one. While, like many interactionists, he presents his explanation in softened terms – using words like 'influence', 'implication' and 'reinforcement' rather than 'causality' or 'determination' – effectively his argument is that the character of the working consensus which a teacher negotiates with his/her class, itself determined by the coping strategies of teacher and pupils, determines the level and nature of social differentiation among the pupils. He compares the 'good formal regime' of Mrs Rothwell's class with the 'progressive' working consensus of Mr Harman's class. He investigates the level of social differentiation among pupils in the two classes, using reading levels, seating position, and patterns of sociometric choice as indicators. And he concludes that the formal regime seems to produce a stronger correlation between academic and social differentiation than does the informal regime.

For the purposes of this discussion, I shall focus upon just one of the variables Pollard discusses: the progressive–traditional dimension along which teaching style varies.[8] He presents descriptions of the perspectives and practices of Mrs Rothwell and Mr Harman, and, in trying to show that these two teachers represent contrasting positions on the dimension, he uses several types of evidence:

(a) *Information about the teachers and classes presumably derived from documents, interviews or observation, but without the source being indicated.* For example:

> Mrs Rothwell felt a sincere caring duty towards the children in her class whom she believed came from generally poor and unstable home backgrounds (p. 36).

> . . . Mr Harman's control techniques were based on principles which forsook all physical sanctions and extrinsic inducements (p. 43).

(b) *Time-generalized observer description.* Here we are provided with a summary of the behaviour of teacher and pupils over time, of their typical behaviour in respects relating to the working consensus. For instance:

> Mrs Rothwell used classwork for almost everything – during craft activities everyone made a flower in the way they were shown, in writing practice everyone copied the patterns from the board, in number lessons everyone chanted their 2-times, 3-times, 5-times and 10-times tables, in poetry times children spoke verses chorally, in creative English everyone wrote on the subject suggested using the words written on the blackboard. These examples occurred consistently and regularly (p. 37).

> In Mr Harman's classroom the tables were arranged for children to work in small groups of five or six. Each child had an official seat at one of the six separate tables and this official seat was for registration and for the first and most 'work'-intensive lesson period of the day (p. 44).

(c) *Frequency-specified, time-generalized observer description.* As with (b), but this time the frequencies of the behaviours are provided. Thus Pollard provides a table indicating the percentage of teacher–pupil contacts initiated by each party and the percentages of each type of contact:

Table 7.1   Teacher-child contacts (%)

	Child-initiated		Teacher-initiated		
	Work-related	Other	Work-related	Other	Advisory
Mrs Rothwell's class	12	15	27	11	35
total		27		73	
Mr Harman's class	20	32	18	17	13
total		52		48	

After Pollard (1984, p. 36).

(d) *Time-specific observer description.* Here the researcher provides a description of behaviour on one particular occasion which is taken to be typical, or significant in some other way. For example, Pollard cites the following in support of his claim that 'collaboration was far from unusual and was an active process':

Mrs Rothwell:	Today we are going to try to do two sorts of sums at once, we'll try to do the take-away ones and the add-up ones, but I'm going to try and trick you by mixing them up . . . (writes sums on board) . . . this is my day for tricking people

(The children work. A little later . . .)

Janet:	She hasn't caught me out yet
Sandra:	She hasn't caught me out yet
Nigel:	She hasn't caught me out yet – has she . . .?
Janet:	She has – you're caught – she's caught him out!
Nigel:	Why?
Janet:	He's got two 'ten take-aways' . . .
Nigel:	I think she has caught me out
Duncan:	Nigel, I think you'd better copy off me, or you'll make a messy job. Ten take away nought makes ten
Sandra:	Ten take away nought makes ten?
Janet:	You've done the second one wrong, you've done the second one wrong
Nigel:	I haven't
Janet:	You have – oh, there shouldn't be a four there should there?
Duncan:	There should
Janet:	Should there? (Janet alters the answer)
Nigel:	Yes, oh yes, that's right
Sandra:	You've done it wrong, there shouldn't be a four there. (Children change answers)
Duncan:	Mine's right
Nigel:	So's mine
Janet:	Mine is
Janet:	Everybody knows ten add ten makes twenty
Nigel:	Ten add ten makes twenty
Nigel:	What's ten add nothing?
Duncan:	Nothing
Sandra:	Ten add nothing is nothing – it's nothing
Nigel:	Janet's done it wrong, she's done ten
Sandra:	Mine are right
Duncan:	They are tricky – oh Sandra, you've done that one wrong, no, look. (Shows and Sandra alters)
Duncan:	That's it

(pp. 40–1)

(e) *Quotations from participants' accounts.* These can be used in two ways:

(i) To document perspectives: For instance:

Mrs Rothwell had a clear image of her ideal pupil (Becker, 1952) but felt a type of resigned concern towards many of those who could not match up to this image. As she put it:

> It really is rewarding when you get a child who is bright, one who you can really talk to and rely on, but we don't get many of those . . . most of them here really do need a lot of help. We do what we can for them but some of them are very hard to help even when you want to do your best for them.
>
> (p. 37)

(ii) As a source of description of events: For example:

In their reception class the children had been used to a daily routine of 'work' in the morning, 'activities' in the afternoon. Mr Harman initially aimed to integrate the two.

> I tried to establish not 'work' and 'play' time but just 'inclass' time – but I totally failed. This distinction between work time and choosing time was forced on me, early on, when I realised they *expected* to do work in the morning. They couldn't cope with the idea of someone 'playing' (in their terms) whilst they were 'working'. I had groups in sand, water, painting, Maths, writing etc . . . they kept asking 'what are those children doing?' They got confused and didn't know what they were meant to do. I found myself policing all the time, checking on what they had and hadn't done. So I've established this system of 'work periods', which they found acceptable and I found productive, and also 'choosing periods' in which I am able to have groups, and gradually I'm getting this idea that some kids can be working when others are choosing.
>
> (pp. 45–6)

This range of data used by Pollard is probably a representative sample of the kinds of information ethnographers usually employ. I want now to look at some of the problems involved in the use of these different types of evidence.

Accuracy of description

There are two, not clearly distinguishable, aspects of accuracy. At the most basic level, we need to be sure that the teacher or pupils did actually do, say or write what Pollard describes. In the case of quotes from audio-recordings this is a matter of whether the transcription is accurate and whether the verbalization was authored by the person to whom it is attributed. This is a fairly straightforward matter, though if the recordings are of poor quality there can be serious difficulties. Where quotations are recorded by means of field notes, the dangers of inaccuracy are rather greater but still probably minor.

The case of non-verbal elements of action is more difficult. To the extent that these are recorded in detail, what is required is accurate portrayal of patterns of physical movement. Unless still photography, or video or film recording, is used, the problems of mapping physical movement are combined with those intrinsic to the writing of field notes, in particular the immediacy and rapid process of the situation being observed, and the limitations of memory.

However, we are not interested in this etic level of physical sounds and movement for its own sake, but rather to document emic patterns of perspective and action. And here there arises the problem of interpretation given such emphasis by ethnomethodologists.[9] While I do not accept the arguments of ethnomethodologists *in toto*, there is no doubt that the attribution of intentions and attitudes on the basis of what people say or do can involve serious problems, and that it is not always handled effectively by ethnographers. For instance, let us look again at one of Pollard's descriptions:

> Mrs Rothwell felt a sincere caring duty towards the children in her class whom she believed came from generally poor and unstable home backgrounds (p. 36).

How do we know that the attribution to Mrs Rothwell of a 'sincere caring duty' and of a belief that the children in her class came from 'generally poor and unstable home backgrounds' represents an accurate interpretation? Pollard does not tell us the grounds for these imputations, and as a result we have no basis for judging their accuracy. Moreover, we can imagine that there might be room for considerable disagreement among observers over this interpretation.

In other cases, Pollard provides at least some evidence. As an instance of time-specific observer description, we cited Pollard's use of an account of a conversation among pupils to support his claim that pupils collaborated among themselves over answers (p. 39). Here we are able to assess the relation between the concept of collaboration and the pattern of activity that the pupils are engaging in, as described by Pollard: comparing one another's answers, trying to understand the discrepancies, altering their answers, etc. There seems to be little serious doubt that what we have here is an instance of collaboration. Pollard does not provide a clear definition of the concept, but those activities would seem likely to fall under most definitions of the term.

The problem of accuracy is perhaps at its most severe when we have to rely upon participants' accounts as a source of descriptions of events. Here the threats to accuracy operate at one remove from the ethnographer as well as in her or his interpretation of the data, and for this reason it may be particularly difficult to get much purchase upon them. The use of multiple accounts, in other words triangulation, is one strategy; but it is no panacea.[10]

The generalizability of the descriptions

Pollard, like other ethnographers, makes claims about the stable perspectives and typical behaviour of the people he studied, within some (unspecified) time limits. Clearly, whatever the data used, we need to ask whether they reflect accurately what these people do across different occasions.[11] With accounts, time-specific descriptions and non-frequency time-generalized descriptions, we have to rely upon the researcher's judgement, on the basis of whatever evidence was available, that the opinion or behaviour was typical. This is unsatisfactory because it seems likely that informal estimates of frequency are open to such large errors that estimates of all but the most extreme variations are of questionable accuracy. Reliance upon such estimates is perhaps the most serious defect of ethnographic measurement.

However, for one item Pollard does provide a frequency description. This is fairly unusual for an ethnographer, though by no means unique. Pollard's table (above) illustrates both the value and some of the problems involved in providing frequency descriptions. The value is that we can see *how* typical the behaviour is of each teacher's teaching, and the scale of difference between the teachers in this respect. The problems are manifold, and to varying degrees are to be found in 'systematic observation' studies too.[12] In the case of Pollard's table, we need to know:

1. The period over which the observation of teacher–pupil contacts was carried out; whether it was continuous; and its size relative to the time-span over which generalization is being made?
2. How rigorously were teacher–child contacts identified? Pollard provides no information about this. Yet variations in identification procedure over the course of observation are a source of error and we need to know how large this error is. This covers both the question of how clear and concrete the identification criteria were and how effectively, practically speaking, these criteria were applied. For example, was the measurement done by live coding or on the basis of video-recording?
3. How rigorously were the child/teacher initiative and work-related/other/ advisory distinctions made? Again, we need to know how closely specified the categories were and how effective the counting of instances was, given practical constraints.

There are serious difficulties involved in devising well-specified category schemes and in applying them rigorously and considerable error can be created by variations in definition, coding procedure and practice.[13] Without information about these matters, even the generalizability of Pollard's frequency description is difficult to judge.

Content validity

By content validity[14] I mean the extent to which the evidence which Pollard uses to document the teachers' perspectives represents all the components of his definition of traditionalism/progressivism (for example, didactic versus discovery pedagogy, use of intrinsic versus extrinsic motivation, etc.). In order to assess this we need a clear definition of traditionalism/progressivism. Unfortunately, Pollard does not provide one. This failure to provide adequate definitions of key concepts is by no means unusual in ethnographic work.

Of course, in the absence of such definitions, we could try to explicate the concepts ourselves, or draw on other accounts such as those of Barth, Berlak and Berlak, Bennett, and Hammersley.[15] However, what we are interested in is not what people typically refer to as progressive or traditional teaching, but those aspects of teaching that have the effects (variation in social differentiation) in which Pollard is interested. Alternatively, we could try to retrieve the components of traditionalism/progressivism, as defined by Pollard, from the data he gives. But that undercuts the very possibility of assessing content validity.[16]

Given this lack of clarity about the concepts employed, characteristic of much ethnography, it is impossible to assess the content validity of the indicators Pollard uses for traditionalism/progressivism.

Construct validity

An equally important aspect of measurement is what is often termed 'construct validity': the extent to which an indicator accurately measures the concept or component of a concept it is supposed to measure. In other words, how far do variations in the indicator – for instance, frequency of recitation of tables – actually reflect variations in the variable being measured – didactic pedagogy. Once again, we are faced with the problem that there is no clear definition of 'working consensus', nor of the traditional and progressive versions of it. But putting this on one side, there are several reasons why the construct validity of such measures as frequency of the recitation of tables may not be high. For example, a teacher might regard knowledge of tables as an important prerequisite for discovery learning in mathematics, and thus recitation of tables may not be accompanied by other features of didactic pedagogy. Alternatively, there may be other factors which generate recitation of tables besides commitment to traditionalism, for example the imminence of school-wide maths tests, a forthcoming visit by HMI or even the presence of the observer. We are not told how long Pollard spent observing these classrooms, but clearly the longer the time period the less serious the danger from some of these threats to validity.

Another threat to construct validity is idiosyncratic and/or *ad hoc* use of indicators for traditionalism and progressivism. In order to assess the construct validity of indicators for each component of traditionalism/progressivism, besides trying to ensure a representative sample of teaching over time, we might use the stability of interpretations of the data across observers: given the identification criteria developed to recognize the indicators, would another observer, or even Pollard himself on another occasion, have interpreted the events in the same way? The aim here is to assess the effects of random variations, as well as systematic error resulting, for example, from bias on the part of the observer. As another check on systematic error we might try to assess the degree to which the various indicators of traditionalism and progressivism which Pollard uses correlate with one another, and do not correlate with aspects of teacher behaviour which the theory would lead us to expect them *not* to correlate with.[17]

Conclusion

Starting from the assumption that ethnographers have failed to develop any viable alternative to the 'standard measurement model', in this chapter I have explored some of the implications of the application of that model to ethnographic work. In doing this, I took an article by Pollard as an example. I chose this article because he explicitly presents a theory and uses a wide variety of data, including quantitative indices, to support his claims. I have identified four problems of measurement, two of which (accuracy and generalizability) concern the relationship between descriptions and the events described, and the other two (content and construct validity) involving the relationship between descriptions and theoretical variables or concepts.

In evaluating any study, it is useful to keep three things distinct:

1. Whether the descriptions and explanations provided are correct.
2. Whether the researcher has taken the best precautions and made the best checks so as to maximize the chances of the validity of descriptive and explanatory claims, given available methodology.
3. Whether the researcher provides the reader with the necessary information about the precautions taken and the checks made for an assessment to be made of their effectiveness.

As regards the correctness of the descriptions and explanations, neither the researcher nor, even less, the reader can know this with certainty, one way or the other. Thus, the reader is forced back on assessing whether proper precautions were taken and checks carried out.

The problems I have highlighted are severe and Pollard, like most other ethnographers, gives little indication that he has attended to them. He certainly does not provide the reader with the information necessary to decide whether his treatment of them was effective. Of course, I am not pretending that such

Appendix

Background characteristics of the two teachers

Background	Mrs R.	Mr H.
Sex	F	M
Qualifications	T. Cert.	Soc. Sc. Degree and T. Cert.
Age	Late 30s	25
Experience	12 years	2.5 years
Marital status	M	Unknown
Children	2	Unknown
Residence	Pleasant village outside town	Unknown
Religion	Practising Christian	Unknown
Attitude to school	Unknown	Isolation and disagreement
Origin of perspective	Unknown	Reference groups outside school

Perspective and practice regarding pedagogy

	Mrs R.	Mr H.
Aim	Provision of moral standards and efficient transmission of knowledge and skills	Facilitating learning how to think and how to learn
Transmission and practice *vs* asking questions and verbal discussion	Transmission	Asking the right questions
Extrinsic *vs* intrinsic motivation	Extrinsic	Intrinsic
Physical sanctions	Unknown	No
Careful planning and presentation	Yes	Unknown
More *vs* less structured timetable	More	Less
More *vs* less differentiated curriculum	Less	More
More *vs* less fixed seating	More	Less
More *vs* less grouping by ability	More	Less

Perspective on pupils

	Mrs R.	Mr H.
Model	Family	Personal validity of children's perspectives
Criteria	Ability and behaviour	Oral rapport
Cultural deprivation	Yes	No

problems can be solved easily, or indeed that they can ever be solved perfectly. What I *am* arguing is that they are important, and that they can be dealt with much more effectively than they are at present. My aim in this chapter has been to clarify these problems so that ethnographers might address them directly and systematically.

8 Ethnography and the Cumulative Development of Theory: A Discussion of Woods' Proposal for 'Phase Two' Research[1]

The last chapter in this book takes up issues raised in the previous two about the need for ethnographers to focus their work on the development of theory and what is involved in this. I look closely at Peter Woods' treatment of this issue, arguing both that he is too complacent about the degree of progress so far and that his conception of what is required if cumulative development of theory is to be achieved is mistaken at several points. (For a response to this article by Woods, and a reply, see the issue of the British Educational Research Journal *from which this article is reprinted.)*

The last 20 years have witnessed a sharp growth in the amount of ethnographic research on schools, in Britain and North America.[2] However, most of this research has been relatively exploratory and descriptive, and diverse in focus, opening up new areas rather than systematically investigating those where work has already begun. Reflecting on this, several writers have recently called for a concerted effort to develop and test theory.[3] However, they are not in agreement about what the cumulative development of theory involves and about how much has already taken place. In this chapter I want to examine one of the most influential statements about this issue in the sociology of education: Peter Woods' argument for what he calls 'phase-2' ethnographic research.[4] I shall argue that his proposals do not go nearly far enough to bring about the cumulation of theory in this field.

Woods argues that what is required now is phase-2 work which cultivates 'leaps of (theoretical) imagination' (p. 52). It is necessary to move away from merely 'descriptive' to 'sensitizing' concepts, to develop and fill in existing theory and to formulate new theories (p. 57). At the same time, though, Woods also sees phase-2 studies as involving 'hypothesis formation and testing' and the process of analytic induction (p. 58).

Woods does not regard phase-2 research as a complete break with the past, but rather as an extension of what has already occurred in some areas. As an illustration of an area where some theoretical cumulation has already taken place, he cites work on teachers' strategies:

> In some areas there has been cumulative work which illustrates the promise in maintaining the dialectic between theory and data collection. One of these areas is that of 'social' (Lacey, 1977), 'coping' (A. Hargreaves, 1978), or 'survival' (Woods, 1979) strategies. It is interesting that these three approaches to essentially the same phenomenon were all made, in the first instance, independently of and unknown to the others. In my study, I documented and categorised teacher 'survival' strategies, a particular form of 'social' or 'coping strategy' at one end of a continuum governed by resources and policy. Hargreaves was interested in developing the theoretical base behind the notion of 'coping' as it was acted out at the intersection of micro-interaction and macro-structures; while Lacey was concerned to fill out a balanced model which allowed for consideration of personal redefinition of situations as well as situational redefinition of persons . . .
>
> A further example of what might be regarded as 'phase 2' work was then provided by Pollard (1982), who, in considering the Hargreaves analysis of coping, found it stronger on the macro end of the dimension than the micro. As Lacey had done, Pollard found an *imbalance* in existing work, and sought to strengthen the weaker area. He did this by developing my work on teacher survival, through the notions of 'self' and 'interests-at-hand' (the latter well-documented in his own ethnographic work – Pollard, 1979; 1980). Thus where Hargreaves tended to approach coping from the macro side, from the point of view of what had to be coped with, Pollard concentrated on the subjective meaning of coping, and emphasized the importance of teacher biography, while attempting to pull all the relevant factors together in a theoretical model.[5]

Woods also identifies the study of pupil cultures as a field where cumulation has occurred:

> Ethnography can contribute to certain theoretical areas as a corrective. Here, research may not be designed to test an existing theory, but material is discovered that raises questions about it, without entirely invalidating it. Rather, it acts as a 'synthesizer'. A useful illustration is within the field of pupil cultures. Work here reflects developments within both sociology and education, and reminds us that the *historical* element has to be taken into account in the construction of theory. In the 1960s Hargreaves (1967) and Lacey (1970) posited their differentiation/polarisation model of two pupil subcultures, one pro- and one anti-school. These were linked to social class, but fostered by the school streaming structure. Differential norms and values were generated, to which individuals gravitated. This subcultural model was too restrictive for my own Lowfield study, which revealed a wider variety of responses, which underwent change along temporal and situational dimensions. I had recourse to an adaptational

model as reworked by Wakeford (1969) on a Mertonian basis, and extended this in accordance with my data. This model rests on adaptations to official goals and means. All inmates are required to make a response to these, even if it is to reject both, but it assumes a priority which may actually misrepresent many pupils – and teachers. This was picked up by interactionists working closer to the fine detail of the lived moment. Furlong (1976), strongly criticising Hargreaves for not taking pupil knowledge into account, developed his notion of 'interaction set', a more amorphous and transient grouping than a subculture, in and out of which pupils shaded; and Hammersley and Turner (1980) considered the pupil's adjustment to school primarily in terms of his or her own interests, revealing the problematic nature of 'conformist' and 'deviant' labels. Whether pupils conform, they argue, depends on whether the school has the resources to meet their interests.

I would argue that this represents a cumulative sequence, though not all the contributors to it might agree, and though the studies involved are pitched at different levels of generality and abstraction. It is distinguished again by the search for *balance*, and this particular series of studies does inhibit a certain roundedness. Theoretical purchase is immediately gained by selection of an *appropriate* area where there is a body of non-ethnographic theory available, in an area where ethnography can make a signal contribution. The ethnographic studies were undertaken first in a spirit of challenge and *critique*, focusing first on the deficiencies of previous theories in directing data collection toward their repair. This, in turn, created a new imbalance, which itself found one kind of rectification in the *synthesis* offered by Ball (1981), where he shows that the major bipolar cultures still exist, but that a range of adaptations exists within them.[6]

The work in these two areas, then, serves for Woods as an exemplar of phase-2 research. I shall look at this work in some detail below. Before doing so, however, I want to deal with the question of what we mean by the terms 'theoretical cumulation' or 'theoretical development'. (I shall treat these terms as synonymous for the purposes of my argument.) Woods does not provide clear definitions of these terms, but their meaning is crucial to his argument.

The minimum requirement for a theory, as I shall use the term, is that it makes explanatory claims in the form: given the occurrence of $(A_1 \ldots A_n)$ then $(B_1 \ldots B_n)$ will probably occur. Such claims are generally causal in nature, and symbolic interactionists like Woods have sometimes been critical of causal explanations of a 'deterministic' nature.[7] However, the implications of this critique are obscure. It is not clear whether it is explanations which do not include reference to people's situational interpretations which are being criticized, or whether causal explanations of *any* kind relating to human behaviour are being rejected. If we look at interactionist empirical work, it does seem that the explanations offered are causal rather than hermeneutic, despite the use of euphemisms for causal relations like 'fosters', 'impinges upon', 'shapes', 'influences', 'generates', etc. These explanations are translatable into the minimum form for explanation outlined above without apparent distortion. And, indeed, at one point in his article, Woods defines a theory as something which will '*explain* teacher behaviour, and (. . .) *predict* the possibilities . . .'.[8] From this it seems that what I am suggesting here may not be too far from what he intends.

Theory development surely involves the following types of activity:

1. Addition of new concepts/variables and relations (or elimination of unnecessary ones.)
2. Clarification and development of concepts/variables and their relations.
3. Developing and testing measures for variables.
4. Testing relations between theoretical variables.

Woods mentions some of these activities, notably the addition of new concepts and the testing of theories. Whether he would accept the other two is less clear.

I now want to examine the research that Woods offers as paradigmatic for his conception of theory development. I shall begin with the area of teachers' strategies, looking at whether any of the activities I have listed can be found there.

Teachers' strategies

Adding new concepts and relations

Hargreaves, Lacey and Pollard certainly do introduce new variables, and so there is at least a *prima facie* case for theory development having taken place in this respect. Let us look in detail at Woods' strategy theory and at the concepts Hargreaves, Lacey and Pollard add.

Woods' discussion of teachers' strategies is presented in a discursive form, but we can reconstruct it in a more summary manner. Woods is primarily concerned with teaching in British secondary schools during the 1960s and early 1970s, and he argues that during this period teachers in these schools have increasingly come to employ what he calls 'survival strategies'. He defines survival strategies as actions directed towards securing the teacher's own security and ease, and he contrasts them with teaching, defined as actions designed to encourage learning on the part of pupils.[9] Woods outlines a large number of survival strategies: socialization, domination, negotiation, fraternization, absence or removal, ritual and routine, occupational therapy and morale-boosting. He identifies two sets of factors which, in combination, generate these strategies:

1. Changes in teachers' working conditions:
   (a) Increased demands made upon teachers:
      (i) the raising of the school-leaving age;
      (ii) the increasing tendency for schools and thus teachers to be judged in terms of examination success and the increasing numbers of pupils taking examinations;
      (iii) worsening pupil–teacher ratios;
      (iv) increased public expectations of schools, generated by educationalists.
   (b) Increasing recalcitrance on the part of pupils to teaching.

2. The high levels of commitment of teachers to their occupation. Generally being untrained for any other job, teachers have no escape from the pressures outlined in 1.

What Woods seems to be identifying here is displacement of goals, rather than the adoption of alternative strategies in pursuit of the same goal. He does not seek to explain why teachers might adopt one survival strategy instead of another. Rather, his explanation addresses the issue of why teachers engage in survival strategies at the expense of teaching.

In his study of the socialization of student teachers, Colin Lacey introduces the concept of social strategy as a way of expressing 'the autonomy of the individual' while yet recognizing the effects of 'coercive social pressures'.[10] He notes how the behaviour of the student teachers, while shaped by existing social structures, notably the institutionalization of subject subcultures, varied between contexts. The concept of social strategy is designed to allow conceptualization of the complex process by which situated human activity is generated. Lacey identifies three types of social strategy, though he indicates that his typology is not intended to be exhaustive. Two types of strategy represent forms of situational adjustment: strategic compliance and internalized adjustment. The other type involves a challenge to situational requirements: strategic redefinition. Lacey also introduces a separate typology of what he calls 'observed' strategies, complementing the earlier 'theoretical' typology. Here he distinguishes between privatizing and collectivizing accounts, and between the upward and downward displacement of blame. Lacey identifies two main orientations in questionnaire responses from students in a sample of university departments of education in England: the radical and the professional. And he proposes that a number of factors push student teachers and probationary teachers in the direction of the professional orientation. Initially, the pressures of the classroom do this, and so, subsequently, do the demands for conformity which must be met if promotion within the school is to be achieved.

Andy Hargreaves begins from the concept of 'coping strategy', which he sees as providing a way of conceptualizing the impact of macro social forces upon teachers while at the same time not representing teachers as simply controlled by or passively responding to those forces. Thus, his concept of strategy is similar to that of Woods and Lacey. Hargreaves defines *coping* strategies as 'adaptive', as 'successfully' dealing with experienced constraints, from the teacher's point of view. He contrasts coping strategies with 'transformative' strategies, which set out to transform the constraints under which the teachers find themselves working.[11] This typology seems similar to Lacey's distinction between situational adjustment and strategic redefinition.

Hargreaves identifies a number of factors which he believes generated the coping strategies he identified in the middle schools he studied:

1. The fundamentally contradictory goals of the education system in capitalist society.
2. The effects of scarcity of material resources, exacerbated by the prevalence of decision making in terms of 'administrative convenience'.

3. The proliferation of and changes in influence of educational ideologies, such as progressivism and Great Debate traditionalism.

Finally, Andrew Pollard sets out to develop Hargreaves' work to make it 'rather more balanced and complete in terms of the duality of structure and action'.[12] He believes that in giving attention to the macro level forces operating upon teachers, partly in reaction against Woods' 'situationism',[13] Hargreaves neglected the level of 'the individualized teacher/actor'. Pollard identifies the creative responses of the teacher to the pupils, to teacher culture, to the social organization of the school (what he calls 'institutional bias'), and to biographical factors as key factors underplayed by Hargreaves. In reconstructing Hargreaves' coping strategy model Pollard draws on Woods' conception of survival, elaborating it in terms of the idea that teachers 'juggle' interests at hand.[14] He summarizes his revised model in the form of a diagram (see Fig. 8.1).[15]

While it is clear that Lacey, Hargreaves and Pollard do indeed add concepts beyond those present in Woods' account, we must ask what the criteria are for

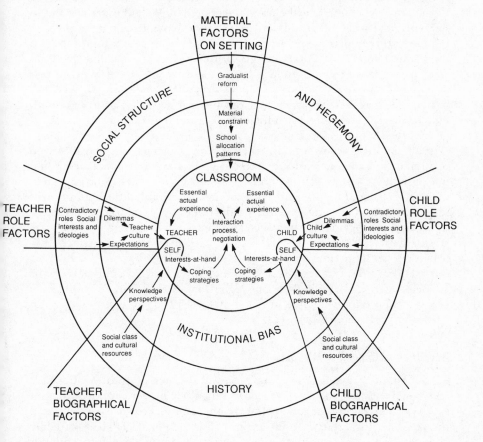

Figure 8.1 (Pollard, 1985, p. 157).

accepting a new concept as an addition to a theory. Presumably one criterion is that the new concept relates to the explanation of the same phenomenon as the original theory, or at least to some transformation of it produced by analytic induction. However, there is doubt about whether this is the case with these authors' work, despite Woods' claim that they are 'approaches to essentially the same phenomenon'.[16] Whereas Woods set out to explain why teachers adopt survival rather than teaching strategies, none of the others adopt the distinction between teaching and survival. Instead, their concern is with situational adjustment and challenge. These two typologies (teaching/survival; coping/transformation) do not seem to be isomorphic. Given this difference in focus, it is perhaps not surprising that Lacey, Hargreaves and Pollard should also appeal to rather different explanatory factors to those cited by Woods. It seems that we are dealing with different theories not with a single overarching one.

Of course, it might be suggested that my argument misses the point: that despite the differences I have identified, all these theories seek to explain teachers' behaviour, so that the object of explanation is the same for all of them. This, for example, is the position adopted by Pollard in his attempt to synthesize the work of Woods and Hargreaves. Now, it may be possible to produce a theory that will explain all aspects of teacher behaviour; though I think this is open to serious doubt. What I believe is beyond question, though, is that we cannot produce such a theory from scratch, without first developing and testing theories about particular aspects of teachers' behaviour: such as their tendency to adopt survival strategies; or to cope with rather than transform their circumstances. The result of attempts to produce a general theory of this kind, *ab initio*, are well illustrated by Pollard's model. Despite important contributions, for example in seeking to relate teacher and pupil strategies, the model that he produces is so comprehensive that it could not possibly be tested. It is an array of factors all of which probably affect teachers' behaviour, in one respect or another. We can all probably agree that such behaviour is in some sense the product of macro level factors, organizational factors, biographical factors, etc. The question is, though, in what ways and to what extent do particular factors at each level shape teachers' behaviour. Pollard provides no hypotheses about this. In this respect, it seems to me that Pollard's synthesis represents not progress beyond the work of Woods, Lacey and Hargreaves, but regression. Woods' theory is relatively specific and economic and, in principle at least, it is open to test. This is not true of Pollard's model.

Theoretical clarification and development

The question of whether the four pieces of research Woods mentions are concerned with one theory or several is difficult to answer because in all four cases, not untypically for much ethnographic and indeed sociological work, the concepts and their relations are not clearly defined. There is certainly considerable scope, then, for theoretical clarification and development in this area.

All the authors Woods refers to share basically the same concept of strategy, founded on the idea that actions are constructed by people over time and on the basis of interpretations of the situations they face; rather than being mere responses to a context, generated by previous socialization. However, Woods' treatment of this concept of strategy is vague in important respects.[17] First, it is unclear what other types of action there are that contrast with strategy. Indeed, it may be an ontological assumption of symbolic interactionism that *all* action is strategic.[18] If so, then we must ask whether there are any forms of human behaviour that do not fall under the heading of action, and whether they are all non-strategic. Only by asking these questions can we clarify what the term 'strategy' means. Woods provides no clear answer to such questions in his work. And neither do Hargreaves, Lacey and Pollard.

A related area requiring clarification concerns whether strategies are always consciously adopted by the actors concerned.[19] If they are, then it does seem that a considerable amount of human behaviour falls outside the scope of the concept of strategy, and that this includes much teacher behaviour. Jackson and Doyle have emphasized the immediacy and complexity of the classroom environment.[20] It is likely that this would lead to much teacher behaviour becoming routinized, and this does indeed seem to be the case.[21] Thus, we need to examine the relationship between strategic action on this definition and other types of teacher behaviour.

If the concept of strategy does *not* necessarily imply conscious deliberation, then strategy explanations are equivalent to functionalist explanation and inherit its well-known problems.[22] In particular, if strategies are not the product of conscious decision-making processes, they must be generated by some other feedback process. This is not to dismiss this type of explanation; there are good arguments for the legitimacy of functionalist accounts.[23] However, the problems need to be dealt with.[24] They are not addressed by Woods, nor have they been tackled by subsequent research on teachers' strategies.

In some ways the use of the term 'strategy' in the research cited by Woods is misleading. That term implies that the primary concern is with how different courses of action are used to achieve a particular goal. In fact, however, these authors are concerned with the displacement of goals (Woods) or with adaptation to conflicting role demands (Lacey and Hargreaves). Moreover, the typologies they present are in a very rudimentary state of development. They suffer from what Lofland terms analytic interruptus: their development has not been carried through to its conclusion.[25] Indeed, in this respect they contrast unfavourably, for example, with Merton's model of individual adaptations.[26] That model, for all its weaknesses, at least makes the dimensions underlying it explicit and presents the full range of types of adaptation produced by substruction.[27] Interestingly, Merton's model covers some of the same ground as this work on teachers' strategies; yet while it has been applied to pupils' adaptations, by Woods himself, surprisingly it has not been used in the study of teachers.[28]

In short, then, there are major issues requiring clarification and developmental work in strategy theory, but these have not been tackled. In this respect, too, little progress seems to have been made.

Measurement

In common with most ethnographers, Woods gives very little attention to measurement issues;[29] and yet there are some difficult problems here. For example, there is the task of distinguishing between teachers' actions directed towards teaching and those concerned with survival. The trouble is that the same action might serve both purposes simultaneously. This is not a problem in principle. What Woods seems to be claiming is that, under the conditions specified, survival dominates teaching as a criterion for selecting courses of action. This could be true even where particular courses of action are multi-functional; though teaching and survival would have to be clearly demarcated by teachers as criteria for assessing actions. There is clearly a methodological problem, however, in gaining access to the selection criteria to check whether Woods' theory is correct. Woods attempts to read off these criteria from what he takes to be the design characteristics of observed teachers' actions. The fact that the same action might serve both purposes constitutes a serious obstacle here, especially given the room for error involved in reading back from actions to intentions or functions. Woods provides no criteria for distinguishing between instances of teaching and of survival. Yet it seems clear that, for example, negotiation may be used as a teaching strategy or to establish the conditions for teaching to take place, as well as for survival. And the same applies to many of the other strategies he cites. Furthermore, even in clear cases where teaching does not seem a plausible reading we need to check that these instances are typical: perhaps emphasis on teaching or survival varies over time. Indeed, commonsense knowledge about teachers would suggest that this is so: there are time cycles within days, weeks, terms and years.[30] To establish the dominance of survival considerations, then, we would need to ensure that we had a representative sample of teachers' behaviour, as well as that our coding of teacher behaviour was consistent and accurate. Woods does not address these problems, and Hargreaves', Lacey's and Pollard's work involves no advance in this respect. For example, they too do not provide explicit criteria for identifying types of social strategy, or for recognizing instances of coping strategies, interests at hand, etc. Nor do they engage in systematic sampling over time.

Testing causal relationships

Woods seems to see this as an important aspect of theory development. In addition, he obviously believes that his own work and that of Hargreaves, Lacey and Pollard has tested the strategy model. He argues that the fact that he, Hargreaves, and Lacey produced their accounts of teachers' strategies independently constitutes evidence that they are true:

> That this (the production of the concept of 'strategy' and its theoretical refinement) should occur contemporaneously in three independent studies was itself a *test* and *confirmation* of the concept, as well as an indication of the influence of the general approach – in this case symbolic interaction – leading people in the same direction.[31]

However, even putting aside the fact that what the three studies produced were *different* strategy theories, this is not a convincing argument. There are two reasons. First, that these three accounts of teachers' strategies were produced independently is only true in a restricted sense. As Woods himself notes, the concept of strategy is intrinsic to interactionism;[32] and all the authors recognize this. Moreover, there had been some use of the concept in the area of education before the studies of Woods, Lacey and Hargreaves, notably the work of Waller, and of Westbury and his student Abrahamson.[33] Much of this work was known to most, if not all, of the authors Woods cites. Given this background, it is not very surprising that the concept of 'teacher strategy' should be used in all three studies.

The second point is that even if it were true that the same theory had been invented by several people simultaneously, this does not constitute a test of that theory. That Woods should believe it to be reflects, I think, an inductivist conception of theory production not uncommon among ethnographers, where the fact that a theory is produced in the process of analysing data is felt to validate it. Glaser and Strauss support their conception of 'grounded theorising' in these terms.[34] From this point of view, if multiple researchers generate the same theory independently on the basis of different data sets, this may seem like strong evidence that the theory is true. However, as Woods himself recognizes elsewhere, theory construction is a creative process, theories cannot be logically derived from data.[35] There are strong philosophical arguments against inductivism.[36] It relies upon a conception of the theory-independence of evidence that would be difficult to defend, and one which owes more to British empiricism than to the American pragmatism which interactionism claims as its ancestor.[37]

Whether one adopts the perspective of Peirce or Popper, testing involves checking whether the evidence supports the theoretical claims being made, and in particular whether it supports those claims better than competing theories. The classic technique here of course is the experiment, where implications are derived from the theory and tested by holding constant, or eliminating by randomization, other factors that might affect the dependent variable. But the experiment is only a special case of the comparative method, and comparative analysis is often taken to be a key element of ethnography.

None of the authors cited by Woods, nor anyone else as far as I know, has used the comparative method to test a theory about teachers' strategies. Yet this is essential if we are to understand which social factors cause particular patterns of teacher action in the classroom. In order to test *his* explanation, Woods would need to compare the incidence of survival strategies before and after the increase in the explanatory variables he appeals to; or he would have to compare Britain with another setting in which these factors do not operate, or operate at much lower levels. This would be a first step. But since Woods' theory concerns *strategic* responses, rather than simply the *effects* of the factors he cites on teachers' behaviour, other kinds of evidence would also be necessary. Ideally, to show that the teachers' behaviour was concerned with survival, it would be necessary to specify the range of courses of action available to them in particular circumstances, to rank these in terms of their survival payoff, and then to investigate whether it was indeed the case that those with the highest survival value were adopted.

This would be very difficult to do, at least in the present state of development of the theory: given, for example, the very broad definition of 'survival' that Woods adopts; and the fact that ordinal measurement of the survival value of strategies would be required. It may be possible to overcome the latter problem by longitudinal studies of student teachers on teaching practice or of probationary teachers. If Woods' theory is correct, over time, in a stable environment, teachers would increasingly select strategies with a high survival value and reject those with a low survival value. If we could identify samples of strategies with high and low survival value used by students and/or probationary teachers, we could then plot their differential rates of persistence or repetition, to test whether those with survival value were indeed abandoned and those with high survival value retained. Among experienced teachers one would presumably expect the process of selection to have become highly efficient, so that few low survival strategies would occur. However, the process of selection might be accessible in circumstances of great change, where teachers have to reconstruct their teaching in a major way.

Testing Woods' theory would be difficult, but not impossible. However, subsequent studies of teachers' strategies have not begun to do this, nor do they report tests of the theories they present. Given this, the case for progress having taken place in theory testing remains unconvincing.

Pupil culture

The other area where Woods argues that theoretical cumulation has occurred is in the study of pupil cultures. I shall deal with this more briefly since the same arguments apply here as to research on teachers' strategies. Woods claims that his own model of pupil adaptations represents a corrective to the differentiation-polarization model produced by D. Hargreaves and Lacey; and that the work of Furlong and my own work with Turner constitutes a subsequent phase of cumulative correction culminating in the synthesis produced by Ball.[38] I have argued elsewhere that the research of David Hargreaves, Colin Lacey and Stephen Ball represents an example of cumulative development.[39] But the set of studies Woods collects together here is quite different. Once again, what we have is *not* the development of a single theory but a collection of studies referring to one another, but concerned with the explanation of different things. Differentiation-polarization theory focuses upon explaining why the attitudes and behaviour of pupils in a school, and within a school class, are ranged along a dimension from pro- to anti-school values. It claims that this is, in part at least, the product of differentiation at the level of the school (streaming, banding) and at the level of the classroom. Woods' adaptation model, on the other hand, is not an explanation for this, or for anything else. It is a set of categories for describing the orientations of pupils in school. It does not explain either why particular pupils adopt particular orientations or why particular patterns of adaptation occur in particular schools or year groups. Merton's original model was itself primarily taxonomic, though he did indicate possible explanations for why the working class might be over-represented among 'innovators', while the lower middle class would be over-represented among 'ritualists'.[40] With the development of the taxonomy, via Harary, Wakeford and Woods, even these rudimentary explanatory speculations have been dropped.[41]

In much the same way, Furlong and later Glenn Turner and I,[42] despite our claims, were not correcting or replacing the differentiation-polarization and adaptation models. Rather, what was involved was a shift in focus. As with Woods, the work of these authors is primarily descriptive, but they adopt a more micro focus than he does. They criticize D. Hargreaves, Lacey and Woods for using concepts which do not capture the full complexity of patterns of behaviour among pupils. They draw attention to the fact, for example, that the same pupils may display varying attitudes and behaviour across different contexts. This is undoubtedly true, and indeed was pointed out by the authors they criticize. However, this fact is not incompatible with sharp differences *among* pupils in attitudes and behaviour. We may need a different theory to explain these two phenomena. We certainly cannot *assume* that they have the same causes. Nor can we assume that, because differentiation-polarization theory does not explain variation in the behaviour of pupils between contexts, it is not a satisfactory theory.

Briefly turning to the other aspects of theory development, the basic concepts in the field of pupil culture − culture, adaptation, etc. − are as poorly defined as those in the area of teacher strategies. And in this area too there has been little or no progress in measurement and no systematic testing of theories.

Conclusion

It is encouraging that there is some agreement among ethnographers working on school processes that theory development is now a priority. It seems clear, however, that there is not yet agreement about exactly what is required to achieve this goal.

Woods stresses the creative generation of theoretical ideas. There is no doubt that this is an important condition for theoretical development. However, in my view and contrary to Woods, this is not an area that has been seriously neglected by ethnographers; certainly not by comparison with other aspects of theory development. Work on teachers' strategies and on pupils' cultures, both cited by Woods and other studies,[43] displays a plethora of theoretical concepts.

Unlike Woods, both David Hargreaves and John Scarth, Sue Webb and I[44] place primary emphasis on the systematic development and testing of theories. For us it is the neglect of this that explains the non-cumulative nature of research in the sociology of education in general, and in the ethnography of schooling in particular. Referring to the recent history of the sociology of education, Hargreaves comments:

As times goes by, theories do not become better, by which I mean broader in scope and more economical in content, either as a result of careful testing or as a result of subsuming earlier theories. Theories simply 'lie around' in the field, relatively vague and relatively untested.[45]

This certainly seems to be true in the area of teacher strategies and pupil cultures.

While Woods underlines the importance of theory development and testing, it is not exemplified in his two paradigm cases, nor does he give any indication of what would be required for it to occur. In particular, he fails to explain how ethnographic practice will have to change to facilitate it. Indeed, the overwhelming impression one gets from what he writes is that ethnographers, or some of them anyway, need only continue working much as before. In my view, however, unless there is a major reassessment and reconstruction of ethnographic practice the cumulative development of theory will not take place.

Postscript

As I noted in the Preface, this final article does not represent a terminus, but only one more way-stage on a continuing journey. This is not a journey back to positivism, as Louis Smith suggests in his Critical Introduction; though it can easily be mistaken for that. It certainly does transgress the boundaries of what is conventionally regarded as the ethnographic paradigm. But I have always accepted the validity of most of the criticisms directed by ethnographers against 'positivistic' research on classrooms. There would be no justification for a return to such work in its earlier forms. At the same time, I have tried to show that serious methodological questions must be asked about the ways in which ethnography is currently practised; especially about its claim to produce theory and to ground concepts in data. These problems have not yet been resolved, and it is impossible to tell where my own attempts to deal with them may lead. What *is* very likely, though, is that they will go beyond at least some of the conclusions reached in these essays.

Notes and References

Preface

1. There had been some ethnographic research in schools, both in Britain (Hargreaves 1967; Lacey 1970) and in the United States (notably Smith and Geoffrey 1968). However, I dismissed these as theoretically and methodologically naive. I have since revised my views about who was naive.
2. Young 1971.
3. For further details of these various types of work, see Atkinson *et al.* (1988).
4. See Hammersley 1980c and 1982, Delamont 1976a and Woods 1983 for overviews of this research. Hammersley and Hargreaves 1983, Hargreaves and Woods 1984, Hammersley and Woods 1984 and Ball and Goodson 1984 include many of the key studies.
5. Hammersley 1974, 1976, 1977a, 1980a, 1981b, 1983, 1984b and 1984e.
6. Secondary moderns became established in England and Wales in the 1950s as schools suitable for those who had not been selected for the grammar schools and who were therefore regarded as non-academic and destined for manual and routine non-manual occupations.
7. Hammersley *et al.* 1985; Hammersley and Scarth 1986; Scarth and Hammersley 1988, Chapter 4 in this volume.
8. Hammersley 1984e.
9. Hammersley 1974 and 1977a, Chapters 1 and 3 in this volume.
10. Open University 1979.
11. Hammersley and Atkinson 1983.
12. Hammersley 1981a, Chapter 5 in this volume; 1980b; 1984a; Hammersley and Turner 1980.
13. Hammersley 1985 and 1987a, Chapters 6 and 8 in this volume; Hammersley 1986 and 1989a; see also Woods 1987 and Hammersley 1987b.
14. Hammersley 1989b.
15. Hammersley 1987a.
16. Weber 1949.

Critical Introduction

1. Special thanks are due to the author's colleagues and students in Education 5292.

'Field Methods in the Study of Groups, Organizations and Communities' for their reading, discussion and elaboration of the ideas presented here. By name they are: Benerjee, M.; Beyer, K.; Billet, B.; Brown, C.; Clay, W.; Coyle, C.; Greathouse, K.; Harris, L.; Klass, C.; Klinedinst, L.; Lefton, C.; Mitchell-Miller, J.; Orange, C.; Osburg, J.; Pike, B.; Treffeisen, S.; Uljee, L.; Wells, L.; Wells, W.; and Wolfmeyer, J.

2. Hammersley and Atkinson 1983; Woods and Hammersley 1977.
3. Goetz and LeCompte 1984.
4. Homans 1950.
5. Smith and Geoffrey 1968.
6. Arensberg and Kimball 1940.
7. Roethlisberger and Dickson 1939.
8. Willis 1977.
9. Whyte 1955.
10. Geertz 1983.
11. Arensberg and MacGregor 1942.
12. Homans 1962.
13. Geertz 1973.
14. Becker *et al*. 1961; Peshkin 1982.
15. Jacob 1987; Atkinson *et al*. 1988.
16. Glaser and Strauss 1967.
17. Zetterberg 1963.
18. Smith and Kleine 1969.
19. Merton 1957.
20. Kesey 1962.
21. Redl and Wineman 1957; Redl and Wattenberg 1962.
22. Kounin 1970.
23. Smith 1958.
24. Beittel 1973.
25. Smith and Brock 1970; Brock and Smith 1981.
26. Smith and Keith 1971.
27. Smith and Pohland 1974; Campbell and Fiske 1959; Cronbach and Meehl 1956; Denzin 1970.
28. Kaplan 1964.
29. Redfield 1955; Mills 1959.
30. Smith *et al* 1986, 1987 and 1988.
31. Geertz 1983.
32. Hammersley and Atkinson 1983.

Chapter 1: The Organization of Pupil Participation

1. I would like to thank Isabel Emmet, Phil Harris and Joan Hammersley for comments on an earlier version of this chapter.
2. Comments made about teachers and pupils in this chapter are intended to apply only to this school. Though my aim is not to depict this school in its uniqueness, further generalization will require careful comparison with the work of other teachers in other schools. Little can be said about methods of fieldwork here other than that, while I have provided extracts from tape transcriptions to give some indication of the kinds of evidence I have used and the way I have used it, the reader is inevitably reliant on my observation and reporting. See Hammersley (1984e) for an account of the fieldwork.

3. I cannot provide conclusive evidence for the reader that my description of teachers' activities is applicable to all the teachers in the school. Even full reproduction of all the transcriptions would be inadequate since, while I observed most of the teachers at work at one time or another, my observations and tape-recordings were largely focused on four of them. There were differences between even these four, but the differences between all the teachers seemed to be in technique rather than in basic concerns – for instance, some of them used speaker selection far more strictly than others.

4. The enthusiasm to answer questions was less among the older than the younger pupils in the school, but even pupils towards the end of the third year still competed to answer questions, 'shouting out' answers simultaneously. (My data on fourth i.e. final year pupils is inadequate for a judgement on this issue.) There was no streaming in the school, though in the third year 'those willing to work' had been creamed into a separate class and in the second year there was setting for maths, and English. There seemed to be little difference in clamour to answer questions between classes in the same year that I observed. However, I must stress that the way in which pupils' orientations in the classroom change as they progress through the school was not a central research topic and therefore this footnote is tentative and superficial.

5. Mean average class size for the lessons I observed was 17 and the range was from 7 to 30. This is on the low side for any school, particularly a secondary modern, though the task which the teachers set themselves of making seventeen pupils behave as one party to the interaction is probably not much less difficult than making even more behave in the same way.

6. Besides unofficial answers and initiatives directed at the teacher, there is always some pupil to pupil communication in any lesson, varying considerably between lessons and teachers, but this is usually at a low volume level and is directed to someone sitting close by. Shouts across the room are relatively infrequent while the teacher is present and unofficial pupil address of the whole class even rarer.

7. My evidence for this orientation is difficult to specify but basically lies in the following observation: pupils often laughed at what they regarded as 'silly answers' or laughed themselves while providing an answer, presumably to distance themselves from it in case it turned out to be 'silly'; yet they appeared to invest written work with much less importance, whereas that seemed to be regarded as, if anything, more important by the teachers. Of course, this orientation was not adopted by all the pupils or by any pupil all the time.

8. I am not suggesting by implication that this claimed authority is illegitimate – that is not my concern here – nor is it a question to which I find any easy answers. Rather what I am arguing is that if for any reason and at any point in his school career a pupil sees teacher authority as illegitimate and acts on that belief, he will tend to be seen as lacking in 'intelligence' by the teachers in this school. Even if the teachers decide that a pupil is 'more intelligent' than his school work would imply, that does not in itself alter the 'standard' of his school work.

Chapter 2: School Learning: The Cultural Resources Required to Answer a Teacher's Question

1. I would like to thank Frankie Todd, Douglas Barnes and their seminar group on Communication and Learning in Small Groups for comments on earlier versions of this chapter. Thanks must also go to the staff and pupils of the school studied for making the research possible.

2. See Halsey *et al.* 1961; Hopper 1971.
3. Hargreaves 1967; Lacey 1970.
4. The lesson was not chosen on any principled basis. I assume that processes relevant to selection and socialization will occur in one form or another in all lessons. To what extent this is true and how the processes in this school compare with those in others awaits further research. The lesson was certainly not chosen as an example of good or bad teaching. I am not concerned with the technical or moral evaluation of the teaching in this lesson.
5. These excerpts represent over two-thirds of the lesson, most of the rest being taken up with the reading of the story.
6. In the course of this he also ignores a pupil initiative which is tied to the previous lesson's topic, and he deals with some pupil deviance, indicating and reinforcing the nature of 'proper pupil behaviour'.
7. Getting answers to his questions is crucial for the teacher to get through 'what is to be taught this lesson'.
8. I shall show the significance of such considerations in the course of this chapter.
9. Once again, I hope to establish this implication later in the chapter.
10. The evidence for this is that he has the example of a tall story waiting. I shall discuss the pitching of lessons later.
11. Even earlier than this he reverts momentarily to immediate evaluation, in lines 63–6, 73–94 and 111–27.
12. Note that the pupil is probably thinking of the term 'spy-glass'.
13. It is perhaps necessary to reinforce the point that there is no implication here that this is a bad thing. I am simply pointing to a feature of the lesson.
14. Whether the model of knowledge and thinking embedded in this lesson is the same as that involved in other lessons remains to be seen, as does the issue of whether pupils actually incorporate this model into their perspectives.
15. It may be that in other lessons in this sequence of lessons on types of story the teacher does discuss the category system as a whole. I have data on some of these other lessons and this does not seem to be the case.
16. See, for instance, Collingwood 1952; Barnes 1974; Harris 1970.
17. For instance, long or short (depending on the standard), rambling, a lie, boastful, nautical, a war story, a historical tale, an adventure story, etc.
18. Note that the argument that they will be familiar with many other stories in and out of school and that therefore the evidence available to them is greater than I have suggested is invalid – while they will know other stories they will not know what type of stories these are (in the teacher's terms), whether any of them are tall stories, for instance. Indeed, the teacher at one point disputes a pupil's assessment of what is a joke (line 63).
19. For the teacher to provide even a reasonable amount of evidence to make induction feasible would probably take a number of lessons and would very heavily cut down the material that teachers could try to 'get across' to pupils. The problems are heightened in this case because what is to be induced is simply a matter of conventional usage.
20. This idea derives from the older notion of the hermeneutic circle (see Radnitzky 1973: 215ff.). For an unusually clear account of ethnomethodology and an example of its application to education, see Payne (1976).
21. This is derived from the work of Harvey Sacks. For an account of his work, see Speier (1973).
22. Partridge 1963.
23. Schutz 1962.
24. There are of course a variety of ways within the organization of conversation to express distance and/or superiority without actually abandoning that interactional medium.

25. Without the use of a gun, for instance, which would transform the situation into something else.
26. See Goffman 1968.
27. Who are not in fact treated in terms of the 'stranger' category.
28. They are asked by others but, apart from quiz-show questioners, not routinely.
29. Though to set out to produce an answer that fits the relevances of the questioner is to recognize his or her right to ask such a question.
30. Or rather the fact that this is known to be the case by pupils does this.
31. If they believe themselves to be stupid, of course, they may not operate on this assumption. This makes pupil self-confidence and their own assessment of their capabilities crucial to school achievement.
32. This is one explanation for apparently stupid pupil answers.
33. Unless the question can be seen as designed to test their attention. This points to another important consideration pupils must bear in mind when attempting to answer teacher questions: there are at least two fundamentally different types of teacher questions. Some are intended to test attention, some to test understanding. In this chapter I am concerned with the latter, the former are formulated to be easy and therefore to test attention *not* understanding, ability, etc. (see Hammersley 1976).
34. On retrospective-prospective interpretation, see Garfinkel (1967). Note that the teacher is not teaching retrospective-prospective interpretation – he has no need to – but is using that device to make relevant a particular feature of the story.
35. The teacher disguises this process, for instance in lines 199–207, by challenging some of the pupils' doubts about the possibility of one of the 'tall' incidents. Perhaps this is a covering move designed to ensure that the conclusion that the story is 'unbelievable' comes out later rather than at that point. On covering and uncovering moves, see Atkinson and Delamont (1976).
36. Goffman 1961.
37. Hammersley 1976.
38. Or at least as an individual variation on a common theme. The feature I have been discussing here also seems to occur in classrooms where the teacher seeks to encourage 'discovery learning' (Atkinson and Delamont 1976).
39. There are other, very different and competing, ways of setting out to explain this phenomenon, for instance to see it as part of 'doing teaching', a form of life which is self-constituting and self-justifying (see Payne 1976), or as an alienated and alienating mode of discourse (see Torode 1977). However, these various alternatives are so radically distinct that it is difficult to know how to begin to evaluate them and this is certainly not the place to begin that task.

Chapter 3: Pupil Culture and Classroom Order at Downtown

1. Willis 1977; Anyon 1981.
2. Webb 1962; Willis 1977; Corrigan 1979.
3. See Hammersley 1980a and 1983.
4. Corrigan 1979: 51–2.
5. Coser 1959.
6. McDermott 1976.
7. Teachers often play on this ambiguity for rhetorical effect. Researchers sometimes do likewise, but in the reverse manner: demonstrating that pupil deviance is not 'really' disorderly (McDermott 1976; Marsh *et al.* 1978).
8. In fact the course of classroom deviance is often all too predictable for the teacher!
9. Sinclair and Coulthard 1975; McHoul 1978; Mehan 1979.

10. All but one of the teachers at Downtown were male and I did not observe the teaching of the part-time, female, music teacher. For this reason I cannot generalize my findings to her. She was extremely marginal to the teacher culture at Downtown.
11. Hammersley 1974, Chapter 1 in this volume, and 1976.
12. Hargreaves *et al.* 1975.
13. Berlak *et al.* 1975.
14. Willis 1977; Marsh *et al.* 1978; Woods 1979; Corrigan 1979.
15. Anyon 1981.
16. Hargreaves *et al.* 1975; Pollard 1979 and 1980.
17. In my view, the teachers' staffroom comments do not represent realistic judgements about the threat of violence: they serve a variety of functions that result in exaggeration (see Hammersley 1980a).
18. Willis 1977: 12–13.
19. Willis (1977), and to some degree Corrigan (1979), treat such pupils as representing an advanced form of working-class consciousness. The criterion of statistical representativeness is put aside in favour of an alternative approach which trades on an idealized notion of 'working-class consciousness' similar in form (though not content!) to that found in the writings of Lenin and Lukacs. Thus, Willis provides no evidence that 'the lads' were in some empirical sense more working class than the 'ear 'oles'. Instead, the orientations of the two groups are implicitly judged as more or less 'working class' according to the degree to which they match what is presumed to be 'true' working-class consciousness. Whether or not it flows from a correct reading of Marx (McCarney, 1980), this argument is not open to empirical test and thus falls outside the scope of social science. The evidence I have presented bears out the teachers' staffroom view that their problems centre on a few particularly troublesome pupils. However, this is not to suggest that their explanations as to why these pupils are more of a problem than others – appealing to immaturity, mental instability, etc. – are correct. Indeed, the same argument applies to those psychological theories as I shall apply below to macro research which fails to investigate the local contexts of pupil activities. In contrast to the way in which accounts are presented in the staffroom, where context is cut out (Hammersley, 1980a), pupil behaviour must be examined as shaped by and to the particular circumstances in which it occurs. Psychological factors only have their effects through the ways in which those circumstances are perceived and responded to.
20. This lack of an inverse relationship between status accorded by the school and informal status among pupils conforms to the findings of Werthman (1963), but differs from those of Hargreaves (1967), Lacey (1970) and Ball (1981).
21. My knowledge of the status hierarchy within 2n is impressionistic, based on observation of who among the pupils successfully initiated group action, who deferred to whom, etc.
22. Willis 1977: 11.
23. This commitment to school achievement occurs despite the usual reluctance to be found among pupils to be picked out as 'hard-working':

(Walker: English)
T: What makes some of you always wanting to jump about and waste time like our gentleman here (Crabtree) while others are studious and want to sit quietly and get on with their work like our gentleman there (Smith)
Smith: (protests) Me sir?

Smith was ranked low in the informal status hierarchy and was near the top of the class. He clearly felt it necessary to distance himself from the image of the 'swot' (Turner 1981).

24. Willis 1977: 60–1.
25. It is interesting that at Downtown, in general, 'the lads' or 'troublemakers' seemed to be white and, if Wilson is representative, like Willis's lads, harboured racist views. Even in the case of Downtown (Hammersley 1980a), it seems unlikely that this racism was a product of the influence of the teachers. They did not generally voice their views to, or in front of, pupils and there were of course other possible sources of racist views, such as parents and peers.
26. Hargreaves 1967; Lacey 1970.
27. Delamont 1976a; Hammersley and Turner 1980.
28. Woods 1979.
29. Woods 1979: 74.
30. Woods 1979: 74.
31. Woods 1979: 76.
32. Woods 1979: 78.
33. Hammersley and Turner 1980.
34. Werthman 1963; Furlong 1976 and 1977; Gannaway 1976; Delamont 1976a; Turner 1981.
35. Hammersley 1981a.
36. For an exception, see Pollard 1984.
37. Corrigan 1979.
38. Woods 1979.
39. I only witnessed its use by Holton (several times) and Baldwin (once); though it was threatened, and no doubt used, by other teachers.
40. The use of irony in this example is significant: it both trades on pupil knowledge of 'correct' behaviour and reinforces the unquestionable character of that knowledge. The same technique is used by the teachers in the staffroom with the same effect.
41. Goffman 1968.
42. Woods 1975. Of course, even physical punishments gain much of their power from the identity they impose: they too involve an element of 'showing up'.
43. Ball 1972.
44. The oft-noted tendency of teachers to formulate demands and orders in the form of requests – as in the ubiquitous 'Can I have your attention please' – also reflects the use of this rhetoric.
45. Sacks *et al.* 1974.
46. Furlong 1976 and 1977; Marsh *et al.* 1978.
47. Had the pupils been committed to a strong counter-culture, they might have been immune to the use of these rhetorics, possessing a contrasting conception of male adulthood and intelligence. Without that, it seems likely that they were highly vulnerable. While it is correct to see the use of these rhetorics as a form of 'divide and rule', it must be remembered that the pupils are divided to start with, not only, at the very least, latently in terms of ethnicity, but also manifestly according to friendship networks.
48. Woods 1980a.
49. Sharp and Green 1975; Woods 1979.
50. Hammersley 1977b and 1980a.
51. Woods 1979; A. Hargreaves 1978.
52. Stebbins 1975; Hargreaves *et al.* 1975; A. Hargreaves 1979.
53. Hammersley 1980a.
53. Hammersley 1980a.
55. Bird 1980.
56. But note some of the pupils' desire for 'more discipline' (p. 58 above).

57. Werthman 1963; Hargreaves 1967; Lacey 1970; Reynolds 1976a and 1976b; Reynolds and Sullivan 1979; Ball 1981.
58. Becker and Geer 1960.
59. Matza 1961.
60. Bourdieu and Passeron 1977; Willis 1977.

Chapter 4: Examinations and Teaching: An Exploratory Study

1. Nuttall 1984; Macintosh 1985; Torrance 1985; Horton 1987.
2. Secondary Examinations Council 1986; Scarth 1987.
3. Scarth 1986a.
4. Hammersley and Scarth 1986.
5. Roach 1971: 242.
6. Mackenzie 1982: 10.
7. Department of Education and Science 1979: 248.
8. See, for example, Hartog and Rhodes 1935; Connaughton and Skurnik 1969; Nuttall and Skurnik 1969; Nuttall and Willmott 1972; Macintosh 1974.
9. Whitty 1976 and 1978; Bowe and Whitty 1983 and 1984; Scarth 1983, 1984 and 1986b.
10. Turner 1983; Lewin 1984.
11. Turner 1984: 51.
12. Turner 1984: 52.
13. Turner 1984: 52.
14. Quoted in Turner 1984: 52.
15. Lewin 1984.
16. Scottish Education Department 1969; Mee *et al.* 1971; Lewin 1984: 133.
17. Lewin 1984: 18.
18. Lewin 1984: 140.
19. Lewin 1984, Table 4.16, p. 141.
20. Lewin 1984, Table 4.17, p. 141.
21. Lewin 1984: 141–2.
22. Scarth and Hammersley 1986a.
23. See, for example, Hammersley and Scarth 1986: appendix B.
24. We argued that if teachers were more concerned with fact-transmission on examination-assessed courses we could expect them to take up a higher proportion of public classroom talk in lessons on these courses than in other lessons. This corresponds to the frequently made criticism of examinations that they lead to increased lecturing. For further information about the measures we used, including our procedures for timing teacher and pupil talk and the consistency of our application of these procedures, see Hammersley and Scarth (1986: ch. 3 and appendix C).
25. We have used the correlation ratio to assess the strength of the relationship between our independent variables (qualification-dispensing assessment and examinations) and our dependent variable (fact-transmission teaching). The correlation ratio is a measure of the confidence that we can have in claiming that teaching on courses with different assessment regimes show diferent levels of fact-transmission. Without such a measure we have little guidance about the strength of the correlation between independent and dependent variables. The scores for the correlation ratio range from 0 to 1. If the correlation ratio between a second-year course and a fifth-year course for the proportion of pupil talk were 1, this would indicate that there is no internal variation in the scores for each course and also that the scores are not the same. (This would be the case, for instance, if the percentages of pupil

talk for lessons in a second-year course were 2, 2, 2, 2, and 2, and the corres-
ponding percentage scores for lessons in a fifth-year course were 3, 3, 3, 3 and 3.)
One would be able to predict with perfect accuracy whether a lesson with a
percentage score of, say, 2% came from the second- or the fifth-year course. A
correlation ratio of 0 would indicate that the scores for each course are identical.
There is no requirement here that the scores within each course should be the
same. (For example, if the fifth-year scores on the above example were also all
2%, this would produce a correlation ratio of 0. Similarly, if *both* courses had
scores of, say, 1, 2, 3, 4 and 5, then the correlation would again be 0.) In this case,
knowing that a score for a particular lesson was 2% would *not* enable one to
predict accurately which course the lesson came from. Such extreme values of
the correlation ratio are seldom, if ever, achieved. The value is usually *between* 0
and 1. But these are the principles on which correlation ratios are calculated. The
nearer the ratio approaches 1 the less likely will error be involved in predicting
which course the score came from and thus the stronger the correlation. It is
normally accepted that values of 0.4 and below on the correlation ratio indicate
that little or no correlation exists. For further information about the correlation
ratio, see Mueller *et al.* (1977).
26. The Integrated Humanities CSE examination in the school studied had a 40/50
balance in favour of coursework, with 10% for oral work. However, the examination was internally set and marked by teachers and demanded very little memoriz-
ing on the part of pupils.
27. The lesson scores for teacher and pupil talk can obviously be affected by the
amount of written work in lessons (which reduces the amount of public talk and
hence opportunity for public pupil talk). We controlled for this by calculating
pupil talk as a proportion of a standard unit of public talk. We have used periods of
1000 seconds for this purpose. All correlation ratios are based on scores for 1000-
second periods.
28. Inter-coder agreement was 98.5%, and intra-coder agreement was 99.7% (see
Hammersley and Scarth 1986: appendix C for further details).
29. The work of Wragg (1973), Morrison (1973) and Delamont (1976b) has also
suggested that Flanders' two-thirds rule may be an underestimate of teacher talk in
British secondary schools.

Chapter 5: Putting Competence into Action: Some Sociological Notes on a Model of Classroom Interaction

1. For an outline and discussion of this tradition see Hamilton and Delamont (1974).
   For a more detailed account see Walker (1971).
2. They would not trouble all sociologists, of course, but only those committed to
   what, in this chapter, I call action theory.
3. Incidentally, I recognize the perilous nature of this enterprise. It is very easy to
   misunderstand work in other disciplines – for example, because one is unaware of
   some crucial qualification which underlies all work in a discipline, or because one
   fails to allow for differences in purpose between disciplines. I trust my criticism will
   be taken in the tentative, constructive spirit in which it is intended.
4. These are convenience labels and may be misleading from the point of view of
   linguistics where the contrast to competence is performance. I am rather uncertain
   about the relationship between this distinction and the one I am proposing here. As
   I see it at the moment, the action approach would argue that the competence-
   performance distinction can only be made for particular points in the development

of a sequence of social interaction, since performance is continually modifying competence in marginal respects, and sometimes in major ways.

5. Hymes 1977.
6. Austin 1962 and Searle 1965.
7. Sudnow 1972; Turner 1974; Schenkein 1978. Conversational analysis is a difficult case. While in terms of ethnomethodological principles it escapes most of the problems I shall document here – though at enormous cost – in practice conversational analysts often seem to deviate from these principles in ways which leave their work open to these criticisms.
8. Sinclair and Coulthard 1975 and Coulthard 1977.
9. For examples concerned with classrooms, see Berlak *et al.* 1975, Woods 1977, A. Hargreaves 1979 and Hammersley 1974 and 1976.
10. There is no work in this tradition on classrooms, but see Kapferer (1976).
11. Berger and Luckmann 1967 and Schutz and Luckmann 1974. Hargreaves, Hester and Mellor (1975) represents an approach to classroom interaction which spans the interactionist and phenomenological approaches and also shows traces of a competence approach.
12. Gonos (1977) argues that Goffman's work has been misunderstood, that it is not interactionist but structuralist (i.e. not an action but a competence theory). However, this is rather unfair on Goffman's commentators since there seem to be elements of both approaches in his work (compare *The Presentation of Self* with *Frame Analysis*, for example), though I think it is probably correct to say that structuralism of a kind is dominant at least in his later work.
13. For the distinction between 'order' and 'control' theories see Dawe (1970).
14. This criticism is much less true of the phenomenologists but this approach has resulted in very little empirical work. For an expansion of these criticisms, see Hammersley (1978).
15. Sinclair and Coulthard 1975. The only other work at a similar level of development, this time influenced by conversational analysis, is that of Mehan (1979).
16. With, as I remarked earlier, the partial exception of conversational analysis which, when it does avoid these problems, does only at an exorbitant cost: that of restricting the focus of research to 'possible methods' for producing accounts of social phenomena.
17. I am using 'functionalism' here in its sociological, not its psychological or linguistic, sense. That there should be such a similarity is not altogether surprising in the case of Sinclair and Coulthard's work, if one remembers the links between Malinowski, one of the founders of functionalist anthropology, and Firth; and, perhaps more significantly, between Durkheim and Saussure.
18. There are versions of functionalism which seek to avoid this problem, such as that of Merton (1957), but in my view their strategies for doing this undermine the functionalist scheme.
19. Sinclair and Coulthard 1975: 6.
20. Coulthard 1977: 161.
21. Sinclair & Coulthard 1975: 51.
22. Sinclair and Coulthard 1975: 50.
23. For example, D.H. Hargreaves (1967) and Lacey (1970).
24. Furlong (1976).
25. Sinclair and Coulthard 1975: 20.
26. Sinclair and Coulthard 1975: 19.
27. Incidentally, this tendency also appears in speech act analysis where what are in fact elements of social acts become designated as *speech* acts.
28. Having made this criticism, I suppose I ought to provide an alternative basis for

distinguishing directives from elicitations. My current view is that directives demand compliance to a rule implied, or spelt out in, the utterance, where compliance is assumed to be within the capabilities of the target actor; and failure to comply, at least in the absence of a disclaimer (Hewitt and Stokes, 1975) or remedial action (Goffman, 1972; Lyman and Scott, 1970), will be read as unwillingness and/or deviance. An elicitation, on the other hand, requires the production of a sign (not necessarily verbal) which fills in a frame implied or present in the utterance (see Schutz, 1962, for the concept of sign as used here). Ability to provide this is not necessarily assumed and failure to provide an 'appropriate' answer is not necessarily treated as deviance, though ignorance can sometimes be treated as indicating incompetence or stupidity. There is a complicating factor, however: elicitations always presuppose a directive, and refusal to answer the question will be treated as deviance.

29. Sinclair and Coulthard 1975: 27–8, original emphasis.
30. It is, of course, possible to identify further patterns which seem to fit this notion of linguistic patterning: for example, one can distinguish between teacher questions designed solely to test attention or demonstrate the inattention of pupils, and those which are concerned with testing learning or knowledge. This is not in itself a criticism – this is the kind of distinction which can be picked up with increased delicacy. See Hammersley (1976).
31. Sinclair and Coulthard 1975: 34–5, original emphasis.
32. This is the notion of triangulation which originated with Webb, Campbell, Schwartz and Sechrest (1966). For an account of the role of triangulation within ethnographic research, see Hammersley (1979).
33. I stress in the first place because I do believe it is possible to talk of unintended functions.

Chapter 6: From Ethnography to Theory: A Programme and a Paradigm in the Sociology of Education

1. I am grateful to Stephen Ball, John Gee, Andy Hargreaves, David Hargreaves, Colin Lacey, Audrey Lambart, Donald Mackinnon, John Scarth, Peter Woods, and to three anonymous reviewers for their comments on earlier versions of this chapter.
2. For a discussion of one aspect of this over-reaction, see Hammersley and Atkinson (1983: ch 1).
3. Willer 1967; Cohen 1980.
4. Freese (1980) contains some useful discussions of cumulation. For a powerful presentation of the case for theory-testing in one area of the sociology of education, see Hargreaves (1981).
5. Hammersley 1982.
6. Lacey 1966 and 1970; Hargreaves 1967.
7. Ball 1981.
8. There are, of course, versions of ethnography which stress the goal of theory, notably Glaser and Strauss (1967). However, there are few examples of ethnographic work explicitly following this model, apart from the work of Glaser and Strauss themselves. I should add that their conception of theory, and of the process of theorizing, is rather different from that presented here. Much closer is the older approach of Lindesmith (1937 and 1968) and Cressey (1953). See Hammersley et al. (1985).
9. For a discussion of the background to this development, see Frankenberg (1982).
10. Lambart did not adopt this focus, not least because strong differentiation was not to be found at Mereside. For this reason, I have excluded her work from my discussion.

11. Hargreaves 1967: methodological appendix; Lacey 1970.
12. Ball 1984.
13. Ball 1983b.
14. Cohen 1980.
15. Berger (1970) and Cohen (1980) call this the historical strategy, contrasting it with the generalizing strategy concerned with theory.
16. This view of theorizing is a development of the work of logical positivists like Hempel (1965) and Nagel (1961). See Cohen (1980), Willer (1967), Willer and Heckathorn (1980) and Freese (1980). Interestingly, though, it differs almost as sharply from the conception of theory that underlies most work in sociology which is regarded as positivist (for example, Blalock 1961) as it does from the ideas about theory characteristic of ethnographers. It has been subjected to considerable criticism (Winch 1958; Scriven 1959; Keat and Urry 1975). But it has also been effectively defended (Hempel 1965; Scheffler 1967; Newton-Smith 1981). While there remain problems with this view of the nature of theory, in my opinion these are less serious than those accompanying available alternatives.
17. 'Differentiation' and 'polarization' are terms used by the authors themselves; though Hargreaves, in particular, is rather inconsistent in his usage of them.
18. Hargreaves, Lacey and Ball do not clearly detach differentiation-polarization theory from the other factors that they mention, such as the role of social class. Nor do they make explicit the fact that they are testing the theory simultaneously at two different levels: those of the school as a whole and the individual class. In Berger's (1970) and Cohen's (1980) terms their approach is more historical than generalizing. What I am presenting is a rational reconstruction (Reichenbach 1938; Kaplan 1964) of their work from a generalizing perspective.
19. Quine 1974; Musgrove 1979: 42–8.
20. It is important to be clear about what is involved in the process of testing differentiation-polarization theory. It is *not* a matter of showing that differentiation always produces polarization or that *only* differentiation produces polarization. My concern is whether the relationship holds under some conditions, and if so what those conditions are.
21. Rescher 1978.
22. The consequences would, of course, depend upon many factors. Of interest here is Lacey's analysis of the effects of destreaming at Hightown Grammar (Lacey 1974).
23. Goldthorpe 1980; Halsey *et al.* 1980.
24. Cohen 1955.
25. This idea bears similarities to Cloward and Ohlin's (1960) theory of delinquency.
26. Scarth 1986b: ch. 5.
27. Glaser and Strauss 1967.
28. Kuhn 1970.
29. Homans 1967.
30. There are some other examples of such theories within sociology generally, for instance the work of Lindesmith (1968) on addiction and Cressey (1953) on financial trust violation. Robinson's (1969) critique of these studies is well-founded but does not undercut the promise of the theories proposed. Turner's (1969) critique, while illuminating in several respects, is committed to a view of theory which requires that it encompass all the factors producing a phenomenon. See Cohen (1980) in particular for arguments against this conception of theory. Probably the most developed example of a theory of this kind is that concerning status characteristics and social interaction developed by Berger, Cohen, Zelditch and others (Berger *et al.* 1977).
31. Scriven 1959.

32. Miller 1958; Willis 1977; Humphries 1981; Anyon 1981. It should be pointed out, though, that these two theories are not *logically* incompatible. What I mean by this is that there is nothing in either which denies the validity of the other, they could both be true. Thus, what I have said about differentiation-polarization theory does not in any way imply that a research programme based on class subculture theory would not be valuable; indeed, I suspect it would be.
33. As indicated earlier, what I am advocating is a particular interpretation of the positivist model. See note 15 above.
34. Hammersley and Turner 1980.
35. Sharp 1981.
36. Fortunately, neither of these seems to be required for the development of theory. The first is unnecessary because theories only deal with *particular aspects* of institutions or behaviour. The second is unnecessary because theory can operate at many diferent levels along the macro–micro scale (Hammersley, 1984c). Indeed, differentiation-polarization theory itself may operate at several different levels: the individual class, the school and the education system as a whole.
37. Hammersley *et al.* 1985.
38. In fact, in Freese's (1980) terms, the three studies represent lateral cumulation rather than real cumulation: they show more concern with how the theory applies to particular cases than with systematically developing it.
39. Hargreaves 1967: vii.
40. I include my own work in this judgement.
41. See Reilly 1970; Rescher 1978; and Almeder 1980.
42. Hammersley 1984c.
43. Becker 1970.
44. Willer 1967.
45. In fact, of course, Lacey began his study before Hargreaves.
46. For the distinction between selecting cases for study and sampling within them, see Hammersley and Atkinson (1983: ch. 2).
47. For an example, see Hammersley 1984e.
48. I leave aside the issue of the appropriateness of the use of such tests (Morrison and Henkel 1970).
49. Though see McCall 1969.
50. Hammersley 1986.
51. Both Lacey (1976) and Hargreaves (1967) treat quantitative data as more objective than qualitative data.
52. Lacey 1970: chs 4 and 7.
53. Hammersley 1984c; Hammersley *et al.* 1985.

Chapter 7: Measurement in Ethnography: The Case of Pollard on Teaching Style

1. This is represented in sociology by, for example, Blalock (1968).
2. Douglas 1967.
3. Mehan 1973.
4. See, for example, McCall and Simmons 1969.
5. Blumer 1969; Cicourel 1964.
6. Hammersley 1989a.
7. Pollard 1984.
8. Pollard uses the term 'working consensus' rather than 'teaching style' to indicate that what he is interested in is not just a characteristic of the teacher but a product

of the interaction of teacher and pupil strategies. For the purposes of my argument here, these terms can be treated as synonyms.

9. Garfinkel 1967; Heritage 1985.
10. Hammersley and Atkinson 1983.
11. Strictly speaking, we need to ensure that both the teachers have been given an equal opportunity to display 'progressive' and 'traditional' behaviours of the various kinds. While in non-experimental research we have to rely upon the natural occurrence of such opportunities, it may be that we could identify such opportunities and sample them. However, at the moment this seems a remote possibility.
12. Scarth and Hammersley 1986a.
13. Scarth and Hammersley 1986b.
14. This is a rather free interpretation of the concept of content validity, but I hope it might prove useful.
15. Barth 1972; Berlak and Berlak 1981; Bennett 1976; Hammersley 1977b.
16. There are, in any event, areas where we have information on one teacher but not on the other. See the Appendix to this chapter.
17. Evans 1983.

Chapter 8: Ethnography and the Cumulative Development of Theory: A Discussion of Woods' Proposal for 'Phase Two' Research

1. I am grateful to Barry Cooper, Donald Mackinnon, John Scarth and Peter Woods for comments on an earlier draft of this chapter.
2. Hammersley 1980c; Delamont 1981; Woods 1983.
3. Hargreaves 1981; Woods 1985a; Hammersley *et al.* 1985.
4. Woods 1985a. `
5. Woods 1985a: 60–1.
6. Woods 1985a: 63–4.
7. Blumer 1969.
8. Woods 1985a: 62.
9. Woods 1979: 147.
10. Lacey 1977: 67.
11. Hargreaves 1985.
12. Pollard 1982: 22.
13. Hargreaves 1980.
14. Abrahamson 1974.
15. Subsequently, Peter Woods (personal communication) has argued that there have been further developments, for example in the work of Nias (1980 and 1984) and his own research on teachers' biographies (Sikes *et al.* 1985). However, it seems to me that my argument applies as much to this more recent work as it does to that of Woods, Lacey, Hargreaves and Pollard.
16. Woods 1985a: 60.
17. Woods 1979, 1980a and 1980b.
18. Lofland 1976.
19. Woods (1980a) seems to argue that teachers' strategies are conscious most of the time because circumstances are constantly changing, but he does mention the possibility of routinized strategies.
20. Jackson 1968; Doyle 1977.
21. Hammersley 1981a; Sinclair and Coulthard 1975; Mehan 1979.
22. Demerath and Peterson 1967.
23. Cohen 1978; van Parijs 1981.

24. The most promising option here is what van Parijs (1981) calls reinforcement-evolutionary explanation, modelled on the concept of reinforcement in learning theory (Skinner 1953). For an outline of how this model might apply to teachers' strategies, see Hammersley and Scarth (1986).
25. Lofland 1970.
26. Merton 1957: ch. 4.
27. Lazarsfeld 1937.
28. Woods 1979.
29. Hammersley 1986.
30. Ball 1983a.
31. Woods 1985a: 61.
32. Lofland 1976.
33. Westbury 1973; Abrahamson 1974. Indeed, Abrahamson and Westbury use the concepts of 'coping strategy' and 'survival'.
34. Glaser and Strauss 1967: 5–6.
35. Woods 1985b.
36. Popper 1962.
37. See Skagestad 1981 on Peirce; Mead 1917; Lindesmith 1937.
38. Ball 1981.
39. Hammersley 1985.
40. Merton 1957.
41. Harary 1966; Wakeford 1969. In seeking to explain pupils' orientations, Woods appeals to a range of factors, including the process of differentiation-polarization. But no links are offered between the explanatory factors mentioned and the categories of pupil response distinctive to his model. As a result, he does not show what relevance those categories have for the explanation of pupils' attitudes and behaviour.
42. Furlong 1976; Hammersley and Turner 1980.
43. Woods 1983.
44. Hargreaves 1981; Hammersley *et al.* 1985.
45. Hargreaves 1981: 10.

Bibliography

Abrahamson, J.H. (1974). *Classroom Constraints and Teacher Coping Strategies: A way to conceptualise the teaching task*. Unpublished Ph.D. thesis, University of Chicago.

Almeder, R. (1980). *The Philosophy of Charles S. Peirce*. Oxford, Blackwell.

Anyon, J. (1981). 'Social class and school knowledge'. *Curriculum Inquiry*, **11**, 1, pp. 3–41.

Arensberg, C.M. and Kimball, S.T. (1940). *Family and Community in Ireland*, Cambridge, Mass., Harvard University Press.

Arensberg, C.M. and MacGregor, D. (1942). 'Determination of morale in an industrial company'. *Applied Anthropology*, **1**, pp. 12–34.

Atkinson, P. and Delamont, S. (1976). 'Mock-ups and cock-ups: The stage management of guided discovery learning'. In P. Woods and M. Hammersley (eds), *School Experience*. London, Croom Helm.

Atkinson, P., Delamont, S. and Hammersley, M. (1988). 'Qualitative research traditions: A British response to Jacob'. *Review of Educational Research*, **58**, 2, pp. 231–50.

Austin, J.L. (1962). *How to Do Things with Words*. Oxford, Oxford University Press.

Ball, D. (1972). 'Self and identity in the context of deviance: The case of criminal abortion'. In R.A. Scott and J.D. Douglas (eds), *Theoretical Perspectives on Deviance*. New York, Basic Books, pp. 158–86.

Ball, S. (1981). *Beachside Comprehensive*. Cambridge, Cambridge University Press.

Ball, S.J. (1983a). 'Case study research in education'. In M. Hammersley (ed.), *The Ethnography of Schooling*. Driffield, Yorks, Nafferton.

Ball, S.J. (1983b). 'Beachside: A study in ethnography'. Audio-cassette 3, side 2, *E205 Conflict and Change in Education*. Milton Keynes, Open University.

Ball, S.J. (1984). 'Beachside reconsidered: Reflections on a methodological apprenticeship'. In R.G. Burgess (ed.) *The Research Process in Educational Settings*. Lewes, Falmer Press.

Ball, S.J. and Goodson, I. (eds) (1984). *Teachers' Lives and Careers*. Lewes, Falmer Press.

Barnes, B. (1974). *Scientific Knowledge and Sociological Theory*. London, Routledge and Kegan Paul.

Barnes, D. (1976). *From Communication to Curriculum*. Harmondsworth, Penguin.

Barth, R. (1972). *Open Education and the American School*. New York, Agathon Press.

Becker, H.S. (1970). *Sociological Work*. Chicago, Aldine.

Becker, H.S. and Geer, B. (1960). 'Latent culture: A note on the theory of latent social roles'. *Administrative Science Quarterly*, **5**, pp. 304–13.

Becker, H.S., Geer, B., Hughes, E.C. and Strauss, A.L. (1961). *Boys in White: Student culture in medical school*. Chicago, University of Chicago Press.

Beittel, K.R. (1973). *Alternatives for Art Education Research*. Dubuque, Ia., Brown.

Bennett, N. (1976). *Teaching Styles and Pupil Progress*. London, Open Books.

Berger, J. (1970). 'Elements of a sociological self-image'. In I.L. Horowitz (ed.), *Sociological Self-images*. Oxford, Pergamon.

Berger, J., Fisek, M.H., Norman, R.Z. and Zelditch, M. (1977). *Status Characteristics and Social Interaction*. New York, Elsevier.

Berger, P. and Luckmann, T. (1967). *The Social Construction of Reality*. Harmondsworth, Penguin.

Berlak, A. and Berlak, H. (1981). *Dilemmas of Schooling*. London, Methuen.

Berlak, A. *et al.* (1975). 'Teaching and learning in English primary schools'. *School Review*, **83**, 2, pp. 215–43.

Bird, C. (1980). 'Deviant labelling in school: The pupils' perspective'. In P. Woods (ed.), *Pupil Strategies*. London, Croom Helm.

Blalock, H.M. (1961). *Causal Inferences in Nonexperimental Research*. Chapel Hill, University of North Carolina Press.

Blalock, H.M. (1968). 'The measurement problem'. In H.M. Blalock and A. Blalock (eds), *Methodology in Social Research*. New York, McGraw-Hill.

Blumer, H. (1969). *Symbolic Interactionism*. Englewood Cliffs, N.J., Prentice-Hall.

Bourdieu, P. and Passeron, J. (1977). *Reproduction in Education and Society*. London, Sage.

Bowe, R. and Whitty, G. (1983). 'A question of content and control: Recent conflicts over the nature of school examinations at 16+'. In M. Hammersley and A. Hargreaves (eds), *Curriculum Practice: Some sociological case studies*. Lewes, Falmer Press.

Bowe, R. and Whitty, G. (1984). 'Teachers, boards and standards: The attack on school-based assessments in English public examinations at 16+'. In P. Broadfoot (ed.), *Selection, Certification, and Control*. Lewes, Falmer Press.

Brock, J.A.M. and Smith, L.M. (1981). *Teaching Tales and Theories: A story and commentary on a general science classroom*. St. Louis, Mo., CEMREL.

Brooke, N. and Oxenham, J. (1984). 'The influence of certification and selection on teaching and learning'. In J. Oxenham (ed.), *Education versus Qualifications?* London, Allen and Unwin.

Campbell, D.T. and Fiske, D.W. (1959). 'Convergent and discriminant validation by the multitrait-multimethod matrix'. *Psychological Bulletin*, **56**, pp. 81–105.

Campbell, D.T. and Stanley, J.C. (1963). *Experimental and Quasi-Experimental Designs for Research*. Chicago, Rand McNally.

Cicourel, A.V. (1964). *Method and Measurement in Sociology*. New York, Free Press.

Cloward, R. and Ohlin, L. (1960). *Delinquency and Opportunity*. Chicago, Free Press.

Cohen, A.K. (1955). *Delinquent Boys*. Chicago, Free Press.

Cohen, B.P. (1980). *Developing Sociological Theory*. Englewood Cliffs, N.J., Prentice-Hall.

Cohen, G.A. (1978). *Karl Marx's Theory of History*. Oxford, Oxford University Press.

Collingwood, R.G. (1952). *An Autobiography*. Oxford, Oxford University Press.

Connaughton, I.M. and Skurnik, L.S. (1969). 'The comparative effects of several short cut item analysis procedures'. *British Journal of Educational Psychology*, **39**, pp. 225–32.

Corrigan, P. (1979). *Schooling the Smash Street Kids*. London, Macmillan.

Coser, R. (1959). 'Some social functions of laughter'. *Human Relations*, **12**.

Coulthard, M. (1977). *An Introduction to Discourse Analysis*. London, Longman.

Cressey, D. (1953). *Other People's Money*. New York, Free Press.

Cronbach, L.J. and Meehl, P.E. (1956). 'Construct validity in psychological tests'. In H. Feigl and M. Scriven (eds), *The Foundations of Science and the Concepts of Psychology and Psychoanalysis*. Minneapolis, University of Minnesota Press.

Dawe, A. (1970). 'The two sociologies'. *British Journal of Sociolgy*, **21**, 2, pp. 207–18.
Delamont, S. (1976a). *Interaction in the Classroom* (2nd edn 1983). London, Methuen.
Delamont, S. (1976b). 'Beyond Flanders' fields'. In M. Stubbs and S. Delamont (eds), *Explorations in Classroom Observation*. Chichester, John Wiley.
Delamont, S. (1981). 'All too familiar? A decade of classroom research'. *Educational Analysis*, **3**, 1.
Delamont, S. and Hamilton, D. (1984). 'Revisiting classroom research: A continuing cautionary tale'. In S. Delamont (ed.), *Readings on Interaction in the Classroom*. London, Methuen.
Demerath, N.J. and Peterson, R.A. (eds) (1967). *System, Change and Conflict*. New York, Free Press.
Denzin, N.K. (1970). *The Research Act*. Chicago, Aldine.
Department of Education and Science (1979). *Aspects of Secondary Education in England: A survey by HM Inspectorate*. London, HMSO.
Douglas, J.D. (1967). *The Social Meanings of Suicide*. Princeton, Princeton University Press.
Doyle, W. (1977). 'Learning the classroom environment'. *Journal of Teacher Education*, **28**, pp. 51–5.
Evans, J. (1983). 'Criteria of validity in social research'. In M. Hammersley (ed.), *The Ethnography of Schooling*. Driffield, Nafferton.
Flanders, N. (1970). *Analyzing Teacher Behaviour*. Reading, Mass., Addison-Wesley.
Frankenberg, R. (ed.) (1982). *Custom and Conflict in British Society*. Manchester, Manchester University Press.
Freese, L. (ed.) (1980). *Theoretical Models in Sociology*. Pittsburgh, University of Pittsburgh Press.
Furlong, V.J. (1976). 'Interaction sets in the classroom'. In M. Stubbs and S. Delamont (eds), *Explorations in Classroom Observation*. Chichester, John Wiley.
Furlong, V.J. (1977). 'Anancy goes to school: A case study of pupils' knowledge of their teachers'. In P. Woods and M. Hammersley (eds), *School Experience*. London, Croom Helm.
Gannaway, H. (1976). 'Making sense out of school'. In M. Stubbs and S. Delamont (eds), *Explorations in Classroom Observation*. Chichester, John Wiley.
Gardiner, P. (ed.) (1959). *Theories of History*. New York, Free Press.
Garfinkel, H. (1967). *Studies in Ethnomethodology*. Englewood Cliffs, N.J., Prentice-Hall.
Geertz, C. (1973). *The Interpretation of Cultures*. New York, Basic Books.
Geertz, C. (1983). *Local Knowledge*. New York, Basic Books.
Glaser, B.G. and Strauss, A. (1967). *The Discovery of Grounded Theory*. Chicago, Aldine.
Goetz, J. and LeCompte, M. (1984). *Ethnography and Qualitative Design in Educational Research*. London, Academic Press.
Goffman, E. (1961). 'Role distance'. In E. Goffman, *Encounters*. Indianapolis, Bobbs-Merrill.
Goffman, E. (1968). *Asylums*. Harmondsworth, Penguin.
Goffman, E. (1971). *The Presentation of Self in Everyday Life*. Harmondsworth, Penguin.
Goffman, E. (1972). *Relations in Public*. Harmondsworth, Penguin.
Goffman, E. (1975). *Frame Analysis*. Harmondsworth, Penguin.
Goldthorpe, J.H. (1980). *Social Mobility and Class Structure in Modern Britain*. Oxford, Clarendon Press.
Gonos, G. (1977). 'Situation versus frame'. *American Sociological Review*, **42**, 6, pp. 854–67.
Halsey, A.H., Floud, J. and Anderson, C.A. (1961). *Education, Economy and Society*. New York, Free Press.

Halsey, A.H., Heath, A.H. and Ridge, J.M. (1980). *Origins and Destinations*. Oxford, Clarendon Press.

Hamilton, D. and Delamont, S. (1974). 'Classroom research: A cautionary tale'. *Research in Education*, **11**, pp. 1–15.

Hammersley, M. (1974). 'The organisation of pupil participation'. *Sociological Review*, **22**, 3, pp. 355–68.

Hammersley, M. (1976). 'The mobilisation of pupil attention'. In M. Hammersley and P. Woods (eds) *The Process of Schooling*. London, Routledge and Kegan Paul, pp. 104–15.

Hammersley, M. (1977a). 'School learning: The cultural resources required to answer a teacher's question'. In P. Woods and M. Hammersley (eds), *School Experience*. London, Croom Helm, pp. 58–86.

Hammersley, M. (1977b). 'Teacher perspectives', units 9 and 10, E202 *Schooling and Society*. Milton Keynes, Open University Press.

Hammersley, M. (1978). 'What is a strategy?' Unpublished paper.

Hammersley, M. (1979). *Data Collection in Ethnographic Research*. Block 4, in Open University course DE304.

Hammersley, M. (1980a). *A Peculiar World: Teaching and learning in an inner-city school*. Ph.D. thesis, University of Manchester.

Hammersley, M. (1980b). 'On interactionist empiricism'. In P. Woods (ed.), *Pupil Strategies*. London, Croom Helm, pp. 198–213.

Hammersley, M. (1980c). 'Classroom ethnography'. *Educational Analysis*, **2**, 2.

Hammersley, M. (1981a). 'Putting competence into action'. In P. French and M. MacLure (eds), *Adult–Child Conversation*. London, Croom Helm.

Hammersley, M. (1981b). 'Ideology in the staffroom: A critique of false consciousness'. In L. Barton and S. Walker (eds), *Schools, Teachers and Teaching*. London, Falmer Press.

Hammersley, M. (1982). 'The sociology of classrooms'. In A. Hartnett (ed.), *The Social Sciences in Educational Studies*. London, Heinemann.

Hammersley, M. (1983). 'Staffroom news'. In A. Hargreaves and P. Woods (eds), *Classrooms and Staffrooms*. Milton Keynes, Open University Press.

Hammersley, M. (1984a). 'The paradigmatic mentality: A diagnosis'. In L. Barton and S. Walker (eds), *Social Crisis and Educational Research*. London, Croom Helm.

Hammersley, M. (1984b). 'Staffroom news'. In A. Hargreaves and P. Woods (eds).

Hammersley, M. (1984c). 'Making a vice of our virtues: Some notes on theory in history and ethnography'. In S. Ball and I. Goodson (eds), *Defining the Curriculum*, Lewes, Falmer Press.

Hammersley, M. (1984d). 'Is there a macro–micro problem in the sociology of education?' *Sociological Review*, **32**, 2, pp. 316–24.

Hammersley, M. (1984e). 'The researcher exposed: A natural history'. In R.G. Burgess (ed.), *The Research Process in Educational Settings*. London, Falmer Press.

Hammersley, M. (1985). 'From ethnography to theory: A programme and paradigm for case study research in the sociology of education'. *Sociology*, **19**, 2, pp. 244–59.

Hammersley, M. (1986). 'Measurement in ethnography: The case of Pollard on teaching style'. In M. Hammersley (ed.), *Case Studies in Classroom Research*. Milton Keynes, Open University Press.

Hammersley, M. (1987a). 'Ethnography and the cumulative development of theory'. *British Educational Research Journal*, **13**, 3, pp. 283–95.

Hammersley, M. (1987b). 'Ethnography for survival? A response to Woods'. *British Educational Research Journal*, **13**, 3.

Hammersley, M. (1989a). 'The problem of the concept: Herbert Blumer and the relation between concepts and data'. *Journal of Contemporary Ethnography*, **18**, 2.

Hammersley, M. (1989b). *The Dilemma of Qualitative Method: Herbert Blumer and the Chicago tradition.* London, Routledge.

Hammersley, M. and Atkinson, P. (1983). *Ethnography: Principles in Practice.* London, Tavistock.

Hammersley, M. and Hargreaves, A. (1983). *Curriculum Practice: Some sociological case studies.* London, Falmer Press.

Hammersley, M. and Scarth, J. (1986). *The Impact of Examinations on Secondary School Teaching.* School of Education, Open University.

Hammersley, M. and Turner, G. (1980). 'Conformist pupils?' In P. Woods (ed.), *Pupil Strategies.* London, Croom Helm.

Hammersley, M. and Woods, P. (1984). *Life in School.* Milton Keynes, Open University Press.

Hammersley, M., Scarth, J. and Webb, S. (1985). 'Developing and testing theory: The case of research on examinations and pupil learning'. In R.G. Burgess (ed.), *Issues in Educational Research.* London, Falmer Press.

Harary, F. (1966). 'Merton revisited: A new classification for deviant behaviour'. *American Sociological Review,* **31**, 5.

Hargreaves, A. (1978). 'The significance of classroom coping strategies'. In L. Barton and R. Meighan (eds), *Sociological Interpretations of Schooling and Classrooms.* Driffield, Nafferton.

Hargreaves, A. (1979). 'Strategies, decisions and control'. In J. Eggleston (ed.), *Teacher Decision-making in the Classroom.* London, Routledge and Kegan Paul.

Hargreaves, A. (1980). 'Synthesis and the study of strategies: A project for the sociological imagination'. In P. Woods (ed.), *Pupil Strategies.* London, Croom Helm.

Hargreaves, A. (1985). *English Middle Schools: An historical and ethnographic study.* Unpublished Ph.D. thesis, University of Leeds.

Hargreaves, A. and Woods, P. (1984). *Classrooms and Staffrooms.* Milton Keynes, Open University Press.

Hargreaves, D. (1967). *Social Relations in the Secondary School.* London, Routledge and Kegan Paul.

Hargreaves, D. (1981). 'Schooling for delinquency'. In L. Barton and S. Walker (eds), *Schools, Teachers and Teaching.* Lewes, Falmer Press.

Hargreaves, D., Hester, S. and Mellor, F. (1975). *Deviance in the Classroom.* London, Routledge and Kegan Paul.

Harris, E. (1970). *Hypothesis and Perception.* London, Allen and Unwin.

Hartog, P. and Rhodes, E.C. (1935). *An Examination of Examinations.* Basingstoke, Macmillan.

Hempel, C.G. (1965). *Aspects of Scientific Explanation.* New York, Free Press.

Heritage, J. (1985). *Garfinkel and Ethnomethodology.* Cambridge, Polity.

Hewitt, J.P. and Stokes, R. (1975). 'Disclaimers'. *American Sociological Review,* **40**, pp. 1–11.

Homans, G. (1950). *The Human Group.* New York, Harcourt Brace Jovanovich.

Homans, G. (1962). *Sentiments and Activities.* New York, Free Press.

Homans, G. (1967). *The Nature of Social Science.* New York, Harcourt Brace Jovanovich.

Hopper, E. (1971). *Readings in the Theory of Educational Systems.* London, Hutchinson.

Horton, T. (ed.) (1987). *The GCSE: Examining the new system.* London, Harper and Row.

Humphries, S. (1981). *Hooligans or Rebels?* Oxford, Blackwell.

Hymes, D.H. (1977). *Foundations in Sociolinguistics.* London, Tavistock.

Jackson, P. (1968). *Life in Classrooms.* New York, Holt, Rinehart and Winston.

Jacob, E. (1987). 'Qualitative research traditions: a review'. *Review of Educational Research,* **57**, 1, pp. 1–50.

Jacob, E. (1988). 'Clarifying qualitative research: A focus on traditions'. *Educational Researcher*, **17**, pp. 16–24.

Kapferer, B. (1976). *Transaction and Meaning*. Philadelphia Institute for the Study of Human Issues.

Kaplan, A. (1964). *The Conduct of Inquiry*. San Francisco, Chandler.

Keat, R. and Urry, J. (1975). *Social Theory as Science*. London, Routledge and Kegan Paul.

Kesey, K. (1962). *One Flew Over the Cuckoo's Nest*. New York, Viking.

Kounin, J.S. (1970). *Discipline and Group Management in Classrooms*. New York, Holt, Rinehart and Winston.

Kounin, J.S. *et al.* (1961). 'Explorations in classroom management'. *Journal of Teacher Education*, **12**, pp. 235–46.

Kuhn, T.S. (1970). *The Structure of Scientific Revolutions*, 2nd edn. Chicago, University of Chicago Press.

Lacey, C. (1966). 'Some sociological concomitants of academic streaming in a grammar school'. *British Journal of Sociology*, **XVII**, 3, pp. 245–62.

Lacey, C. (1970). *Hightown Grammar*. Manchester, Manchester University Press.

Lacey, C. (1974). 'Destreaming in a "pressured" academic environment'. In J. Eggleston (ed.), *Contemporary Research in the Sociology of Education*. London, Methuen.

Lacey, C. (1976). 'Problems of sociological fieldwork: A review of the methodology of "Hightown Grammar" '. In M. Shipman (ed.), *The Organisation and Impact of Social Research*. London, Routledge and Kegan Paul.

Lacey, C. (1977). *The Socialisation of Teachers*. London, Methuen.

Lambart, A. (1976). 'The sisterhood'. In M. Hammersley and P. Woods (eds), *The Process of Schooling*. London, Routledge and Kegan Paul.

Lambart, A. (1982). 'Expulsion in context: A school as a system in action'. In R. Frankenberg (ed.), *Custom and Conflict in British Society*. Manchester, Manchester University Press.

Lazarsfeld, P.F. (1937). 'Some remarks on typological procedures in social research'. Translated from the German. In P.F. Lazarsfeld, A. Pasanella and M. Rosenberg (eds), *Continuities in the Language of Social Research*. New York, Free Press, 1972.

Lewin, K. (1984). 'Selection and curriculum reform'. In J. Oxenham (ed.), *Education versus Qualifications*. London, Allen and Unwin.

Lindesmith, A.R. (1937). *The Nature of Opiate Addiction*. Chicago, University of Chicago Libraries.

Lindesmith, A.R. (1968). *Addiction and Opiates*. Chicago, Aldine.

Lofland, J. (1970). 'Interactionist imagery and analytic interruptus'. In T. Shibutani (ed.), *Human Nature and Collective Behaviour: Papers in honour of Herbert Blumer*. Englewood Cliffs N.J., Prentice-Hall.

Lofland, J. (1976). *Doing Social Life*. John Wiley.

Lyman, S.M. and Scott, M.B. (1970). *A Sociology of the Absurd*. New York, Appleton-Century-Crofts.

McCall, G. (1969). 'The problem of indicators in participant observation research'. In G. McCall and J.L. Simmons (eds), *Issues in Participant Observation*. Reading, Mass., Addison-Wesley.

McCall, G. and Simmons, J.L. (1969). *Issues in Participant Observation*. Reading, Mass., Addison-Wesley.

McCarney, J. (1980). *The Real World of Ideology*. Brighton, Harvester.

McDermott, R.P. (1976). *Kids Make Sense: An ethnographic account of the interactional management of success and failure in one first grade classroom*. Ph.D. Thesis, Stanford University.

McHoul, A. (1978). 'The organisation of turns at formal talk in the classroom'. *Language in Society*, **7**, pp. 183–213.

Macintosh, H.G. (ed.) (1974). *Techniques and Problems of Assessment*. London, Arnold.

Macintosh, H.G. (1985). 'The GCSE and the future'. *Forum, 28*, pp. 7–9.

Mackenzie, R.F. (1982). 'High priests and ikons: Examinations vs knowledge'. *The Head*, 1, 7, pp. 10–11.

Marsh, P., Rosser, E. and Harré, R. (1978). *The Rules of Disorder*. London, Routledge and Kegan Paul.

Matza, D. (1961). *Delinquency and Drift*. New York, John Wiley.

Mead, G.H. (1917). 'Scientific method and the individual thinker'. In J. Dewey *et al.*, *Creative Intelligence: Essays in the pragmatic attitude*. New York, Henry Holt.

Mee, A. *et al.* (1971). *Science for the 70s*. Teachers' Guide, Books 1 and 2. London, Heinemann.

Mehan, H. (1973). 'Assessing children's school performance'. In H.P. Dreitzel (ed.), *Childhood and Socialization, Recent Sociology No. 5*. New York, Collier Macmillan.

Mehan, H. (1979). *Learning Lessons*. Cambridge, Mass., Harvard University Press.

Merton, R. (1957). *Social Theory and Social Structure*. New York, Free Press.

Miller, W.B. (1958). 'Lower class culture as a generating milieu of gang delinquency'. *Journal of Social Issues, 14*, pp. 5–19.

Mills, C.W. (1959). *The Sociological Imagination*. Oxford, Oxford University Press.

Morrison, A. (1973). 'The teaching of international affairs in secondary schools in Scotland'. *MOST, 2*.

Morrison, D.E. and Henkel, R.E. (1970). *The Significance Test Controversy*. Chicago, Aldine.

Mueller, J.H., Schuessler, K.F. and Costner, H.L. (1977). *Statistical Reasoning in Sociology*, 3rd edn. Boston, Houghton Mifflin.

Musgrove, F. (1979). *School and the Social Order*. Chichester, John Wiley.

Nagel, E. (1961). *The Structure of Science*. London, Routledge and Kegan Paul.

Newton-Smith, W.H. (1981). *Rationality of Science*. London, Routledge and Kegan Paul.

Nias, J. (1980). 'Commitment and motivation in primary school teachers'. *Educational Review, 33*, pp. 181–90.

Nias, J. (1984). 'The definition and maintenance of self in primary teachers'. *British Journal of Sociology of Education, 5*, 3, pp. 167–80.

Nuttall, D.L. and Skurnik, L.S. (1969). *Examination and Item Analysis Manual*. Slough, NFER.

Nuttall, D.L. (1984). 'Doomsday or a new dawn? The prospects for a common system of examining at 16+.' In P. Broadfoot (ed.) *Selection, Certification and Control: Social issues in educational assessment*, Lewes, Falmer Press.

Nuttall, D.L. and Willmott, A.S. (1972). *British Examinations: Techniques of analysis*. Slough, NFER.

Open University (1979). *DE304 Research Methods in Education and the Social Sciences*. Milton Keynes, Open University Press.

Parijs, P. van (1981). *Evolutionary Explanation in the Social Sciences*. London, Tavistock.

Partridge, E. (1963). *Usage and Abusage*. Harmondsworth, Penguin.

Payne, G.C.F. (1976). 'Making a lesson happen: An ethnomethodological analysis'. In M. Hammersley and P. Woods (eds), *The Process of Schooling*. London, Routledge and Kegan Paul.

Peshkin, A. (1982). *The Imperfect Union: School consolidation and community conflict*. Chicago, University of Chicago Press.

Pollard, A. (1979). 'Negotiating deviance and "getting done" in primary school classrooms'. In L. Barton and R. Meighan (eds), *Schools, Pupils and Deviance*. Driffield, Nafferton.

Pollard, A. (1980). 'Teacher interests and changing situations of survival threat in primary school classrooms'. In P. Woods (ed.), *Teacher Strategies*. London, Croom Helm.

Pollard, A. (1982). 'A model of coping strategies'. *British Journal of the Sociology of Education*, **3**, 1, pp. 19–37.

Pollard, A. (1984). 'Coping strategies and the multiplication of differentiation in infant classrooms'. *British Educational Research Journal*, **10**, 1, pp. 33–48.

Pollard, A. (1985). *The Social World of the Primary School*. London, Methuen.

Popper, K.R. (1962). *Conjectures and Refutations*. London, Routledge and Kegan Paul.

Quine, W.G. (1974). 'Polarised cultures in comprehensive schools'. *Research in Education*, **12**, pp. 9–25.

Radnitzky, G. (1973). *Contemporary Schools of Metascience*. Chicago, Henry Regnery.

Redfield, R. (1955). *The Little Community*. Chicago, University of Chicago Press.

Redl, F. and Wattenberg, W. (1951). *Mental Hygiene in Teaching*. New York, Harcourt Brace Jovanovich.

Redl, F. and Wineman, D. (1957). *The Aggressive Child*. Glencoe, Ill., Free Press.

Reichenbach, H. (1938). *Experience and Prediction*. Chicago, University of Chicago Press.

Reilly, F. (1970). *Charles Peirce's Theory of Scientific Method*. New York, Fordham University Press.

Rescher, N. (1978). *Peirce's Philosophy of Science*. Notre Dame, University of Notre Dame Press.

Reynolds, D. (1976a). 'The delinquent school'. In M. Hammersley and P. Woods (eds), *The Process of Schooling*. London, Routledge and Kegan Paul.

Reynolds, D. (1976b). 'When teachers and pupils refuse a truce'. In G. Mungham and G. Pearson (eds), *Working Class Youth Culture*. London, Routledge and Kegan Paul.

Reynolds, D. and Sullivan, M. (1979). 'Bringing schools back in'. In L. Barton and R. Meighan (eds), *Schools, Pupils and Deviance*. Driffield, Nafferton.

Roach, J. (1971). *Public Examinations in England 1850–1900*. Cambridge, Cambridge University Press.

Robinson, W.S. (1969). 'The logical structure of analytic induction'. In G. McCall and J.L. Simmons (eds), *Issues in Participant Observation*. Reading, Mass., Addison-Wesley.

Roethlisberger, F. and Dickson, W. (1939). *Management and the Worker*. Cambridge, Mass., Harvard University Press.

Sacks, H., Schegloff, E. and Jefferson, G. (1974). 'A simplest systematics for the organization of turn-taking in conversation'. *Language*, **50**, pp. 696–735.

Scarth, J. (1983). 'Teachers' school-based experiences of examining'. In M. Hammersley and A. Hargreaves (eds), *Curriculum Practice*. Lewes, Falmer Press.

Scarth, J. (1984). 'Teachers' attitudes to examining'. In P. Broadfoot (ed.), *Selection, Certification and Control*. Lewes, Falmer Press.

Scarth, J. (1986a). 'Some notes on the concept of fact transmission in teaching'. Unpublished paper.

Scarth, J. (1986b). *The Influence of Examinations on Whole-school Curriculum Decision-making: A case study*. Unpublished Ph.D. theses, University of Lancaster.

Scarth, J. (1987). 'Teaching to the exam? The case of the Schools Council History Project'. In T. Horton (ed.), *The GCSE: Examining the new system*. London, Harper and Row.

Scarth, J. and Hammersley, M. (1986a). 'Questioning ORACLE'. *Educational Research*, **28**, 3, pp. 174–84.

Scarth, J. and Hammersley, M. (1986b). 'Some problems in assessing the closedness of tasks'. In M. Hammersley (ed.), *Case Studies in Classroom Research*. Milton Keynes, Open University Press.

Scarth, J. and Hammersley, M. (1988). 'Examinations and teaching'. *British Educational Research Journal*, **14**, 3, pp. 231–49.

Scheffler, I. (1967). *Science and Subjectivity*. Indianapolis, Bobbs-Merrill.

Schenkein, J. (1978). *Studies in the Organisation of Conversational Interaction*. London, Academic Press.

Schutz, A. (1962). *Collected Papers*, Vol. 1. The Hague, Martinus Nijhoff.

Schutz, A. and Luckmann, T. (1974). *The Structures of the Lifeworld*. London, Heinemann.

Scottish Education Department (1969). *Science for a General Education*. Curriculum Paper No. 7. London/Edinburgh, HMSO.

Scriven, M. (1959). 'Truisms as the grounds for historical explanations'. In P. Gardiner (ed.), *Theories of History*. New York, Free Press.

Searle, J. (1965). 'What is a speech act?' In M. Black (ed.), *Philosophy in America*. London, Allen and Unwin.

Secondary Examinations Council (1986). *History GCSE: A guide for teachers*. Milton Keynes, Open University Press.

Sharp, R. (1981). 'Review of Stephen Ball's "Beachside Comprehensive" '. *British Journal of Sociology of Education,* **2**, 3, pp. 278–85.

Sharp, R. and Green, A. (1975). *Education and Social Control*. London, Routledge and Kegan Paul.

Sikes, P., Measor, L. and Woods, P. (1985). *Teacher Careers: Crises and continuities*. London, Falmer Press.

Sinclair, J. McH. and Coulthard, M. (1975). *Towards an Analysis of Discourse*. Oxford, Oxford University Press.

Skagestad, P. (1981). *The Road of Inquiry: Charles Peirce's pragmatic realism*. New York, Columbia University Press.

Skinner, B.F. (1953). *Science and Human Behaviour*. New York, Free Press, 1965.

Smith, L.M. (1958). 'The concurrent validity of six personality and adjustment tests for children'. *Psychological Monographs,* **77**, p. 457.

Smith, L.M. and Brock, J.A.M. (1970). *'Go, Bug, Go': Methodological issues in classroom observational research*. Occasional Paper Series No. 5. St. Ann, Mo., CEMREL.

Smith, L.M. and Geoffrey, W. (1968). *The Complexities of an Urban Classroom*. New York, Holt, Rinehart and Winston.

Smith, L.M. and Keith, P. (1971). *Anatomy of Educational Innovation*. New York, John Wiley.

Smith, L.M. and Kleine, P. (1969). 'Teacher awareness: Social cognition in the classroom'. *School Review,* **77**, pp. 245–56.

Smith, L.M. and Pohland, P.A. (1974). 'Education, technology and the rural highlands'. In D. Sjogren (ed.), *Four Evaluation Examples: Anthropological, economic, narrative and portrayal*. Chicago, Rand McNally.

Smith, L.M., Kleine, P.F., Prunty, J.J. and Dwyer, D.C. (1986). *Educational Innovators: Then and now*. London, Falmer Press.

Smith, L.M., Prunty, J.J., Dwyer, D.C. and Kleine, P.F. (1987). *The Fate of an Innovative School: The history and present status of the Kensington School*. London, Falmer Press.

Smith, L.M., Dwyer, D.C., Prunty, J.J. and Kleine, F.F. (1988). *Innovation and Change in Schooling: History, politics and agency*. London, Falmer Press.

Speier, M. (1973). *How to Observe Face-To-Face Communication*. Pacific Palisades, Goodyear.

Stebbins, R. (1975). *Teachers and Meaning: Definitions of classroom situations*. Leiden, E.J. Brill.

Sudnow, D. (1972). *Studies in Social Interaction*. New York, Free Press.

Torode, B. (1977). 'Interrupting intersubjectivity'. In P. Woods and M. Hammersley (eds), *School Experience*. London, Croom Helm.

Torrance, H. (1985). 'Current prospects for school-based examining'. *Educational Review,* **37**, pp. 39–51.

Turner, G. (1981). *The Social World of the Comprehensive School.* London, Croom Helm.

Turner, J. (1983). *Integrated Humanities and the Public Examination System.* Unpublished M.Ed. thesis, University of Leicester.

Turner, J. (1984). 'Teacher-controlled assessment and integrated humanities'. *Forum,* Spring, pp. 50–2.

Turner, R. (1974). *Ethnomethodology.* Harmondsworth, Penguin.

Turner, R.H. (1969). 'The quest for universals'. In G. McCall and J.L. Simmons (eds), *Issues in Participant Observation.* Reading, Mass., Addison-Wesley.

Wakeford, J. (1969). *The Cloistered Elite: A Sociological analysis of the English public boarding school.* London, Macmillan.

Walker, R. (1971). *The Social Setting of the Classroom: A review of observational studies and research.* Unpublished M.Phil thesis, University of London.

Waller, W. (1932). *The Sociology of Teaching.* New York, John Wiley.

Webb, E.J., Campbell, D.T., Schwartz, R. and Sechrest, L. (1966). *Unobtrusive Measures.* Chicago, Rand McNally.

Webb, J. (1962). 'The sociology of a school'. *British Journal of Sociology,* **13**, 3, pp. 264–72.

Weber, M. (1949). *The Methodology of the Social Sciences.* New York, Free Press.

Werthman, C. (1963). 'Delinquents in school'. *Berkeley Journal of Sociology,* **8**, 1, pp. 39–60.

Westbury, I. (1973). 'Conventional classrooms, "open" classrooms and the technology of teaching'. *Journal of Curriculum Studies,* **V**, pp. 91–121.

Whitty, G. (1976). 'Teachers and examiners'. In G. Whitty and M.F.D. Young (eds), *Explorations in the Politics of School Knowledge.* Driffield, Nafferton.

Whitty, G. (1978). 'School examinations and the politics of school knowledge'. In L. Barton and S. Walker (eds), *Sociological Interpretations of Schooling and Classrooms: A reappraisal.* Driffield, Nafferton.

Whyte, W.F. (1955). *Street Corner Society,* rev. edn. Chicago, University of Chicago Press.

Willer, D. (1967). *Scientific Sociology.* Englewood Cliffs, N.J., Prentice-Hall.

Willer, D. and Heckathorn, D. (1980). 'Cumulation; explanation and prediction'. In L. Freese (ed.), *Theoretical Models in Sociology.* Pittsburgh, University of Pittsburgh Press.

Willis, P. (1977). *Learning to Labour.* Farnborough, Saxon House.

Winch, P. (1958). *The Idea of a Social Science and its Relation to Philosophy.* London, Routledge and Kegan Paul.

Woods, P. (1975). 'Showing them up in secondary school'. In G. Chanan and S. Delamont (eds), *Frontiers in Classroom Research.* Slough, National Foundation for Educational Research.

Woods, P. (1977). 'Teaching for survival'. In P. Woods and M. Hammersley (eds), *School Experience.* London, Croom Helm.

Woods, P. (1979). *The Divided School.* London, Routledge and Kegan Paul.

Woods, P. (1980a). 'Strategies in teaching and learning'. In P. Woods (ed.), *Teacher Strategies.* London, Croom Helm.

Woods, P. (1980b). 'The development of pupil strategies'. In P. Woods (ed.), *Pupil Strategies.* London, Croom Helm.

Woods, P. (1980c). 'Introduction'. In P. Woods (ed.), *Teacher Strategies.* London, Croom Helm.

Woods, P. (1983). *Sociology and the School.* London, Routledge and Kegan Paul.

Woods, P. (1985a). 'Ethnography and theory construction in educational research'. In R.G. Burgess (ed.), *Field Methods in the Study of Education,* Lewes, Falmer Press.

Woods, P. (1985b). 'Creativity and technique in writing up qualitative research'. In R.G. Burgess (ed.), *Issues in Educational Research: Qualitative methods*. London, Falmer Press.

Woods, P. (1987). 'Ethnography at the crossroads: A reply to Hammersley'. *British Educational Research Journal*, **13**, 3.

Woods, P. and Hammersley, M. (1977). *School Experience*. London, Croom Helm.

Wragg, E.C. (1973). 'A study of student teachers in the classroom'. In G. Chanan and S. Delamont (eds), *Towards a Science of Teaching*. Slough, NFER.

Young, M.F.D. (1971). *Knowledge and Control*. London, Collier-Macmillan.

Zetterberg, H. (1963). *On Theory and Verification in Sociology*. Totowa, N.J., Bedminster Press.

Author Index

Subject Index